Legal Problem Solving

Reasoning, Research & Writing

Fourth Edition

Maureen F. Fitzgerald
Ph.D., B.Comm., LL.B., LL.M.

with
Melinda Renner

LexisNexis®

Legal Problem Solving: Reasoning, Research & Writing, Fourth Edition
© LexisNexis Canada Inc. 2007
August 2007

Members of the LexisNexis Group worldwide

Canada	LexisNexis Canada Inc, 123 Commerce Valley Drive East, MARKHAM, Ontario
Argentina	Abeledo Perrot, Jurisprudencia Argentina and Depalma, BUENOS AIRES
Australia	Butterworths, a Division of Reed International Books Australia Pty Ltd, CHATSWOOD, New South Wales
Austria	ARD Betriebsdienst and Verlag Orac, VIENNA
Chile	Publitecsa and Conosur Ltda, SANTIAGO DE CHILE
Czech Republic	Orac sro, PRAGUE
France	Éditions du Juris-Classeur SA, PARIS
Hong Kong	Butterworths Asia (Hong Kong), HONG KONG
Hungary	Hvg Orac, BUDAPEST
India	Butterworths India, NEW DELHI
Ireland	Butterworths (Ireland) Ltd, DUBLIN
Italy	Giuffré, MILAN
Malaysia	Malayan Law Journal Sdn Bhd, KUALA LUMPUR
New Zealand	Butterworths of New Zealand, WELLINGTON
Poland	Wydawnictwa Prawnicze PWN, WARSAW
Singapore	Butterworths Asia, SINGAPORE
South Africa	Butterworth Publishers (Pty) Ltd, DURBAN
Switzerland	Stämpfli Verlag AG, BERNE
United Kingdom	Butterworths Tolley, a Division of Reed Elsevier (UK), LONDON, WC2A
USA	LexisNexis, DAYTON, Ohio

Library and Archives Canada Cataloguing in Publication

Fitzgerald, Maureen F.
     Legal problem solving : reasoning, research & writing / Maureen F. Fitzgerald. — 4th ed.

Includes index.
ISBN 978-0-433-45707-7

     1. Legal research—Canada. 2. Legal research. 3. Legal composition.
I. Title.

KE250.F57 2007   340'.072071   C2007-903929-4
KF240.F57 2007

Printed and bound in Canada.

To my life partner Paul Clay Quinn

MFF

To the memory of my mother, Dot

MR

Preface

Legal problem solving is the backbone to all that lawyers do. Every lawyer is engaged in some form of legal problem solving, every day. Without the skills to be able to solve legal problems, lawyers would be unable to access or understand the law. Every law school in Canada teaches legal problem solving through a first-year legal research and writing course.

This book was designed as a textbook for that course. Unlike other textbooks, this book:

- places legal research in the context of solving legal problems;
- teaches the fundamental steps to all legal research;
- provides enough detail to enable any researcher to solve a legal problem from beginning to end;
- introduces a step-by-step problem-solving process (FILAC) to make research more systematic and memorable; and
- includes learning objectives, examples, and exercises to engage students in their learning.

Fifteen years ago I created the concept of FILAC — a problem-solving technique to teach legal research and writing — after several years of teaching Legal Research and Writing at both the University of Victoria and the University of British Columbia. As a lawyer I understood the importance of making student learning relevant and immediately applicable. I decided that I would teach them the whole process of legal problem solving.

At that time in Canada the course was taught primarily by librarians and the content was essentially about how to find laws in books in a law library. The critical piece that was missing was context. I discovered over the years that to make learning most effective, students needed to understand **why** they were looking for the books and **what** they would do with the books once they located them. I slowly began to understand how to better teach the course and translated this knowledge into this book.

Who This Book Is For

This book can be used by anyone who wishes to solve a legal problem. This includes lawyers, law students, legal assistants, and the general public. It is written in a way that should be easily understandable to those who are not familiar with the law.

The Format of This Book

This book teaches the entire process of legal research. All research begins with a set of facts or circumstances. The researcher's task is to analyze facts, determine legal issues, find relevant law, analyze the law, apply the law to the facts, and communicate the results.

Each chapter begins with a set of learning objectives and ends with a self test. This enables the reader to quickly see what is covered in each chapter and understand the learning expectations.

Since the skills of factual analysis, issue identification, finding the law, legal analysis, and legal writing are learned best through repeated practice, examples and problem-based exercises have been included. In addition to doing these exercises, researchers should practise the skills on their own time or in small groups where the skills can be simulated and feedback can be received.

Enjoy the learning!

Maureen F. Fitzgerald
Vancouver, April 2007

Acknowledgments

When I wrote this book almost 15 years ago I did not imagine that it would go into a fourth edition. I am deeply honoured to be able to help law students learn about this very important skill. Even though my law practice has evolved into one of conflict resolution exclusively, I still believe that legal research is one of the most important skills a lawyer can possess. It's not so much about finding books as it is about *thinking about what you need to solve a problem and how you will use that information once you find it*. It is about being effective and efficient and not simply about finding relevant cases and statutes. Even today I go back to the fundamentals contained in this book and have the confidence of knowing that I have all the information I need to solve my legal problem.

I have not wavered from my thinking that legal research is necessarily about legal problem solving and I am proud to say that the success of this book is in the fact that so many law faculty are using it to teach their Legal Research and Writing courses. I have received many complimentary e-mails from students, faculty, law librarians, and legal researchers in law firms. Thank you.

I wish to thank those who supported me over the years: Melinda Renner, who truly made this edition possible; Kathleen McIsaac, who never wavers; the students at the University of Victoria and University of British Columbia; Monica Beauregard; John Fairlie; Nancy Hannum; Pat Pitsula; Pat Nelson; Anne Morrison; Joan Honeywell; Joan Fraser; Penny Hazelton; Michael Lee; Emily Quinn; Paige Quinn; Jennifer Leslie and Paul Quinn.

I would also like to thank Michael Silverstein, Ji Hyun (Jenny) Ryu (Thomson Carswell); Mark Bettiol and Tracy Smith (LexisNexis); Mary Mitchell and Anna Holeton (University of British Columbia Law Librarians); and all of the law faculty and legal researchers across Canada who provided me with suggestions for this edition.

Finally, thanks to those publishers who generously granted their permission to reproduce information contained in this book, as well as those organizations that generously provided funding for the first edition in 1996: the Legal Research Foundation (B.C.); the Faculty of Law at the University of Victoria; the Office of the President at the University of Victoria; and the Law Foundation of British Columbia.

I welcome comments and feedback on the book, and can be reached via e-mail at Maureen@CenterPointInc.com.

Maureen F. Fitzgerald
Vancouver, April 2007

I wish to thank my UNB teaching colleagues, Professors Don Fleming and John McEvoy, for their superb assistance as I prepared new sections of this edition that deal with treaties as primary Canadian law sources and aboriginal law, respectively. Thanks go to Janine Miller, Executive Director of CanLII and former Director of the Great Library, Law Society of Upper Canada, for her suggestions regarding the description of CanLII. In addition, I would like to thank my colleague, UNB Head Law Librarian Janet Moss, for her counsel and support during the book's preparation, and to our Library Assistant, Heather Doherty, for her excellent proofreading. Finally, I wish to thank both current UNB Dean of Law Philip Bryden and past Dean of Law Anne Warner La Forest for recognizing the importance of formal legal research training in law school and for championing and supporting it at UNB, and also for their leadership in encouraging all of us within the Faculty of Law to conduct research and to contribute meaningfully to the literature of our professions.

Melinda Renner
Fredericton, April 2007

About the Author

Maureen F. Fitzgerald, Ph.D, B.Comm., LL.B., LL.M., taught legal research and writing at the University of Victoria and the University of British Columbia for several years. She has practised law for over 20 years in both Ontario and British Columbia and built her own conflict resolution practice: CenterPoint — Conflict & Collaboration Inc. (<http://www.CenterPointInc.com>) that is dedicated to transforming conflict and building trusting teams.

She has a doctorate degree from the University of British Columbia on legal education, and a master's degree in law from the London School of Economics, specializing in alternative dispute resolution. She has written many articles and six books, including *Corporate Circles* (2006); *One Circle* (2006); *Hiring, Managing and Keeping the Best* (2002); and *Mission Possible* (2003).

About the Contributor

Melinda Renner, B.A., M.L.I.S., S.L.S., has been Public Services / Reference Librarian at the Gerard V. La Forest Law Library of the University of New Brunswick's Faculty of Law since 1998. She has taught the compulsory legal research course at UNB since 1994 and, prior to joining UNB, held positions with Natural Resources Canada and the U.S. State Department. She directed the research, publishing, client training, and library/information management departments at several private-sector companies and non-profit organizations in the U.S. before moving to Canada. She has been very active in law library associations in Canada and the U.S.

Table of Contents

Chapter 8: How to Find and Update Regulations

Chapter 11: Legal Writing

The Legal Research Process   1

The ultimate goal of legal research is to find solutions to legal problems. In simple terms, this means finding relevant statutes and cases, interpreting them, and applying them to a particular situation. There is no single best way to approach a legal problem; however, all research should be approached systematically.

This book provides a basic introduction, framework, and strategy for conducting legal research. It introduces a step-by-step approach to legal research that can be utilized by newcomers to legal research. It teaches all of the skills necessary to complete any research problem from beginning to end by duplicating the entire research process that lawyers use to solve legal problems. It includes instruction on how to analyze legal problems, design a research plan, locate the law, reason legally, and present research results in an understandable way.

The skills taught here are designed to supplement other legal education and should assist students at law school, during professional legal training, and after call to the Bar. This book should be used as a springboard towards development of expert research skills.

Although the process of legal research has, herein, been broken down into distinct steps for purposes of learning, it must be recognized that legal research is complex and will be shaped by the researcher and the individual problem.

This chapter provides an overview of the entire five-step process of legal problem solving. The remaining chapters discuss these steps in more detail.

LEARNING OBJECTIVES

At the end of this chapter you will be able to:

- Describe the five-step process of legal research
- Explain what is meant by factual analysis
- Explain what is meant by issue determination
- Explain what is meant by legal analysis

THE LEGAL RESEARCH PROCESS (FILAC)

All legal research begins with a legal problem and ends with a solution or conclusion about how the law applies to that problem. The complete process of legal research involves tasks that can be translated into the FILAC five-step approach to legal research:

Step 1:   **F**acts — Analyze the facts
Step 2:   **I**ssues — Determine the legal issues
Step 3:   **L**aw — Find the relevant law
Step 4:   **A**nalysis — Analyze the law and apply it to the facts
Step 5:   **C**ommunication — Communicate the results of the research

These five steps overlap and are repeated over and over as a researcher begins to solve a legal problem. For example, a researcher will analyze the facts initially but will continue to hone the facts as the research continues. Each of the steps is revisited periodically as the research evolves.

The following is a brief description of each step.

Step 1: Analyze the facts — Each new legal problem will have aspects to it that are totally foreign to the legal researcher. The first task, therefore, is to make some sense of the problem by gathering the necessary facts and separating the legally relevant facts from the irrelevant ones. This is called factual analysis.

Step 2: Determine the legal issues — After the facts have been analyzed, the next step is to identify the legal issues raised by the facts. This involves determining the legal questions that need to be examined. This is called issue determination and requires reading about the law generally.

Step 3: Find the relevant law — After the legal issues have been identified, the researcher should visit the library, use online resources or the Internet to locate the relevant cases, statutes, and other legal sources. In order to do this, the researcher must have a basic understanding of what the law is and where it is located. The majority of research time is spent at this stage.

Step 4: Analyze the Law and Apply It to the Facts — Analyzing the law involves reading the relevant law, synthesizing it, and applying it to the facts. Some refer to this step as thinking like a lawyer, legal reasoning, or legal analysis.

Step 5: Communicate the Results of the Research — The last step involves communicating the results of the research to the person in need of the research — such as clients, judges or other lawyers. The results must be communicated either orally or in writing and must be understandable, accurate, clear, and concise. This communication usually takes the form of a memorandum of law or an opinion letter.

The researcher should continually review each of the above steps and confirm the results of each as the law and the problem become clearer. Although the research process has been divided into five steps, it must be emphasized that the process is an art as opposed to a science. Researchers should feel free to develop their own techniques in addition to the basics learned here.

In the FILAC model, as with any research model, the researcher must be systematic. Research should never be approached in an *ad hoc* way. Each step should be planned and the results of the search should be recorded, as the research process sometimes extends over weeks or months.

AN EXAMPLE OF THE RESEARCH PROCESS

The following is a simplified example of the five steps of the legal research process.

Fact Pattern

Ms. Safety

Your client, Ms. Safety, is a security guard for a toy store. One night, after carefully checking the store, she inadvertently locked in Sam, a small boy, who was hiding in the building. The boy was found the next day unharmed. The boy's parents, however, are threatening a false imprisonment suit. Ms. Safety claims she had no intention to confine the boy and would like to know if the boy's parents have a basis for their threatened suit.

Facts: The relevant facts are that Ms. Safety inadvertently locked Sam inside a store. His parents suggest that this is false imprisonment.

Issues: After reading about the law you decide that the legal question to be answered is: Was the inadvertent locking of Sam in the store false imprisonment?

Law: You search the law library and electronic materials and find that there are no statutes that describe the law of false imprisonment, but there are a number of cases. You read these cases and synthesize them. See the example below.

Analysis: After reading the relevant cases, a researcher might synthesize this part of the law into a statement something like this:[1]

> To be found guilty of false imprisonment the person imprisoning the other must have been aware of the imprisonment. If there is no intent to imprison there cannot be false imprisonment.

Applying this law to the facts, it is likely that because Ms. Safety was not aware of the boy hiding in the store, she had no intent to imprison and therefore likely cannot be said to have falsely imprisoned Sam.

Communication: You can tell your client that it is unlikely that her inadvertent locking of Sam in the store would be considered to be false imprisonment.

SELF TEST

The following is a self test based on the information provided in this chapter. The answers to these questions, and the answers to all the other self test questions at the end of chapters, are found at the end of the book in the "Answers to Self Tests" section.

1. What is the five-step process of legal research?
2. What is factual analysis?
3. What is issue determination?
4. What is legal analysis?

---

[1] This is only an example and should not be considered an accurate statement of the law.

Factual Analysis

2

The first step in the legal research process is factual analysis. Every research problem begins with a set of facts or circumstances which must be analyzed in order to determine which legal issues need to be researched. The researcher must read the facts and elicit the legally relevant facts prior to entering the library.

Every new legal problem presents new challenges to students and lawyers alike. No two situations are identical and the variety of situations that clients present to lawyers is infinite. As well, many problems involve multiple legal issues that may not be immediately obvious. It is therefore necessary to develop a method by which to break down the facts. This method may then be used on each new legal problem.

This chapter explains what factual analysis is, describes a method of analyzing facts, and provides an example of factual analysis.

LEARNING OBJECTIVES

At the end of this chapter you will be able to:

- Name the three steps of factual analysis
- Describe what PEC stands for
- Identify legally relevant facts
- Formulate or restate facts

WHAT IS FACTUAL ANALYSIS?

Factual analysis is the task of extricating legally relevant facts from the mass of facts in a legal problem. Legally relevant facts are those with the most legal significance or that raise issues of law. These facts dictate the issues of law to be researched.

The relevant facts are those facts that the courts will take into consideration if the case proceeds to trial. Determining which facts are relevant is a judge's first task when deciding a case. Indeed, every written judgment begins with a recitation of relevant facts.

Although it is difficult to determine the legally relevant facts without some knowledge about the law, an initial attempt at sorting relevant facts from irrelevant ones can provide focus and considerably narrow your research.

HOW TO ANALYZE FACTS

Factual analysis involves figuring out the who, what, where, and why of the problem presented; separating the relevant facts from the irrelevant ones; and restating the facts in a concise fashion. There are a number of ways to analyze facts. The method described here is a recommended systematic approach.

Although there is some skill involved in analyzing the facts of a problem, a researcher who is systematic about the process will find that it soon becomes second nature. Usually a first attempt at factual analysis will not be complete. Factual analysis should continue throughout the research process as the legal issues are defined and narrowed. The process necessitates that researchers return to the facts after looking at the law and revise your statement of the facts accordingly.

There are essentially three steps in factual analysis. They are as follows:

Step 1: Gather and organize the facts
Step 2: Identify the legally relevant facts
Step 3: Formulate the facts

The following fact pattern will be used to explain each of these steps.

Fact Pattern

Paul Quint and Melody Jones

Paul Quint and Melody Jones, after ten years of marriage, are getting divorced. They have two children, Lindsay and Wayne, and have agreed that the children will stay with Melody. However, they cannot reach an agreement as to the division of property. They own a house and a boat on Salty Island. In addition, two years ago, Melody was given a $20,000 gift from her grandmother, which she put into a separate bank account in her own name. She wants to know whether the judge will consider the gift to be a family asset when making a decision about the division of property.

Step 1: Gather and Organize the Facts

The first step in factual analysis is simply to determine what happened. This involves gathering facts and putting them in some kind of order. Researchers should select a method of gathering facts that is easy to use but comprehensive.

In law school, fact patterns are often provided to students in exercises or exams. Therefore, students are often not required to gather facts. Gathering facts, however, is an important step in legal research since the particular facts drive the research and determine the outcome.

Gathering facts usually involves speaking to people such as clients, witnesses, and experts. It also includes gathering information from books or reports and collecting physical evidence such as contracts or weapons.

Typically, fact gathering involves answering who, what, where, when, why, and how. Who is involved or affected? What happened — directly or indirectly? Where and when did it happen? Why did the situation arise? How did it occur? At this initial stage there should be little attempt to control the facts, except to enable the researcher to detect gaps or inconsistencies.

One technique that is frequently used to start thinking about facts is brainstorming. This approach simply requires that the reader think of all possible parties, events, and claims regardless of their significance, relevance, or order.

Although there are a number of ways to gather and organize facts,[1] a recommended method is called the PEC method (Parties, Events, and Claims). In every legal problem there are parties, events, and claims. In each problem presented there is a person or persons with a legal problem, events happen which lead up to the problem, and a claim is made by one or several parties. In analyzing facts, researchers should think about every potential party, every possible event, and any claim that comes to mind.

Some of the questions that should be asked under each of these headings are as follows:

Parties

- Who are the people involved in the problem?
- What are the parties' roles or occupations?
- What are the relationships between the parties?
- What are the parties' special characteristics?

Events

- What occurred?
- When did it occur?
- Where did it occur?
- What is the nature of the location where it occurred?
- How did it occur?

---

[1] Two popular methods used for legal problems are called TAPP (Things, Acts, Persons, and Places) and PAPO (Persons, Actions, Places, and Objects). Both TAPP and PAPO provide four-step tools with which researchers can determine what legally significant events happened.

Claims

- What are the parties complaining of?
- What are the parties claiming?
- What are the injuries or harm?
- What will the defence to the claim likely be?

A researcher should be able to state in non-legal terms the answers to the above questions. At this stage it is important to stay open to as many ideas as possible. There is a danger of defining a problem too narrowly, too early, and rushing into the library.

The following are the facts which were gathered and organized in the Paul Quint and Melody Jones situation:

Parties

Paul Quint:	husband of Melody and father of Lindsay and Wayne
Melody Jones:	wife of Paul and mother of Lindsay and Wayne
Lindsay Jones:	daughter of Paul and Melody
Wayne Quint:	son of Paul and Melody
Grandmother:	mother of Melody

Events

Paul and Melody were married ten years ago and are now divorcing and splitting their property. Two years ago, Melody's grandmother gave her $20,000. Melody held the money in a separate bank account.

Claims

Melody: claims that the $20,000 is hers and should not be part of the family assets, which will be divided upon marriage breakdown.

Paul: claims that the $20,000 is part of the family assets and should be included in the assets to be divided upon marriage breakdown.

Step 2: Identify the Legally Relevant Facts

Once you have gathered and organized the facts, it is necessary to identify which of those facts are legally relevant and which of those facts are irrelevant. The law determines which facts are legally relevant so that is what must be looked at. The following is an example of how to identify the relevant facts in Paul and Melody's situation.

We will assume that initial research of the law pertaining to marital property disclosed that there is a provincial statute called the *Family Property Act* (fictitious). This statute applies to all residents of British Columbia and all marriages that are entered into in British Columbia. It describes particular rules for the division of property upon marriage breakdown. Sections 8–10 provide as follows:

s. 8 Upon marriage breakdown each spouse is entitled to a half interest in the family assets.

s. 9 (1) Property owned by one or both spouses and ordinarily used by a spouse or a minor child of either spouse for a family purpose is a family asset.

(2) Without restricting the generality of subsection (1), the definition of family asset includes:

(*a*) money, including inheritances or gifts, obtained while in the marriage;

(*b*) a right of a spouse under an annuity or a pension, home ownership or retirement savings plan; or

(*c*) a right, share or an interest of a spouse in a venture to which money or money's worth was, directly or indirectly, contributed by or on behalf of the other spouse.

s. 10 Where the provisions for division of property between spouses under section 8 would be unfair having regard to:

(*a*) the duration of the marriage;

(*b*) the duration of the period during which the spouses have lived separate and apart;

(*c*) the date when property was acquired or disposed of;

(*d*) the extent to which the property was acquired by one spouse through inheritance or gift;

(*e*) the needs of each spouse to become or remain economically independent and self sufficient; or

(*f*) any other circumstances relating to the acquisition, preservation, maintenance, improvement or use of property or the capacity or liabilities of a spouse,

a court may order that the property covered by section 8 may be divided into shares fixed by the court.

There is only one case which discussed this statute: *Bogman v. Bregman* (B.C.C.A.) (fictitious). In that case Jill Bogman petitioned for a divorce from her husband, Kevin Bregman, and asked the court to make a determination about the division of assets. The court declared that pursuant to s. 8 of the *Family Property Act* a summer cabin, a camper van, and the contents of the matrimonial home were family assets and were divided equally between Jill and Kevin. A question arose as to whether Jill's registered retirement plan was a family asset. Jill acquired the plan through a monetary gift from her mother and kept it in a separate bank account under her name.

The court held that the retirement savings plan was not to be divided equally between Jill and Kevin. Although the savings plan was automatically included within the definition of family assets under s. 9(2)(*b*) of the *Family Property Act*, the fund was a gift from her mother, not used for family purposes, and was kept in a separate bank account. Therefore, the court exercised its jurisdiction under s. 10 of the *Family Property Act*. Although the court considered the fact that the gift had been received ten years prior and was fairly entrenched in the family assets, this factor was not deemed to be as relevant as the other factors in this particular situation.

The following is a brief summary of the statute and case law:[2]

The law provides that upon marriage breakdown "family assets" must be shared equally between the marriage partners. Family assets include gifts, inheritances, and registered retirement savings plans obtained while in the marriage. However, a court may alter this division if the division would be unfair having regard to a number of factors including "the extent to which property was acquired by one spouse through inheritance or gift" pursuant to s. 10(*d*) of the *Family Property Act*.

A case that interpreted this section (*Bogman v. Bregman*) found that in determining whether the inclusion of a gift is unfair and the extent to which the property was acquired by gift the court would look at the following three factors:

- Whether the gift was kept in a separate bank account;
- Whether it was used for family purposes; and
- How long it had been in the hands of the recipient.

For each component of the law there is a matching legally relevant fact in Paul and Melody's situation. For example, the above law states that family assets include gifts. Thus, one legally relevant fact is that Melody received the money as a gift. Also relevant is the amount of time the gift was held. The following schedule helps to differentiate the legally relevant facts from the law.

---

[2]   See Chapter 4 (Introduction to Law and Legal Materials) for an explanation of case law.

The Legal Questions	The Legally Relevant Facts
1. Is the money a "family asset"?	
(a) Was the gift obtained while in the marriage?	(a) Melody received the gift while she and Paul were married.
2. Would the distribution be unfair?	
(a) What was the extent to which the property was acquired by gift?	(a) Melody received the $20,000 from her grandmother.
(*i*) Was it kept in a separate bank account?	(*i*) Melody kept the money in a separate bank account.
(*ii*) Was it used for family purposes?	(*ii*) The money was not used for family purposes.
(*iii*) How long ago was it received?	(*iii*) Melody received the money two years ago.

Since the only legal issue is whether the $20,000 gift will be considered a family asset, only those facts related to the gift are legally relevant. It is likely, therefore, that the house and the boat are not relevant. It is also likely that the children are not legally relevant. Remember that the relevance of these facts may be revised as the law and the legal issues become clearer.

Step 3: Formulate the Facts

Once you have gathered and organized the facts and determined which ones are legally relevant, it is a good idea to restate or reformulate the facts. This restatement must, of course, include all the relevant facts but will also usually include some facts that help to put the situation into context and enable a reader to understand more clearly what happened.

There are no strict rules for formulating the facts. Some prefer to list the facts chronologically, while others prefer to state a critical fact first. The following are examples of two different approaches to restating the facts in the Paul and Melody situation.

Formulated Facts A

Melody and Paul are divorcing. Melody does not want a gift of $20,000 to be included in the division of family assets. She received the gift two years ago from her grandmother and has kept it in a separate bank account in her name since.

Formulated Facts B

Melody received a gift of $20,000 two years ago from her grandmother. She placed it in a bank account separate from her husband's, under her name. Melody is now divorcing her husband, Paul, and is concerned that the $20,000 will be split equally between she and Paul as part of the division of their family property.

Tips on Reformulating Facts

When restating or reformulating the facts, the following tips should be kept in mind:

- *Often "emotional" facts are irrelevant.* For example, the fact that Melody and Paul may have had a traumatic separation is not legally relevant.

- *Try to use objective language.* Avoid using adjectives or descriptive words. These words tend to make the reading more exciting, but, at the same time, indicate subjectivity or bias. For example, it is preferable not to refer to the home as "beautifully decorated". Later, during advocacy, these words may come in handy, but not at this particular stage.

- *Put the facts in an order that is best suited for the reader.* Writers often gravitate to a chronological description, but be conscious of the fact that a reader may prefer a catchy introductory line which talks about the crux of the issue.

- *Draw attention to any missing facts and their relevance.* Clearly state any necessary assumptions in the facts. If, for example, a critical factor in determining the division of family assets was whether the children had sufficient funds, you would need to either find out about the childrens' finances or make an assumption about their financial status.

- *Do not be afraid to include facts that may not be entirely relevant, but that make the facts readable.* Often a first attempt at restating the facts will be too abbreviated. Facts that are too bald are difficult to understand. Although tabulation of the facts is acceptable, it sometimes comes across as being sterile or too cut-and-dried.

SELF TEST

The following is a self test based on the information provided in this chapter. The answers to these questions are found in the back of the book in the "Answers to Self Tests" section.

1. What are the three steps of factual analysis?
2. What does PEC stand for?

SAMPLE EXERCISE

Do a factual analysis for the following fictitious fact pattern.

Fact Pattern

Ravi, May, and Jan

Ravi and May are being sued jointly by the Regal Bank for $30,000, which was misappropriated from the bank by Jan, their law partner. Unsure of their liability, Ravi and May have asked for your opinion as to the likelihood of successfully defending the action in court. The circumstances leading up to the action are as follows:

Jan, Ravi, and May met and became good friends while they were attending law school in the mid-1980s. They talked often about opening a small firm together some day. All three were interested in blending traditional legal practice with other forms of dispute resolution services. Jan in particular developed a keen interest in mediation while she was at law school.

After being called to the Bar, the three friends decided to form a partnership under the name "JMR Legal Services", to practise law in Toronto. Their partnership agreement included the following terms:

...

14. All profits from the law practice will be shared equally among the partners.
15. Any income or profit received by a partner from business activities, investments, or other sources not forming part of the law practice shall belong to that partner separately, and shall not be subject to sharing under paragraph 14.
16. No partner may use the firm name, letterhead, equipment, or facilities for any purpose not connected with the law practice.

...

In the beginning, the partners worked cooperatively to build their fledgling practice. While all three provided legal representation to clients on a variety of matters, Jan also took some cases as a mediator. She had to keep these roles separate, of course, or she could be in breach of the Law Society's conflict of interest rules. That is, Jan could act *either* as the lawyer for one party to a dispute *or* as a mediator between the parties, but not both.

May and Ravi soon got into the habit of referring some of their clients to Jan when they thought a dispute could be handled more fairly or efficiently through mediation, rather than through adversarial legal action. The troubles began when Jan decided that since her mediation services were separate from her traditional law practice, any profits from mediation should be hers alone to keep. In order to make this clear, Jan began to meet with her mediation clients at home, rather than at JMR's offices, and she arranged for separate bookkeeping, banking, and advertising for "Jan's Mediation Services". Jan continued to take legal clients as well, doing this work at the office and sharing any billings with her partners. Although she bent over backwards to keep the two aspects of her practice separate, Jan occasionally asked the secretary who worked at JMR to type correspondence relating to her mediation files as a personal favour.

Ravi and May were surprised and displeased by Jan's move. In their view, the mediation services were integral to the kind of law practice the three of them had envisioned. Indeed, this was one of the main attractions of going into partnership with Jan. Ravi and May wrote a letter of protest to Jan, in which they argued that mediation profits were subject to sharing under the partnership agreement.

All of this suddenly became irrelevant, however, when Jan was charged with several counts of theft, and admitted that she had misappropriated $30,000 from the Regal Bank. The bank had retained her to provide mediation services in a major dispute with one of its corporate depositors, and she was holding the money in the trust account she had opened for Jan's Mediation Services. Upon discovering that Jan had no assets, the bank sued May and Ravi as partners in the JMR firm.

ANSWERS TO EXERCISE

Step 1: Gather and Organize the Facts

Parties

Ravi:	lawyer and partner of May and Jan
May:	lawyer and partner of Ravi and Jan
Jan:	lawyer and partner of May and Ravi
Bank:	client of Jan for mediation services

Events

- Ravi, May, and Jan formed the law partnership of "JMR Legal Services".
- Their partnership agreement stated that all profits from the law practice were to be shared, and the firm's name and facilities were only to be used for activities related to the law practice.
- Ravi and May regularly referred clients requiring mediation work to Jan.
- Jan started "Jan's Mediation Services", set up her own book-keeping, banking, and advertising, met her mediation clients at home, and kept all the profits generated from this work. She occasionally asked the secretary at JMR Legal Services to type correspondence relating to her mediation work.
- Ravi and May wrote a protest letter to Jan stating that the mediation profits should be shared.
- Jan misappropriated $30,000 from the Regal Bank and held the money in a trust account under the name "Jan's Mediation Services".
- The bank sued Ravi and May as partners in JMR Legal Services.

Claims

- Ravi and May: claim that they do not owe the Regal Bank $30,000 since Jan was working outside the partnership.
- The Regal Bank: claims that Ravi and May owe the Regal Bank $30,000 for the fraud of their partner Jan.

Step 2: Identify the Legally Relevant Facts

The Law

Initial research of the law pertaining to legal partnership and liability of partners disclosed that there is a provincial statute called the *Partnership Act* (fictitious). This statute applies to all partnerships entered into in Ontario. It describes particular rules for the liability of partners. Section 12 of the *Partnership Act* states:

> s. 12 Where by any wrongful act or omission of any partner acting in the ordinary course of the business of the firm, or with the authority of his or her co-partners, loss or injury is caused to any person not being a partner in the firm, or any penalty is incurred, the firm is liable for that loss, injury or penalty to the same extent as the partner so acting or omitting to act.

The following two cases interpreted this section of the *Partnership Act*:

Public Trustee v. Morton (Ont. C.A.) (fictitious)

The defendant, Ms. Morton, a solicitor and partner in a law firm, acted as an executor and trustee of an estate. Morton stole money from the estate. In the course of administering the estate, Morton used the staff and facilities of her law firm. Specifically, Morton used a junior solicitor and the firm's staff for the typing and bookkeeping work on the estate. The executor's fees were included in the firm's revenues. The court found the defendant's partners liable for Morton's wrongful acts because she was acting within the ordinary course of the firm's business. The court outlined several *indicia* as possible ways to separate a partner's activities as an executor of an estate from the ordinary course of the firm's business:

> There would probably be an agreement between the partners to that effect, and one might expect to find that the partner would not charge the estate on an account issued in the firm's name, would personally keep any fees and compensation paid, rather than treat them as revenues of the firm, would keep the funds of the estate in an account separate from her firm's trust account, and would keep a set of accounting records from the estate separate from those of his firm. If she wanted to be careful to make it clear that his work as an executor was not part of the firm's business, she would not use the firm letterhead when writing as an executor.

Kozy v. Pierre (S.C.C.) (fictitious)

Mr. Kozy, a solicitor in a law firm, entered into a business agreement with two clients to form a company and serve as one of its directors. When the company went bankrupt he did not contribute his share of the financing, nor did he help his two clients settle the debts. The court, applying the *Partnership Act*, found Kozy's partners liable for Kozy's wrongful acts because he was acting in the ordinary course of the business of the firm. Kozy acted as the solicitor to the company and, by extension, the directors. He also spent several years working for both clients prior to the company's formation. In addition, all meetings of the company's directors were held in Kozy's law offices. Although there were no profits *per se*, the firm benefited by having Mr. Kozy act as a director of such a prestigious company.

Summary of Statute and Case Law

From the statute and these two cases, the factors that indicate when a partner is acting in the ordinary course of business of a law firm are whether:

- There is an agreement excluding the activity from the firm's business;
- The firm's staff (including lawyers, secretaries, and bookkeepers), facilities (including accounts and offices), and name (including letterhead) are used; and
- The profits from the activity are shared.

The law and the corresponding legally relevant facts could be set out in a diagram as below:

The Law	The Legally Relevant Facts
Words in Statute	
Was the partner acting in the ordinary course of business of the firm?	Ravi, Jan, and Mary carried on business in a partnership called JMR Legal Services to provide legal and mediation services.
Factors from Cases	
1. Is there an agreement excluding the activity from the firm's business?	There is a partnership agreement. It does not exclude mediation from JMR's business, but it states that "all profits from the law practice will be shared equally" and "no partners may use the firm name, letterhead, equipment, or facilities for any purpose not connected with the law practice".
2. Did the partner use the firm's staff (including lawyers, secretaries, and bookkeepers), facilities (including accounts and offices), and name (including letterhead)?	Jan "occasionally" asked the secretary who worked at JMR to type correspondence relating to her mediation files "as a personal favour". Jan kept banking and bookkeeping separate and met mediation clients at her home.
3. Were the profits from the activity shared between the partners?	Jan kept her mediation profits to herself but Ravi and Mary disputed this.

Step 3: Formulate the Facts

The following is a restatement of the facts:

Ravi, May, and Jan formed the law partnership of "JMR Legal Services" (JMR) to provide traditional legal and mediation services. Their partnership agreement stated that all profits from the law practice were to be shared, and that the firm's name and facilities were only to be used for activities related to the law practice.

In building their practice, Ravi and May regularly referred clients requiring mediation work to Jan. However, Jan eventually decided that since her mediation work was separate from the traditional law practice, she would keep the profits generated from this work. Consequently, she started "Jan's Mediation Services" (JMS), set up her own bookkeeping, banking, and advertising, and met her mediation clients at home. Although Jan tried to keep the two areas of her practice separate, she occasionally asked the secretary at JMR to type correspondence relating to her mediation work "as a favour". It is assumed that the secretary did not use JMR letterhead.

Viewing the mediation services as integral to the firm's practice, Ravi and May wrote a protest letter to Jan stating that the mediation profits should be shared. However, before this dispute was resolved, Jan was charged with theft for misappropriating $30,000 from the Regal Bank, which had retained Jan to provide mediation services. During the mediation process, Jan had held the money in a trust account under the JMS name. Since Jan had no assets, the bank sued Ravi and May as partners in JMR. It is assumed that there was no previous relationship between Regal Bank and JMR, and that the bank did not know that Jan was a lawyer.

Note that a few assumptions were made, such as the assumption that the secretary did not use JMR letterhead. Note as well that certain important facts were placed in quotations, indicating their importance.

Issue Determination 3

After you have analyzed the facts, you are in a position to determine the legal issues.

Issue determination involves eliciting relevant legal issues from a set of facts. This takes some skill and an understanding of the law. Defining the legal issues is central to the research process. If you are clear about the issues and ask the correct questions your research will be direct and efficient. Time spent at this stage saves significant time later in the research process.

This chapter explains how to identify legal issues, describes how to formulate legal issues, and provides an example of issue determination.

LEARNING OBJECTIVES

At the end of this chapter you will be able to:

- Name the three steps in determining legal issues
- Name a few techniques to help you think about applicable areas of law
- Name two library sources that might help in defining legal issues
- Distinguish between a legal issue and factual issues

HOW TO DETERMINE LEGAL ISSUES

Issue determination involves translating facts into legal issues. The goal of issue determination is to ask yourself: What are the legal questions that must be answered in order to solve this legal problem?

Since researchers are rarely familiar with all areas of law, they must devise an efficient and effective way to determine the legal issues. A recommended way to do this is to think generally about the areas of law that are likely to apply to the facts, read the law generally in relevant areas, and formulate the legal issues.

Step 1: Determine Applicable Areas of Law

There are some techniques that can help get researchers started in thinking about which areas of law might apply to a set of facts. The methods suggested below are: using the subjects of law courses; brainstorming and word association; and using library sources.

Using Subjects of Law Courses

When determining what the legal issues are, researchers are most likely to attempt to fit the facts into a framework with which they are familiar. Some have past experiences with law and recognize a few areas of law (*e.g.*, criminal or family law). Most, however, have limited experience in law courses. For example, first-year law students typically try to fit issues into the framework of one of their first-year law courses (*e.g.*, torts, contracts, property, etc.).

Using the subjects of law courses to define legal issues may be helpful in situations where the problem fits clearly within the subject area. However, there are two problems with this approach. First, law school courses do not cover the ambit of the law. Second, legal problems rarely fit neatly into these particular divisions. It is important to recognize that law courses are divided into particular subjects for teaching purposes. These divisions are not always helpful when analyzing problems with several dimensions. For example, a situation involving divorce may involve issues of property, contract, tax law, and custody, among others. Therefore, if a researcher categorizes the divorce as involving only an issue of property, other areas of the law may be overlooked.

Brainstorming and Word Association

Brainstorming is another way to start thinking about areas of law that might apply. Brainstorming is a process whereby a few people sit in a group and freely share random ideas about the facts and potential legal issues. Brainstorming results in a list of words or phrases that helps describe possible legal issues. This method is particularly helpful if the people involved have a reasonably good understanding of the law.

Word association is a process similar to brainstorming. Word association involves listing words from the facts presented and creatively thinking of synonyms, antonyms, related words, and categories. This method assists in breaking down pre-established frameworks and assumptions, which can be barriers to creative thinking. Word association enables researchers to think of the issues from different perspectives and avoid narrowing the issues too early in the research process.

As a general rule, when determining issues, researchers should work from the general to the specific like an inverted pyramid: think about broader categories of law first, while working towards narrower subcategories of law. The following is the result of an actual brainstorming session:

Brainstorming Scenario

Facts

Mr. Red and Ms. Green had a birthday party for a close friend and served drinks to most of their guests. Later that night, one of the guests who had been drinking drove into a telephone pole and injured a passenger in the vehicle. Are the hosts liable for the injury?

↓

Results of Brainstorming and Word Association

Hosts, guests, liable, property, alcohol, invitations, driving, drinking, consumption, risk, harm, responsibility, torts, duty of care, joint liability, driver's responsibility, negligence, parties, friends, drunk, inebriated, passenger's responsibility, contributory negligence.

Using Library Sources

A final way to think about potentially applicable areas of law is by using sources in the law library. Every book that describes the law has organized it into various compartments. The following are some library sources that have highly developed categorizations of law and are most helpful in determining applicable areas of law. Each of these are called "secondary materials" and are discussed in more detail later in Chapter 6 (How To Find Secondary Materials).

The Canadian Encyclopedic Digest

The Canadian Encyclopedic Digest (CED) is a comprehensive encyclopedia of Canadian law. It is published by Carswell in two formats: in a paper loose-leaf multi-volume set (in most law libraries), and online from Westlawe Carswell. The CED divides Canadian law into approximately 150 different categories, headings, and subheadings. This categorization is displayed in the first few volumes in the print set.

In the online version, it is presented as a table of contents. If you decide to use the electronic version, it is best to simply look at the main headings in the table of contents first, and then the drop down subheadings. Unless you are fairly sure about what you are looking for you may spend a lot of time looking at topics that are not directly on point. It should be pointed out that, some of the CED's categories are not very current so always check the date it was last updated. See Chapter 6 (How To Find Secondary Materials) for illustrations of the CED.

Halsbury's Laws of Canada

This new comprehensive Canadian encyclopedia was introduced in 2006 by LexisNexis Canada. It is based on the widely used legal encyclopedia *Halsbury's Laws of England,* and upon completion will comprise 57 hardbound topical volumes presenting current commentary on the full range of Canadian law. Each volume is authored by a Canadian expert on the topic and is divided into logical divisions and detailed subheadings about each particular topic. At the end of each volume is a detailed subject index, a recommended list of additional secondary sources for further research, and a glossary of relevant terms. At this time, there is no online equivalent to the printed volumes, which are being sold by subscription and issued when completed.

Textbooks

Every law library has a collection of legal textbooks. Very few of these textbooks are available in electronic form yet. These books include summaries of the law in a number of areas. You can find these books by simply searching a library computer catalogue for your particular subject.

Almost all legal textbooks have tables of contents and subject indices. Both provide examples of the ways in which the law is categorized. For example, a textbook on employment law might have one chapter on unionized employees and one chapter on non-unionized employees. By perusing a table of contents or subject index, researchers can gain ideas about the divisions and categories of the law, which will help determine applicable areas of law.

Periodical Indexes

Legal periodical indexes are published to assist researchers in finding journal articles and other legal sources such as book reviews and reports. These indexes list legal journal articles and other legal sources by subject and author. They therefore have extensive subject categories. These subject categories are extremely well-developed divisions of legal concepts. A researcher can go to the library equipped only with a factual analysis and a list of key words and after perusing these indexes have a good idea about the area of law that might apply and how it is categorized. See Chapter 6 (How To Find Secondary Materials) for more information about periodical indexes.

Each of these three secondary sources categorizes the law in very different ways, so it is best to use them in combination. For example, in the Melody and Paul situation in Chapter 2 (Factual Analysis), the issue of division of family assets was labeled in the following ways in the three sources:

- CED: Family Law
- Textbook on Family Law: Proprietary Rights in Matrimonial Property
- Periodical Index: subject headings of Marriage Law or Marital Property

All of these sources are fairly easy to find and, as you will see, are the first sources that you should look at when you begin to look for the law.

Researchers should be careful to keep open minds about potentially applicable areas of law. It is wise to look at as many areas of law as possible to avoid overlooking relevant areas. Do not delve too deeply into the text of the library sources until you have perused a few. Just look at the indexes of each source until you have a better idea about the specific areas of law that may be relevant. Beware of going off on tangents into areas of law that may be irrelevant.

Step 2: Identify the General Legal Issues

Once you have an idea about the general areas of law that might apply, you can read about these areas generally, and identify the legal issues. This means reading a few secondary materials such as textbooks, the CED or journal articles. You can not identify the legal issues without knowing some law.

Although the process of issue determination is ongoing, you should attempt to identify the broader legal issues early in the research process. This will help you focus your research.

Reading about the subject generally will enable you to formulate the general issues and arrange them in a logical pattern, which will form an outline for your research. For example, if you read about family law, you will learn that there are statutes in most provinces that determine how property is divided upon marriage breakdown. These statutes may then form the starting point for your research.

As you read about the law in more depth you will be able to formulate the legal issues.

Try This Example

Jill's Will

Jill died last night and her daughter, Madeline, found a handwritten will under Jill's bed. Madeline has come to you to find out if the will is valid.

Assume that you read about the law generally and found that there is a provincial statute that regulates the making of wills. You find out as well that in order for a will to be effective it must be in writing and must be witnessed. This is described in case law.

> The first question you will likely want to answer is: Is Jill's will valid? This is a broad legal issue. The next question you might ask is: Did Jill's will have all the necessary requirements of a will? More specifically: Is Jill's handwritten, unwitnessed will valid? These last two questions are more focused legal issues which emerge as you read about the law. This focusing of issues is ongoing throughout the research process.

The more you learn about your particular area, the better you become at drafting legal issues.

Step 3: Formulate the Specific Legal Issues

Only after you have a fairly clear idea about the law will you be able to formulate the specific legal issues. A legal issue is a question arising from the facts that demands an answer in law. The following is an example of a well-drafted legal issue based on the Paul and Melody situation (from Chapter 2):

> Will the $20,000 gift that Melody received from her grandmother two years ago, which she kept in a separate bank account in her name, form part of the family assets to be divided upon marriage break-down?

Because each and every situation is different, each situation has a legal question specific to its particular circumstances. Legal issues should, ideally, include enough information to enable a researcher to go into the library and find the answer to the problem.

Factual Issues vs. Legal Issues

Legal issues combine facts and law into questions. The legal issue must be put into the context of the facts. Without some facts, the issue is incomplete.

The object in drafting issues is to include just enough facts to make the question answerable in that particular situation and no other. Sometimes beginners at research confuse factual issues and legal issues. Factual issues demand a factual answer and can be answered without referring to the law. They do not contain questions about the law. The following are examples of factual issues:

- Why did Melody's grandmother give her the money?
- In whose bank account was the money placed?
- Did Paul know about the money?
- When did Jill write the will?
- Was the will signed?
- Did anyone witness the will?

Sub-issues

There may be more than one issue or one large issue and several sub-issues. Sub-issues emerge through the identification of the larger issues. They usually take the form of necessary components of the larger issues. For example, there are two sub-components of every crime: *mens rea* (intent) and *actus reus* (act). These sub-components will often be the sub-issues of the larger issue of whether the accused is guilty of a crime.

Try This Example

Nancy and Steve

Nancy slipped and fell on Steve's icy driveway today and broke her wrist. Steve had been away on a business trip for a week and there had been a major snow fall over the last three days. Steve was too tired last night to shovel the driveway when he got in from the airport and he was hoping it would warm up overnight and the snow would melt.

Summary of the Law

Negligence law provides that every person has a duty to take reasonable care to prevent foreseeable harm. The duty owed by homeowners to the public is that of the reasonable homeowner in a similar situation (*i.e.*, standard of care).

Possible Main Issue

Is Steve liable for Nancy's fall and broken wrist for failing to clear his driveway of snow for three days?

Possible Sub-Issues

1. Did Steve owe a duty of care to Nancy to clear the driveway? Was it reasonably foreseeable that Steve's failure to shovel the driveway would result in Nancy's slip and fall?
2. Did Steve meet the standard of care required of a reasonable homeowner when he failed to shovel the driveway?
3. Did Steve's failure to shovel the driveway cause Nancy's broken wrist?

Often the sub-issues are elements of a cause of action. For example, the three sub-issues above are the three elements you must prove in a negligence action: duty of care, standard of care, and causation. Each sub-issue should be able to stand on its own as a distinct question of law.

Defining the issues sets the stage for the eventual organization required to write the results of research. Often the logic arising from the formulation of the issues is good logic to follow when explaining the law later.

Although defining the legal issues is important, researchers should not become too concerned about the specific wording of the legal issues too early in the research. It is best to err on the side of defining legal issues too broadly. As the research evolves, these issues will become clearer and more defined. It is wise to review the issues periodically to ensure they are complete and accurate. Often this may not be accomplished until the research is near completion.

SELF TEST

The following is a self test based on the information provided in this chapter. The answers to these questions are found at the end of the book in the "Answers to Self Tests" section.

1. List three steps in determining legal issues.
2. Name a few methods that might assist you in thinking about possible areas of law that might apply to legal problems.
3. What library sources might assist you in determining legal issues?
4. Do correctly formulated legal issues include just facts, just law, or a combination of facts and law?
5. Should legal issues be drafted as questions?

SAMPLE EXERCISE

Instructions

Assume you are given the following fact pattern and you know nothing about this area of law. Do a factual analysis; then go through the three steps for determining legal issues and attempt to formulate the legal issues.

Fact Pattern

Homes and Watson

Sherly Homes asked Mr. Watson, a trusted friend, to assist her in purchasing an automobile. She specified the type and price of automobile Mr. Watson was to search for and stipulated that he was to consult her prior to concluding a deal.

A few weeks later, Mr. Watson found a car suitable for Homes. Unfortunately, he forgot to obtain her prior approval of the vehicle and concluded a deal to purchase the automobile by signing the sale papers in her name.

Before Mr. Watson was able to inform Homes of the purchase, the vendor telephoned him and stated the "the deal is off". Mr. Watson

> then advised Homes of the automobile purchase and the vendor's telephone call. Homes approved Watson's purchase of the automobile.
>   Ms. Homes wants to know if she gets to keep the car.

ANSWERS TO EXERCISE

Factual Analysis

The following is a restatement of the facts:

> Sherly Homes asked Mr. Watson to help her buy a car. She specified the type and price of automobile and stipulated that he was to consult her before concluding a deal.
>   A few weeks later Mr. Watson found a car and, before obtaining Ms. Homes' approval, signed the papers of sale in her name. Before Mr. Watson told Ms. Homes of the purchase, the vendor telephoned him and stated the "the deal is off". Mr. Watson then advised Ms. Homes of the automobile purchase and the vendor's telephone call. Ms. Homes approved Mr. Watson's purchase of the automobile.

Issue Determination

Step 1: Think about possible areas of law that might apply.

- *Law Courses* — Two law courses that could potentially be relevant are Contract Law and Property Law. A review of a typical Contract Law course materials indicates that these facts may fall into the categories of offer, acceptance, and ratification.

- *Brainstorming and Word Association* — Some words that might come to mind during a brainstorm are: contract, car, automobile, ratification, offer, acceptance, agent, principal, on behalf of, authority, apparent authority, and ostensible authority.

- *Library Sources* — There are several textbooks on contracts. Some of the indexes of these texts have chapters devoted to offer and acceptance. The *Canadian Encyclopedic Digest* has a section devoted to contract law.

Step 2: Identify the legal issues by reading the law in more depth; read generally at first. The following three cases describe the relevant law in this area.

Monty's Insurance Co. v. McGill (Alta. C.A.) (fictitious)

An employee of the plaintiff insurance company accepted a promissory note as payment for a policy of insurance. He then entered a notation of the policy on the company's record book. The promissory note was subsequently dishonoured, although no attempt to return the note or to change the notation in the book regarding the policy was made. Several months later, the policy-holder's premises were destroyed by fire. The insurance company refused to honour the insurance policy because the employee did not have authority to accept a promissory note as payment for the policy. The court stated:

> For it cannot be doubted that an agent may bind his principal by acts done within the scope of his general and ostensible authority, although those acts may exceed his actual authority as between himself and his principal; the private instructions which limit that authority, and the circumstances that his acts are in excess of it, being unknown to the person with whom he is dealing.

The court held that by accepting the promissory note, the employee acted outside his scope of authority, as promissory notes were not a recognized method of payment for a policy of insurance. Therefore, the employee did not bind the company to a contract of insurance.

Tillman v. Leader (Sask. C.A.) (fictitious)

Mr. Jones, purporting to act as agent for Mr. Tillman (the plaintiff), contracted with Mr. Leader (the defendant) in the name of Mr. Tillman. Mr. Jones was actually contracting on his own behalf and with fraudulent intent. When the defendant discovered the identity of the agent, he refused to complete the contract. Mr. Tillman, however, then ratified the act of Mr. Jones. The court held that the ratification was valid and stated:

> ... we think that the contracts could be validly ratified by the person in whose name they purported to be made, even although they were in fact made without his actual authority, and although the agent had in his mind some fraudulent intent. ... They were, therefore, contracts which not only purported to be made by him, but which he had the means to carry out. ... It is not found that Tillman the principal was guilty of any fraud. If there was such a finding, the question would be altogether different. ...

Bilder v. Lampton (B.C.C.A.) (fictitious)

The defendant, Lampton, made an offer to the agent of the plaintiff, Bilder, which was accepted by the agent, although the agent had no authority to bind his principal to a contract. The defendant subsequently withdrew the offer. The plaintiff then ratified the acceptance made by his agent. The court held that the contract was binding, and that the ratification went to the date of the acceptance. The court stated:

> The rule as to ratification by a principal of acts done by an assumed agent is that the ratification is thrown back to the date of the act done, and that the agent is put in the same position as if he had authority to do the act at the time the act was done by him.

Step 3: Attempt to articulate the legal issues.

The legal issues appear to be:

Issue 1: Did Mr. Watson have authority to bind Ms. Homes to the purchase of the automobile?

Issue 2: Did Ms. Homes' retroactive ratification of the purchase make the contract binding?

Appendix 3A: Summary of Steps of Issue Determination

The following is a summary of the steps of issue determination:

Step 1: Use the following techniques to think about possible areas of law that might apply to the facts:

    a.   Use law school course subjects (*e.g.*, Tort or Contracts);
    b.   Brainstorm or word associate; and
    c.   Use indices from secondary materials such as the *Canadian Encyclopedic Digest, Haslbury's* or textbooks.

Step 2: Identify the general legal issues by reading the law generally in the relevant areas. The *Canadian Encyclopedic Digests, Halsbury's* or textbooks are a good place to start. Also, check relevant subject headings in periodical indexes to locate articles on point.

Step 3: Formulate the specific legal issues. Read the law in more detail and attempt to articulate the legal issues into questions of law and facts. Remember to continually hone the legal issues as you progress in your research.

Introduction to Law and Legal Materials

4

In order to conduct legal research, you must have a basic understanding of what the law is and how it is made. You must also know about other legal resources, sometimes called secondary materials, and their importance to finding and learning about the law.

This chapter provides a basic introduction to legal systems, the law, and the law-making process. It describes both primary sources such as statutes and cases and secondary materials such as journals and textbooks. This chapter also describes what regulations and municipal bylaws are and how they are made.

Chapter 5 (Law Libraries and Electronic Collections of Law) explains how these legal materials are typically organized in law libraries, on CD-ROMs, online and on the Internet.

LEARNING OBJECTIVES

At the end of the chapter you will be able to:

- Explain the difference between civil and common law systems of law
- Understand the relationship between statutes and cases
- Define what is meant by "the Constitution"
- Describe the law making process
- Describe some secondary materials

SYSTEMS OF LAW

An understanding of legal systems and the way that laws are made is critical to legal research. It assists you in recognizing the relationship between legislation and cases and in understanding why and how law is put in written form, published, and categorized.

There are two types of legal systems that prevail in Canada: the civil law system that applies in Quebec and the common law system that applies in all other provinces and territories. In addition, there is an international system of law that governs the relationship between Canada and other countries in the world.

The Civil Law System

The civil law system is based on a complete set of written laws or a civil code. Unlike the common law system, judge-made cases simply interpret that code and need not be treated as precedents. In practise, however, judges informally recognize precedent and, when cases are appealed, higher courts will not forget what they have said in prior cares. Another feature of the civil law system is that the actual cases are inquisitorial as opposed to adversarial. This means that civil law judges play an active role in eliciting information. They are even permitted to call witnesses and order investigations.

The Common Law System

Canada (with the exception of Quebec) inherited a system of "common law" that originated with travelling courts in England. Because there were few written laws in England, English judges developed a system whereby prior decisions from one area of the country were applied to other areas of the country. These decisions were based on the "common custom" as the judges saw it. These decisions slowly became uniform across the country and were referred to as the "common law".

The common law is, therefore, law made by judges and found in decided cases. Each decided case modifies the law slightly as it is applied to a particular set of circumstances; this system of precedents is called case law. By applying prior case law and interpreting statutes, the courts build upon and revise the law. They clarify ambiguities and elaborate upon the intentions of Parliament as they see them.

Another type of case law is found in the decisions of administrative tribunals. In order to better administer the law, governments create administrative bodies. Governments delegate to these bodies the authority to make decisions but not to pass laws. Although these decisions also form part of the law, they have not been fully integrated into the common law. This is partially because administrative law is not made by judges and, therefore, judges are not compelled to follow it as precedent.

International System of Law

Various international laws also affect Canadians and cannot be overlooked in legal research. These laws include international treaties and covenants, which are agreements signed by the Government of Canada and other countries. The government is ultimately bound by these agreements and Canadians are required to act in accordance with them. These treaties and covenants are sometimes interpreted by Canadian courts and administrative bodies.

WHAT IS THE LAW?

There are essentially two types of written law in Canada: case law and legislation. Case law is judge-made law and legislation is government-made law. Cases and legislation form the law in Canada and are called "primary sources".

Case Law

As described above, case law or court decisions are the written decisions of judges and tribunals. Therefore case law consists of cases from all levels of courts from all jurisdictions, from various provincial courts to international tribunals. The next chapter explains how these cases are published and filed in libraries and databases. Chapter 10 (Introduction to Legal Analysis) explains the hierarchy of these cases and how they are interpreted.

Legislation

Legislation is that part of the law that is made by elected members of Parliament. Legislation is made by each level of government: federal, provincial, and municipal. Federal and provincial legislation is usually in the form of statutes and regulations, whereas municipal legislation is manifested as bylaws.

The main products of legislatures are statutes and regulations. The government is constantly introducing or repealing statutes and thereby creating new law. Although statutes are new law, they are often codifications of case law and are created to clarify case law.

Legislation is introduced primarily to create new laws or to clarify or amend case law. There is rarely a legal problem that is not touched in some way by legislation. Although Canada has a common law legal system based on the rule of precedent or decided cases, it seems that, with the increased creation of statutes, Canada is moving towards a more legislative legal system.

Statutes are published by the federal government and each provincial government. These governments also publish research aids such as indexes of statutes, although many of the tools researchers use to locate statutes are published by commercial publishers.

Statute-making Authority

In Canada, the federal government and provincial governments share governing and, therefore, have separate spheres of law-making powers.

This division between federal and provincial powers is described in ss. 91 and 92 of the *Constitution Act, 1867*.[1] Essentially, the provincial governments regulate provincial matters (*e.g.*, education and property) and the federal government regulates matters that extend across Canada (*e.g.*, banking, national defence, and postal services).

There is often overlap between these two spheres and, therefore, legislation affecting certain matters sometimes appears in both federal and provincial laws. For example, there are both federal statutes and provincial statutes dealing with employment and labour law. As a general rule, the federal laws apply to employees in businesses that cross provincial boundaries and provincial laws apply to employees of businesses of a local or provincial nature; however, this distinction is not always clear. A good researcher will look at both federal and provincial statutes to determine what they cover.

It is a good idea to review ss. 91 and 92 periodically to recall the fundamental divisions and the differing law-making powers.

Regulations and Municipal Bylaws

Because the day-to-day administration of statutes can be time consuming, Parliament and the legislative and territorial assemblies often delegates some of their law-making authority to other government bodies. These more detailed laws, which deal with the implementation of statutes, are called regulations or rules and have as much force in law as statutes.

Regulations and municipal bylaws and ordinances are laws created by a delegated authority and are called subordinate or delegated legislation. Elected representatives delegate their law-making power to other authorities who, in turn, make laws on their behalf.

Regulations describe the day-to-day administration of a statute. They "put meat on the bones" of statutes. For example, while the British Columbia *Name Act*[2] sets out the basic law permitting British Columbians to change their names, the regulations under the *Name Act* describe the process involved in changing names and the cost of doing so. Federal regulations are called statutory instruments (SI) or statutory orders and regulations (SOR).

At the present time, there is no one single online source for Canadian municipal bylaws and ordinances. However, many municipalities post bylaws on their websites.

The Constitution

The most important piece of legislation in Canada is the Constitution. The Constitution will almost always have some effect on a legal problem and thus usually plays a role in research.

---

[1] R.S.C. 1985, Appendix II, No. 5.

[2] R.S.B.C. 1996, c. 328.

The Constitution is the highest law in Canada. All other laws must be consistent with the Constitution or they can be struck down and declared invalid by the courts. Section 52 of the *Constitution Act, 1982*[3] states:

> The Constitution of Canada is the supreme law of Canada, and any law that is inconsistent with the provisions of the Constitution is, to the extent of the inconsistency, of no force or effect.

In simple terms the Constitution describes the rules about how a country governs itself. It specifically describes:

* who can make laws (legislative power);
* who will enforce the laws (executive powers); and
* who interprets the laws (judicial powers).

The Constitution also defines the rights and freedoms of Canadians in the *Canadian Charter of Rights and Freedoms* (the *Charter*).[4] Specifically, it restricts governments from interfering with certain basic rights of individuals. Indeed, there are few areas of law that are not affected in some way by the *Charter*. It protects fundamental freedoms (*e.g.*, speech and religion), democratic rights (*e.g.*, voting), mobility rights (*e.g.*, travel), language rights, equality rights, and legal rights (*e.g.*, consulting a lawyer).

The Constitution of Canada originated as a statute of the United Kingdom entitled the *British North America Act, 1867* (*B.N.A. Act*) (see the *Constitution Act, 1867*). This statute includes ss. 91 and 92, which describe the powers of Parliament and the courts. It established Ontario, Quebec, Nova Scotia, and New Brunswick as the first provinces of Canada. The remaining provinces joined Canada afterwards. Because the *B.N.A. Act* was a statute of the United Kingdom, only the United Kingdom could amend it.

In 1982, that statute was patriated. The United Kingdom introduced the *Canada Act 1982* (U.K.) and its schedule, the new *Constitution Act, 1982*. The *Canada Act 1982* renamed the *B.N.A. Act* to the *Constitution Act, 1867* and contains the amending formula. It gives Canadians sole power over their own constitution and includes the *Charter*. The Act also states that the United Kingdom will not pass any laws affecting Canada.

Therefore, the Constitution consists of a number of documents: the *Canada Act 1982* (U.K.), the *Constitution Act, 1982*[5] and the Acts listed in the schedules to the *Constitution Act*. Part I of the *Constitution Act, 1982* is the *Canadian Charter of Rights and Freedoms* and one of the schedules is the *Constitution Act, 1867*. The constitutional documents can be found in the Appendices volume of Revised Statutes of Canada, 1985.

---

[3] R.S.C. 1985, Appendix II, No. 44.
[4] R.S.C. 1985, Appendix II, No. 44, Sched. B.
[5] R.S.C. 1985, Appendix II, No. 44.

The Constitution is important to legal research for two fundamental reasons: it defines the limits of legislative authority and defines the rights and freedoms of Canadian citizens.

Treaties

In Canada, a treaty is formed with one or more other sovereign states by the federal Executive (the Prime Minister).

Treaties are considered primary legal authority. However, unless a treaty's commitments coincide with existing Canadian law, they are not enforceable in Canada until implemented by statute passed by the appropriate legislative body (federal or provincial) in accordance with the division of powers set out in Canada's Constitution. Hence, when a treaty deals with a provincial power, the Executive will seldom ratify it before obtaining the consent of all the provinces.

Treaties are negotiated by delegates of the Prime Minister and reviewed by the Treaty Section of the Department of Foreign Affairs and International Trade (DFAIT) to ensure that they conform both to the principles of international law and to Canadian practices. Since it stems from the royal prerogative, the power of treaty ratification resides with the Executive. It is carried out by an Order in Council issued by the Governor General in Council.

After being signed, treaties are published by the Treaty Section of DFAIT in the *Canada Treaty Series* which has been published since 1928. DFAIT maintains a free, publicly available searchable resource at <http://www. treaty-accord.gc.ca/> that lists titles, signing dates, other details, and the full text of every bilateral and multilateral treaty to which Canada is a signatory. This website advises that it "also maintains a Registry of many non-treaty arrangements or understandings (MOUs) entered into by the Government of Canada, government departments and agencies, and Canadian provinces". Print copies of individual treaties may be purchased from DFAIT, and an annual print volume for each year is also for sale. DFAIT is responsible for maintaining the original copies of treaties.

Like all other states, Canada adheres to Article 102 of the *United Nations Charter*, which requires that Member states register "every treaty and every international agreement" with the UN Secretariat. As a result, all treaties since the coming into force of the *Canadian Charter of Rights and Freedoms* appear in the *United Nations Treaty Series* (U.N.T.S.).

Aboriginal Law

Aboriginal law consists of the *Indian Act*[6] as well as agreements made between First Nations and governments. The *Indian Act* authorizes band

---

[6]   R.S.C. 1985, c. I-5.

councils to make bylaws governing issues on reserves in relation to local matters such as health, traffic control, zoning, building construction and the residence of band members, as well as to levy property taxes, impose business licences, and regulate the use of intoxicants on reserves. General regulations made by the Governor in Council under the *Indian Act* are published in the *Canada Gazette, Part II*. Until 1987, the index to the *Gazette* also listed individual band bylaws, but the texts themselves were not published in the *Gazette*. Band bylaws are generally available from the bands themselves, sometimes on their websites, or copies may be requested from Indian and Northern Affairs Canada.

First Nations that have entered into land claims and self-government agreements are not subject to the *Indian Act* limitations on the authority of band councils. Such agreements, ratified by each First Nation and then enacted as federal and provincial statutes, define the governmental authority of the First Nation and the relationship of its laws to federal and provincial laws. Examples include the *Nisga'a Final Agreement Act*,[7] and the *Nisga'a Final Agreement Act*.[8]

The *First Nations Gazette*, co-produced since 1997 by the Native Law Centre, University of Saskatchewan, and the Indian Taxation Advisory Board, publishes the full texts of reserve property tax bylaws made under the *Indian Act*, s. 83. This gazette also contains texts of some other finance-related bylaws.

The *Canadian Native Law Reporter* (known as *Canadian Native Law Cases* until 1978), also published by the Native Law Centre, is an excellent and fairly comprehensive resource for full texts of judicial decisions involving Canadian native persons and bands. It also contains occasional secondary legal material such as case comments, articles, and other commentary.

In the area of criminal law, courts have used the sentencing provisions of the *Criminal Code*[9] to authorize alternative forms of sentencing for aboriginal persons, under certain conditions. Forms of restorative justice and community service are being implemented by use of band-based sentencing circles.

The Law-making Process

As described above, statutes and cases combine to form the law of Canada. The law-making process looks something like this:

---

[7]   S.C. 2000, c. 7.
[8]   S.B.C. 1999, c. 2.
[9]   R.S.C. 1985, c. C-46.

Friction in society
↓
Pressure on government to change laws
↓
Government discusses issue
↓
Government creates new law
↓
Law is implemented in society
↓
Courts interpret the law through cases
↓
The government considers the courts' interpretation

If friction exists in society, groups or individuals will often pressure the government for change (*e.g.*, through lobbying). The government will often investigate the issue by setting up commissions or committees. If, after an investigation, the government believes that the conflict can be resolved by creating a new law, it will introduce legislation (*e.g.*, a statute). Eventually, that legislation will be implemented in society. If there is a dispute about the law, it can be challenged in court. If the court finds that the new law is inconsistent with existing law, it will make a decision stating this. Courts interpret the legislation. Each case that is decided affects prior cases and legislation. The following fictional example assists in describing the law-making process.

Example of Law-Making Process

In 2005, research was conducted indicating that the taking of vitamin BX7 prolongs life and general happiness. Activists for preventive medicine pressured the Canadian government to introduce legislation making the use of BX7 mandatory. In 2006, the federal government created a Vitamin Commission, which travelled across Canada gathering data and opinions about the use and effect of BX7. The results were astounding. All those people who had taken BX7 were much happier and appeared to live longer. As a result of this investigation, the government passed legislation, the *Vitamin Act*, requiring that all Canadians take BX7 three times a day. The penalty for non-compliance was ten years in prison. An administrative body was set up to enforce the statute.

Mr. Beauregard, a resident of Vancouver, refused to take BX7 and was imprisoned. He hired a lawyer who brought an action in the courts arguing that Mr. Beauregard's rights and freedoms were violated. The court hearing the case agreed with Mr. Beauregard and stated in its decision that the *Vitamin Act* was inconsistent with Mr. Beauregard's constitutional rights and, therefore, was of no effect. When the government of the day heard about the court decision it decided to repeal the law and remove it from the statute books.

It is important to recognize the interplay between legislation and case law. In Canadian law, neither stands alone and research will always involve a search of both types of law.

It is also important to keep in mind the entire legislative process when researching legislation. Since statutes are only the final product of a long process of consultation and debate, researchers should be aware of documents such as reports of government commissions, which can assist in interpreting statutes or understanding the policy reasons for their introduction.

Secondary Materials

Other types of legal materials are sometimes considered to be part of the law. These are called "secondary materials". They are, however, only aids in interpreting and finding the law; they are not the law. Secondary materials include such things as textbooks, encyclopedias and journal articles. They assist legal researchers in two ways: in understanding the law and in locating the law. For example, encyclopedias and textbooks summarize the law and, in doing so, provide references (*i.e.*, citations) to cases and statutes. They are most frequently used at the beginning of the research process, primarily to gain an understanding of a particular area of law. Chapter 6 (How to Find Secondary Materials) describes these in more detail.

SELF TEST

The following is a self test based on the information provided in this chapter. The answers to these questions are found at the end of the book in the "Answers to Self Tests" section.

1. What are the two types of law in Canada?
2. Where does the term "common law" originate?
3. What is legislation?
4. Describe the law-making process.
5. What is the difference between primary sources and secondary materials?

Law Libraries and Electronic Collections of Law 5

The law and legal resources are available in law libraries and online in electronic collections. The paper version is printed and published in books and stored in law libraries. The electronic form is stored in databases and on CD-ROM. All research involves making appropriate use of both paper and electronic resources.

This chapter explains how information is sorted in libraries and electronically and where these legal materials are typically located. It describes the difference between commercial online services and free public websites, as well as their strengths and weaknesses.

Because computers are used as data retrieval devices, researchers must know what information is available electronically, who owns and provides this information, and how this information can be accessed most effectively and efficiently. Researchers must also be able to use the language of electronic searching in order to instruct the computer to find the information. This chapter covers all of these things, focusing on the two key providers of online services in Canada: LexisNexis, which provides Quicklaw (LN/QL), and WestlaweCARSWELL (WLeC). It also introduces researchers to a number of other important Canadian commercial online providers and free public websites.

LEARNING OBJECTIVES

At the end of the chapter you will be able to:

- Describe the "four doors" of access to a law library
- Describe some of the pros and cons of using electronic research
- Name a few companies and free public websites that provide online Canadian legal information services
- Describe the four steps of electronic legal research
- Construct word searches using Boolean logic

LAW LIBRARY BASICS

Whether you are using a law library or an electronic library, you must always ask yourself three questions:

- What information do you need?
- Where is it likely located?
- Where can you find this information most effectively and efficiently?

For example, if you are looking for cases, you will find them in law libraries, online through service providers and on public access websites. You must decide which is the most cost- and time-effective for your particular search. You should be able to answer the first question about what you need after completing the first few chapters of this book. Your choices will likely be cases, statutes, secondary sources, or all of the above. Unless you have a very clear idea about the exact item you need and where it is located, you will begin your search by reading broadly and narrowing your focus as you refine your problem. In order to continue to stay on track you must continually ask yourself the three questions above.

Why Learn about Print-based Sources and Libraries?

Although many beginning researchers think that electronic sources simply replace law libraries, in reality, physical libraries are still necessary for most research. The most important reason to learn library skills is that the databases you have access to may not include a particular resource or you may not have access to the necessary service. As well, some courts are hesitant to accept electronic versions of cases or statutes because there is still a lack of confidence that the electronic version is completely accurate. This reluctance likely will diminish over time.

Another reason to learn the skills of library research is that print-based research is very similar to electronic research. Many of the companies who publish laws and legal materials in print form are also the publishers who provide the information in electronic form. These publishers collect and organize their print and electronic publications in the same manner. They each develop specially designed tools for use in both the law library and for the electronic version. You may also prefer to turn to a library because of cost and time constraints.

Information Sorting Basics

Each law library sorts its books on the shelves in a particular manner and many create their own search tools. At the same time, publishers publish materials in a certain manner and create their own search tools to be used with their own publications.

In most public libraries, books are sorted by topic, author and call number. This makes sense because most people who are looking for books are usually searching for books on a particular subject or by a particular author. Books on a similar subject are placed in proximity to each other to make subject searches easier. In order to sort by subject, librarians use one of several nationally recognized standard systems of classification and each book is assigned a corresponding call number. These call numbers, subjects, authors' names, etc., are placed in a computer database. This database can then be searched in a variety of ways.

Journals and periodicals are usually sorted in libraries simply by the title of the journal. Comprehensive indexes are compiled to assist researchers in locating articles by subject, author, or title of the article. These journals and indexes are available in print and in electronic form.

A law library is simply a storehouse of the law and other sources relating to the law. Like other libraries, law libraries contain books and journals about a variety of subjects written by various authors. Unlike other libraries, law libraries contain the written laws and specialized tools to assist researchers in both finding and interpreting the law. For example, most governments publish lists of statutes to enable researchers to find the citation (location) of the statute and any revisions to statutes by looking at just one resource.

Books and journals are filed in law libraries in much the same way as they are filed in public libraries. Textbooks and other treatises are filed by subject and call number and journals are filed by the title of the journal. To locate a book, you use a computer catalogue and to locate articles in periodicals, you can use the periodical indexes.

However, legal researchers also need to locate the law itself: cases and legislation. The specific research tools for locating legislation and cases are described in later chapters. Cases, statutes and regulations are kept in distinct places in a law library and are not sorted by subject. Tools have been developed to help researchers locate this law.

In a law library there are four access points: one for general materials such as textbooks; one for journals and periodicals; one for cases; and one for legislation. I refer to access points as the "four doors" to the law library. All four doors should be used for comprehensive legal research.

The Four Doors to the Law Library

Door	What You Are Looking For	Where It Is Shelved	How To Find It	Example
1.	Textbooks	By subject and classification number.	Computer catalogue.	Search the law library catalogue by subject, author, title or keywords.
2.	Journal and periodical articles	By the title of the periodical or journal.	Periodical indexes.	Search for a topic in a periodical index in print or online.

Door	What You Are Looking For	Where It Is Shelved	How To Find It	Example
3.	Legislation	By jurisdiction (federal and each province and territory).	The relevant federal, provincial or territorial table of statutes.	Look in the Federal *Table of Public Statutes* under the letter "L" for the Labour Code.
4.	Cases	By the title of the case reporter (*e.g.*, Dominion Law Reports)	Indexes of cases or case digests.	Look in *Case Digests (Cdn. Abridg.)* under your subject to locate digested cases on that topic.

Novice legal researchers will almost always enter the library first through the first door: the library catalogue, which provides access to most general sources.

The door to journal articles is an important one. Articles are usually ahead of books in terms of currency and new areas of the law because of the relative speed with which articles can be published compared to books. Only after gaining a general understanding of the law will a researcher use the two doors leading to the cases and legislation. Since each law library has its own particular filing scheme, it is best to always look at the floor plan of a library before beginning research.

ELECTRONIC COLLECTIONS OF LAW AND LEGAL INFORMATION

Many organizations collect law and other legal information so that other people can use it. Most of these providers have shifted to web-based interfaces and provide access over the Internet.

There are two main types of providers: commercial providers who provide this information online for a fee and not-for-profit providers who provide legal information on their websites.

Commercial Providers

Commercial providers collect and purchase cases, statutes and other legal resources and put them in electronic form in databases, which grow every single day. In the last few years the key providers have merged so that there are only two main online service providers, in competition with each other: Westlaw*e*CARSWELL (WL*e*C) and Quicklaw through LexisNexis (LN/QL). Initially these providers had very different content but this has changed substantially, and as you will see, the content of these commercial providers' databases is very similar. Now the main differences are in the historic information, privately held information like textbooks, and the research tools, citators, search engines, and user supports that make searching easier.

LN/QL and WL*e*C each maintain their own unique legal information systems and provide a variety of services.

LexisNexis/Quicklaw

The first Canadian online legal research service provider was QL Systems Ltd., which later became Quicklaw Inc. The company was purchased by LexisNexis in 2002 and merged with LexisNexis Butterworths Canada Ltd. to form LexisNexis Canada Inc., provider of the Quicklaw™ service as well as Butterworths print products and the LexisNexis® online services. LexisNexis Canada has been expanding Quicklaw by gathering and compiling cases, legislation and other information for legal practitioners since 1973. Quicklaw can be accessed on the Internet at <http://www.lexisnexis.ca>.

Quicklaw provides access to a comprehensive collection of Canadian cases, statutes, regulations, current services and secondary sources. Users can subscribe to additional collections of premium Canadian, international, and news and business content.

LexisNexis Canada initially negotiated contracts with a number of Canadian publishers to obtain information including digests, headnotes and some full texts of cases. As a result, many of the cases in the Quicklaw sources are identical to the published versions in both form and content.

Quicklaw also contains an online citator, *Quick*CITE™, to help researchers update and note up cases. *Quick*CITE provides parallel citations, case histories, citing cases and judicial treatments.

The most important tool for first-time users is the Quicklaw source directory, available as part of the Quicklaw service. By scanning the directory, you can find the particular source that is likely to contain the information you are looking for. Each source contains different content from one point in time to another. Supreme Court of Canada and Ontario court decisions date back to the 1800s, and full-text cases for most other jurisdictions go back more than 30 years.

Summary of Content on Quicklaw

- **Case law:** An extensive collection of Canadian case law, including headnotes and nearly 660,000 full-text cases dating as far back as 1876. Plus 500,000 full-text cases from more than 100 federal and provincial administrative tribunals.
- **Case digests:** More than 900,000 summaries of court and tribunal decisions.
- **Statutes:** Statutes, regulations and court rules updated regularly for all federal, provincial and territorial jurisdictions. Enhanced collections for Canada (English and French), Alberta, British Columbia and Ontario, offering daily updates, comprehensive

bills services, point-in-time searching and 10 years of historical archives.
- **Citators:** *Quick*CITE™ case citator with links to full-text cases and case law summaries.
- **Secondary sources:** Current awareness services including 88 *NetLetters*™ on 40+ legal topics. Over 50 legal treatises, 30 academic law journals, plus legal newsletters and collections of research papers. The *Index to Canadian Legal Literature* with links to law journal articles, plus other legal indexes.
- **Premium collections:** Forms & Precedents, News & Companies, and international legal content.

A sample Quicklaw search can be found in Appendix 5C.

WestlaweCARSWELL

In 2002 Carswell integrated its online service with United States-based Westlaw to produce WestlaweCARSWELL, an online, web-based service. It is an integrated database that provides online access to most Canadian cases, statutes and rules (plus regulations in specialty areas) and provides access to all the United States and other collections on the Westlaw platform. It can be accessed at <http://www.westlawecarswell.com>.

WestlaweCARSWELL contains Canadian case law, statutes, and secondary materials and includes two of the main Canadian legal research tools: the *Canadian Encyclopedic Digest* (CED) and the *Canadian Abridgment,* including the case digests and citator services, that is, the original *Canadian Abridgment, Case Law Digests,* and *Canadian Case Citations.* You will see in Chapter 9 (How to Find and Update Cases) that these two sources are the main tools for case law research in a library. This also enables researchers to search for cases by using the *Canadian Abridgment* subject classification scheme.

WestlaweCARSWELL is organized by subject into seven services:

LawSource	for all lawyers and legal researchers
FamilySource	for family law practitioners
InsolvencySource	for insolvency law practitioners
SecuritiesSource	for securities law practitioners
CriminalSource	for criminal law practitioners
IPSource	for intellectual property practitioners
Litigator	for civil litigation practitioners

As you can see, five services are designed specifically for practitioners in the areas of family law, insolvency law, securities law, criminal law, and intellectual property law. They are very similar to Carswell's CD-ROM products and include all of the information a busy practitioner might need, including books, loose-leaf services, cases, and legislation on a particular subject, all hypertext linked. These services also provide weekly newsletters, published only electronically.

LawSource is an extremely comprehensive collection of Canadian statutes and case law. It includes a case citator (KeyCite*Canada*) to help researchers update and note up cases, statutes and rules. It contains judicial treatments, parallel citations and case histories. The LawSource service also includes the *Canadian Encyclopedic Digest* (CED), journals, law reviews and the *Index to Canadian Legal Literature* (ICLL).

Litigator is a workflow solution for litigators, providing users with online access to a large collection of litigation resources, including: precedent galleries, quantums, expert directory, lawyer directory, profile awards by judge or counsel, practice guides, commentary and current awareness.

Summary of Content on Westlaw*e*CARSWELL

- **Case law:** Over 550,000 full-text Canadian cases with headnotes. The collection, which may be searched globally, or as broken down by jurisdiction, topic or Carswell law report series, provides decisions from all Canadian courts comprehensively since 1986, with coverage of reported cases generally back to 1977 or earlier for key courts or report series. **Litigator** includes several thousand court filings (pleadings, motions and facta) from important cases in selected areas of law.
- **Case digests:** Over 550,000 case law digests in the *Canadian Abridgment Case Law Digests* collection, covering Canadian reported cases since 1803, and unreported cases since 1986, with links to the full text of all decisions on Westlaw*e*CARSWELL.
- **Legislation:** All federal and common law provincial statutes, plus key Quebec legislation; comprehensive rules of practice; comprehensive regulations for specialties; selected regulations for **Law**Source.
- **Citators:** KeyCite*Canada* based on the print version of the *Canadian Abridgment*, *Canadian Case Citations*, *Canadian Statute Citations*, and *Rules Judicially Considered*, linked to cases and legislation.
- **Secondary sources:** The *Canadian Encyclopedic Digest* (CED), *Index to Canadian Legal Literature* (ICLL), law reviews and journals for **Law**Source; treatises, newsletters and other secondary material for specialty areas; rules annotations and practice guides for Litigator.

A sample Westlaw*e*CARSWELL search can be found in Appendix 5D.

Other Commercial Providers

Although Westlaw*e*CARSWELL and LexisNexis/Quicklaw are generally considered to be the main commercial online providers of Canadian legal resources, there are others that have specialized scope and content.

Maritime Law Book Online

For many years, Maritime Law Book (MLB) has published printed collections of cases (or case reporters) such as Nova Scotia Reports and Alberta Reports, along with their National Reporter (covering Supreme Court of Canada and Federal Court of Appeal cases) and Federal Trial Reports. MLB now provides "mirror images" of their printed reporters in online databases available at <http://www.mlb.nb.ca>. These files of cases are searchable by keyword, judge's name, names of parties, year, *etc.*, but the most helpful feature is the MLB "Key Number System" that assigns a specific, unique classification number to all cases pertaining to the same legal issue, regardless of jurisdiction. Through a "key number" search, you can avoid excessive lists of cases that often result from broad keyword searches and quickly retrieve very similar cases exactly on point.

CCH Canadian Online

CCH publishes specialized books, textbooks and loose-leaf practice manuals. Most of the content of these printed resources is now available online by subscription at <http://www.cch.ca/>. The CCH Canadian search portal has four categories: tax accounting, legal, business, and financial. Of most interest to lawyers is the legal online product group which contains a growing number of subject-based sets of materials, including alternative dispute resolution, environment, family, health, real estate, insurance, technology, and securities. A new tracking service, Legislative Pulse, continuously monitors the progress of all federal and provincial bills and is keyword searchable; users can also set up a profile to track only selected bills of interest. The full text of bills at various stages is also provided.

Canadian Human Rights Reporter Online

All decisions published in the printed reporter Canadian Human Rights Reporter (CHRR) from 1980 to the present are available by subscription through <http://www.cdn-hr-reporter.ca>. These full-text decisions originate from Canadian courts and federal and provincial human rights tribunals and boards of inquiry. Associated with the decisions are summaries and keywords, prepared by human rights specialists, that facilitate speedy research. Researchers can search the full text by year, jurisdiction, adjudicator, legislation cited, or keyword. This service includes a citator to note up decisions, as well as lists of pending and in-process cases that help researchers stay current.

Canada Law Book Online

Canada Law Book, a publisher of law texts, loose-leaf services and reports since 1855 (<http://www.canadalawbook.ca>), now provides subscription-based online comprehensive "libraries" in such specialty areas as criminal, patents, labour, and employment law. It also provides searchable online versions of its printed federal and Ontario statute citators, the annual *Martin's Annotated Criminal Code, Dominion Law*

Reports, O'Brien's Encyclopedia of Forms (11th ed.), *Labour Arbitration Cases*, and other titles, including a fully searchable text of Brown & Beatty's treatise, *Canadian Labour Arbitration* (3d ed.). A recent online addition is Criminal Spectrum, which integrates all available CLB loose-leafs, journals, case reporters, and commentaries into one unified searchable service.

SOQUIJ Online

The Société québécoise d'information juridique, headquartered in Montréal, publishes databases containing over 600,000 documents, including summaries and full text of decisions plus other legal publications. It offers the most comprehensive body of Québec case law available online. Its search engine, AZIMUT, allows searching of summaries and full-text decisions in one unified file or via 13 separate subject databases. SOQUIJ also offers an annotated Civil Code of Québec, searchable Québec court records, and seven current online newsletters, the most well-known of which is the weekly Jurisprudence-Express. See <http://www.info.azimut.soquij.qc.ca/info/> for more information.

World Law Reform Collection

The World Law Reform Collection published by Manas Media (<http://www.manasmedia.com>) provides a searchable online index to over 7,500 law reform commission reports and other publications from common-law countries, including those published by Canadian commissions. These secondary sources are very helpful for determining the state of the law at a point in time, or how experts felt it should have been changed. Such reports may be "prescriptive" in recommending needed reforms. For most reports published after 1999, a link to the full text is also provided.

Free Public Providers

The main providers of free legal material on the Internet are governments and law libraries who continually place materials on their websites. However, over the last few years CanLII has established itself as a substantive key website for free access to Canadian law. Here are some of the more popular free access websites.

Government Websites

The federal government and each of the provinces and territories maintain websites with information on both legislation and case law. Statutes and regulations are usually maintained by the provincial Queen's Printers in each province and territory, and bills are maintained by the legislature. Cases, on the other hand, may be made available by the particular federal court or the various provincial courts. Courts vary greatly in the scope and depth of cases they make publicly available.

A list of the government websites that contain legislation is appended to Chapter 7 (How to Find and Update Statutes) and a list of the court websites that contain cases is appended to Chapter 9 (How to Find and Update Cases).

Here are some selected Canadian government websites that are very good for general legal research, including legislation, government reports, and identifying various agencies and departments:

Seneca Guide to Canadian Federal Bills, Statutes and Regulations
<http://dsp-psd.communication.gc.ca/Reference/seneca-e.html>

Guides to Government Information
<http://dsp-psd.pwgsc.gc.ca/Reference/guides-e.html>

Canada: Departments and Agencies
<http://www.canada.gc.ca/depts/major/depind_e.html>

Canadian Depository Services Program E-Collection
<http://dsp-psd.pwgsc.gc.ca/Epubs/epubs-e.html>

Law Libraries

Another source of law is law library websites. This includes every university law school and most provincial court house libraries. Many of these law library websites are open to the public and their catalogues are searchable through the Internet. As well, more and more information is being placed online to help researchers locate law and other law-related resources. Many public sites have simple instructions about how to find information on their site. Here are some of the better law library websites.

ACJNet: Access to Justice Canada
<http://www.acjnet.org>

Bora Laskin Law Library Legal Resources (University of Toronto)
<http://www.law-lib.utoronto.ca/index.htm>

Cornell Legal Information Institute
<http://www.law.cornell.edu>

York University Law Library
<http://library.osgoode.yorku.ca/>

Gerard V. La Forest Law Library (University of New Brunswick)
<http://lawlibrary.unbf.ca/>

University of British Columbia Law Library
<http://www.library.ubc.ca/law/>

University of Toronto's JURIST CANADA site:
<http://jurist.law.utoronto.ca/legalresearch.htm>

LegalTree
<http://www.legaltree.ca>

CanLII

CanLII is a bilingual, web-based, public legal information resource, accessible at <http://www.canlii.org>, that provides very convenient free access to a growing body of Canadian law. CanLII's aim is to support the legal profession in the performance of its duties and to provide the public with permanent open access to the legal heritage of Canada.

Originally designed as a prototype project by University of Montréal Law Professor Daniel Poulin, the public version of CanLII was created in 2001. CanLII is a non-profit independent corporation managed and funded by the Federation of Law Societies of Canada.

Presently, CanLII provides searchable full-text access to virtually all current consolidated Canadian legislation (federal, provincial and territorial statutes and regulations) and to a very significant and growing number of recent cases from all levels of federal, provincial and territorial courts. The service also contains a number of Canadian board and tribunal decisions, and it provides links to the business of Parliament and the provincial and territorial legislative assemblies, such as progress of bills, debates, and other activities, where available.

CanLII is not a "value-added site" in the sense that it only provides links to the law from the originating sources, without editorial additions and enhancements such as headnotes, summaries, key numbers, or indexes. However, there are key terms, automatically generated, that are associated with every decision retrieved. CanLII provides helpful hypertext linking between case law and legislation and the capability to note up case law.

As noted above, the quality and timeliness of the information to which CanLII links depends completely on the originating source of that data, such as the relevant government legislative assembly, Queen's Printer, or court. CanLII's depth and coverage of case law and decisions of tribunals continues to grow but is understandably somewhat behind that of Canadian for-fee legal resources, due to CanLII's youth relative to longer-established systems. At present, CanLII does not contain secondary sources of commentary on the law such as full-text journals, newsletters, or texts.

CanLII is one of a number of web-based free "legal information institutes" from around the world. See Appendix 5B for a complete list.

Tip When Using Free Sources

As electronic access has evolved, more and more information has become available to the public through various providers and various websites. Therefore it is important to be able to determine the relevance and authenticity of the site and the information you are retrieving from the site. As a general rule, you should always evaluate your Internet source by looking at the following:

- The organization or individual who maintains the site;
- The author of the specific information;
- The scope, accuracy and links; and
- The date of the information.

SOME DRAWBACKS TO USING ELECTRONIC RESOURCES

Computers can access significant legal information and can access it faster than a library search. This is because computer databases often contain information that is not available in libraries, and computers are able to search for specific words and phrases in vast quantities of information at very high speeds. However, there are some drawbacks.

1. Information can be incomplete. Often databases only go back to a certain date. When initially loading information into databases, service providers made certain decisions about what information to put into electronic form. In some instances, information only goes back to the 1980s and some very recent information is not yet available.

    Like legal publishers, commercial providers do not necessarily report all information. Such publishers may decide to only publish digests of cases, as opposed to the full text. Some electronic cases do not include summaries or head notes. Other examples of information that may not be found in electronic form are unreported cases, cases from outside Canada, decisions of some administrative tribunals, and statutes from other countries.

2. Information can be inaccurate. Until recently, there was some question about the accuracy of information from computer databases. Until a few years ago, courts lacked confidence in computer versions of cases or statutes and were hesitant to accept them. As the quality of automated reporting increases, courts are more inclined to accept online versions.

3. The ability of the researcher is critical. Computer searches are limited by the skill of the researcher. Since computers search literally, researchers must be well versed in the terminology connected with a problem. Just as in a print search, the results of

research are only as good as the questions asked or the search conducted. For example, if you search all cases on "cars" you may end up wading through thousands of cases and also have missed several that referred only to "automobiles". This is discussed in detail below.

4. Costs can be high. The cost of computer research can be high if researchers are not skilled at computer research. Commercial providers charge either by use or at a flat rate. An hour-long search can cost hundreds of dollars at the hourly rate. In addition to computer costs, the researcher's time is costly, especially if poor search strategies result in excessive time and therefore costs being billed to a client.

ELECTRONIC RESEARCH IN FOUR STEPS

To retrieve electronic information, a researcher must instruct the computer to find that information. This is done by conducting a word search. A researcher asks the computer to search for a word or words or a phrase, often through a template, and the search engine simply scans all of the information in the databases for the words requested. This is called a literal search. It then provides the researcher with the documents containing those words.

There are four steps to any electronic research. (Note: These steps are condensed into a checklist in Appendix 5A.) Here are the questions you will want to ask at each stage:

1. **Plan your research.**

   • What kind of information do you need?
   • Is the information available in electronic form?
   • Could the information be found more efficiently in a library?
   • What are the legal topics or concepts to be researched?
   • How much time and money do you have?

2. **Select a data source (either a commercial online provider or a free public website).**

   • What information you are looking for? (*e.g.*, cases, statutes, *etc.*)
   • Which sources are available for your use? (*e.g.*, online or website)
   • Which source is most effective and most efficient for your situation?

3. **Select a database.**

   • Which database has the information you are looking for?

- Do the databases provide full text, digests, or indexes?
- Which databases include headnotes, summaries, or annotations?

4. Formulate your search.

- What words or phrases do you want the computer to locate?
- How should the words be grouped?
- Do you want to limit the search by dates?
- Do you want to limit the search by other factors such as judge's name, jurisdiction, or level of court?

Step 1: Plan Your Research

Planning is particularly important for electronic research since computers do only as instructed. If a search is conducted in the wrong database or if it is constructed improperly, the results will be wrong. If the problem is defined too narrowly, the information retrieved will be incomplete. If defined too broadly, too much information will be provided.

As with library research, a researcher must narrow down each problem by analyzing the facts and determining the legal issues before heading to the computer.

What Kind of Information Do You Need?

Different types of information are located in different digital libraries or information systems. Therefore, researchers should know in as much detail as possible what they are searching for. A proper search depends on the information needed. For example, cases and statutes can be found through several commercial providers and free public websites. A choice must be made about where and how to search. Some questions to ask are:

- Are you looking for cases, legislation, or secondary materials?
- Is the information needed from a specific jurisdiction? (*e.g.*, Canada, a province, the United States)
- If you are looking for a case, is the case from a specific court? (*e.g.*, Supreme Court of Canada or British Columbia Court of Appeal)
- Is the information from a specific period of time?

Researchers should read generally about the law, particularly in secondary sources (see Chapters 3 and 6) to determine what specific legal materials are needed.

Is the Information Available in Electronic Form?

Not all print information in libraries is available in electronic form. Information is collected and placed in electronic form at the will of the information providers. Researchers must know what information is available and who provides this information before beginning a computer search. Most commercial online providers provide online and/or printed lists of the information that they have in their databases. It is very important to look at these lists to ensure that they have what you want.

Could the Information Be Found More Efficiently in a Library?

Your decision about whether to use the library will usually be based on the amount of time and money you have and how convenient a well-stocked law library is to you. Library searches tend to take more time, especially if the library is at some distance, but electronic searches tend to require more money. This is an important trade-off that researchers must consider.

As a rule of thumb, the more information you have about what you are looking for, the more efficient electronic research will be. For example, if you have the complete citation of a case or statute, it is fairly easy to find the case by going directly to the case or statute databases.

You should not use electronic sources if you were just beginning to learn about a topic. If you try to do a word search of electronic cases without a clear direction, you will sink into the huge number of cases. The other more significant problem is that you will never know what you do not find. Instead, start your research in secondary sources and let them lead you to the best cases on point.

Another advantage of library sources is that they tend to be easier to read and scan than electronic sources. Researchers can quickly view the whole case or statute instead of just one page at a time.

What Are the Topics or Concepts to Be Researched?

A researcher should have a general idea about the law and the particular legal issues raised in a problem before going into the library or using the computer. Although it is easy to conduct a word search on the computer, the computer search is only as good as the researcher's knowledge and skill at using that particular provider's system. Unless you know exactly what you are looking for, it is best to do some print-based research prior to electronic research, in order to narrow down the issues and learn about the proper terminology. This is discussed further below.

Step 2: Select an Information Source

Once you have planned your research you must decide where you are going to look for the information. In the library? Commercial providers? Free public websites? The main question you must ask is: What are you looking for? Is it cases, statutes, books, journals? Then you must ask which sources are available for your use and which are most effective and efficient. For example, if searching for a federal statute, you could look in a library, on a government website or through a commercial provider. Each has its benefits and drawbacks. When looking for the law you could look at any of the following.

Law	Sample sources
Cases	LN/QL, WL*e*C, CanLII, Fed. or Prov. Court websites
Legislation	LN/QL, WL*e*C, CanLII, Fed. or Prov. Gov. websites
Citators	LN/QL, WL*e*C, to some extent CanLII
Case Digests	LN/QL, WL*e*C
Journals	LN/QL, WL*e*C, HeinOnline, other collections of online journals available to you, often through a law society, courthouse or law school library

Which Sources Are Available for Your Use?

Because access to computer information can be expensive, law libraries and law firms do not necessarily subscribe to all of the information available. A decision is often made to only maintain access through one or two commercial online providers. Some of the questions you must ask when deciding where to look for information are:

1. Which sources do you have access to? (*e.g.*, commercial online providers or free websites)
2. What will it cost for each?
3. Is the information you need online for a fee or in a library for free?
4. Do you know exactly what you are looking for?

Which Source Is Most Effective and Most Efficient?

Effectiveness and efficiency are driven by a host of factors, such as your particular problem, your access to the information, and your skill at searching. Never assume that one method is better than others for all purposes. At this stage you must look not just at the financial and time costs. You must also look at the likelihood that your research will be accurate and complete. If, for example, you are not skilled at constructing word searches then you might be better off starting in the library with secondary sources or printed reporters, or perhaps confirming your computer research in print in a library afterwards. At the end of the day you may decide to contact your library and speak to a librarian. Sometimes this approach is most efficient.

Step 3: Select a Database

If you are using a commercial provider or free website that sorts the information into distinct types of databases, then it is fastest to select — from a drop-down list or template — the particular database that is likely to contain what you are looking for. For example, if you are looking for

Alberta Court of Appeal decisions you would want to select the database or template that covers only cases from that jurisdiction and court level. A search through a database containing Ontario case reports would not prove fruitful.

Each commercial provider has its own particular collection of databases. Like the shelves in a library, each database contains different information. Not all the information is in one database. Selecting a database requires an understanding of exactly what each contains. Each service provider provides a comprehensive list of its databases and their contents. These lists are available online and sometimes in print as well.

Some commercial providers allow researchers to combine databases to make research easier. You can customize your combinations to get what you want with fewer searches. You can click on a description of the contents of each database before you enter it or combine it with others, to ensure that you have picked the right file(s) for your research.

Every database includes information relating to specific jurisdictions, topics, and time spans. Although each provider has its own set of databases, there are essentially three types of legal databases for three types of legal information: cases, legislation, and secondary sources.

Databases of cases are in either full text or digest form. They are sometimes organized in a similar way to the print case reports: by court, jurisdiction, and subject. For example, there is a database on LN/QL for the Supreme Court of Canada Judgments that includes only Supreme Court of Canada decisions. The corresponding print case report is called the Supreme Court of Canada Reports (S.C.R.), which includes only Supreme Court of Canada decisions. Statutes and regulations are also available online, in jurisdiction-specific databases.

Step 4: Formulate Your Search

In order to conduct an effective search you must understand the basics of how the information is stored and retrieved and you must also be able to construct a word or phrase search. Here are some basics about searching, online databases and free public websites, as well as some tips basics on constructing word searches.

Commercial Online Provider Search Basics

When you sign on to use a commercial service you will usually gain access through a web browser. On the web-based interface, the first screen you will see, after you enter your password, usually will display or describe the general contents and provide you with a number of choices such as links or templates. Commands can be completed by easy point-and-click options or selecting the appropriate template.

For example, because lawyers often know the citation of the case they are looking for, on the first screen of Quicklaw you have the option to search for a case by citation. Since new interfaces are created regularly to meet the ever-expanding needs of lawyers, always take your time on the first page. It is always a good idea to familiarize yourself with the tools and look at a map of the site to get a sense of what the site includes. The first step usually involves selecting a database; therefore you must know what information is included in each and most systems search words on the basis of Boolean logic. This means that the computer simply searches for words in different permutations and combinations, explained further in the section below on constructing searches.

Internet Search Basics

Because of the huge amount of information available through the Internet and the increasing capacity of search engines it would be impossible to describe a generic way to conduct an Internet search. For legal research, the best method is to go to a legal site you know, such as those mentioned in this book. The best law sites are those maintained by legal experts or librarians who have selected and sorted legal information in meaningful ways.

In most cases, you can begin with a legal website and use their hyperlinks and list of resources to access other sources of information. The only step you may ever need to think about is which site to go to first. This site will lead to a chain of other sites.

If you decide to conduct a general Internet search, keep in mind some of the limitations of search engines and directories. Although search engines, spiders, or crawlers search through massive amounts of data to locate specific information, they may either be searching the tags on a site or the contents of a specific website.

As well, although they are a very fast way to find information, your search may only be searching through their index — not all that is available on the Internet. Even the biggest search engines only index part of the Internet's public domain. However, they scan sites periodically to update their indexes. Also, all of the search engines use Boolean logic. It uses operators such as AND, OR, and NOT to refine your search. If you do not include Boolean operators the engine will still use Boolean operators automatically. For example, most search engines will interpret the words "mutual funds" as a search for the words mutual AND funds. In other words, it defaults to AND. Therefore is best to use operators when conducting a search.

The main drawback of search engines is that they locate *too much* unsorted information. Another drawback is that they usually do not search inside files or documents such as PDF (Adobe) or proprietary information.

How to Construct a Word Search

The success of your electronic search depends entirely on your ability to construct a proper search. As mentioned above, this in turn depends on your understanding about what the search engine is doing with your request and what information it is searching through.

You must articulate your search in a way that a computer will understand. The skill is in identifying words, concepts, or phrases from a legal problem and arranging them in a way that will direct the computer to the specific information you need. Therefore, like manual research, it is necessary to analyze the facts and determine the legal issues before beginning a search — not only to gain an understanding of the subject matter and determine what information you need, but also to learn the proper terminology. Because computer searches are conducted through words or phrases, a researcher must select words or phrases that best reflect the legal problem.

Although most service providers have templates, these are only as effective as what you place in the correct template.

What Are You Looking For?

The formulation of the search depends on what you are looking for. Careful thought goes into constructing a search. Sometimes it is helpful to think of the document you wish to retrieve. For example, you may imagine a superior court case involving a child who was hit by a train within a municipality where a provincial statute dealing with public land is in effect. Although more search engines are becoming able to understand natural language, some still require that the researcher translate a request into words or phrases found in the databases.

This request is called a query or search. The skill in formulating a search is in arranging the words or phrases in a particular way so that the search will be broad enough to include all relevant information and narrow enough to exclude irrelevant information.

Although most commercial providers and free legal resources have now developed templates to assist in the construction of queries, you will constantly be surprised by what turns up from a search that you thought was very straightforward. Individual commands vary from system to system, but there are also many similarities. Essentially, a search will be either for a single word, alternate words, or multiple words.

Searching for a Single Word

A single word search involves asking a computer to search for a single specific word within a database. Because computers will only search for the exact word requested, if a word is spelled incorrectly, the computer will search for that misspelled word. Consequently, a researcher should be careful of the following:

- Is the word singular or plural?
- Could the word have different prefixes or suffixes?
- Could the word contain a hyphen, parentheses, or other punctuation?

Search engines have remedies specifically designed to combat these potential problems. Many computer systems automatically search for the plural of each word selected. If not, most have a "wild card" or universal character command that instructs the computer to search for *any* letters where a wild card is placed in a query. In many systems the wild card is an asterisk (*) or an exclamation point (!). So, since practice can be spelled two ways — with a "c" or an "s" — a single word search might look like this: practi*e.

Most search engines also allow for the "truncation" of a word. Truncation is a technique used to search for words with the same root. For example, employment, employee, employed all have the same root: employ. In many systems an exclamation mark (!) placed at the end of the word directs a computer to search all words with that root. Therefore, a search for employ! would retrieve sources that include words such as employee, employees, employment and employer. Some systems also handle plurals by retrieving both the singular and plural forms of any searched word.

Searching for Alternate Words

Usually searches will involve words that can be expressed in more than one way (*e.g.,* "car" or "automobile"). Your search depends on selecting the right alternatives or synonyms for that word.

Multiple Word Search

In order not to retrieve too much information, researchers can control or limit searches by combining several words together or doing multiple word searches.

For example, a search for cases with the word "doctor" in them would result in a phenomenal number of cases, whereas a search for cases with the words "doctor" and "cancer" would result in fewer cases being selected. Multiple-word searches involve the use of "connectors" or "proximity indicators".

Connectors

In multiple-word searches, connectors are used between each word. The connectors used are "or", "and", and occasionally "but not". They are linked to the software's system of logic, which is called Boolean logic, described below. This is a system which defines the relationship between concepts by symbols. The example provided is a search for cases dealing with wife assault.

Illustration 5.1
A Picture Description of Boolean Logic

Picture Description	What You Type	Connector
◉◉	wife assault	OR
Alternatively,	Wife assault	May be read as a phrase
◑○	wife AND assault	AND
◉○	wife % assault	BUT NOT
○○	Wife NEAR assault	NEAR

Although computers have language that describes each of these scenarios, often the words "or", "and", and "but not" are used for this purpose. Some systems make "or" implicit. For example, in one system the word "dog" immediately next to the word "food" would be read the same as "dog" or "food", while in another system, the words "dog food", side by side, would be read as the phrase "dog food". It is imperative that a searcher understand the subtle differences in these arrangements. Usually, the service provides tips or hints directly on the search screen that will help you. Also, consult the online or printed user's guide that is available.

The following describes the three connectors seen in the illustration:

- "Or" searches for "wife" *or* "assault". It locates all cases containing either the word "wife" or all cases including the word "assault". Alternatively, some systems will locate all instances of the phrase "wife assault".
- "And" searches for "wife" *and* "assault". It locates cases containing both the word "wife" and the word "assault".
- "But not" (often represented by a per cent sign) searches for "wife" but not "assault". It locates cases containing the word "wife" but not the word "assault". Caution should be used with "but not" since it is nearly impossible to think of all the situations that you do not want. In this case, perhaps a better search would be just the word "wife".
- "Near" locates words within a certain proximity of each other. Usually it is interpreted to be within eight to ten words of each other.

Proximity Indicators

Other connectors placed between words will limit a search even further. Being specific with your searching can yield great success. Researchers can search for specific phrases or for words that are part of a sentence or paragraph. By placing "proximity indicators" between words, researchers can request those cases where a word is found within a certain distance of another word. These searches involve searching for one word and another word within a certain number of words or within the same paragraph of that word. The following are some examples of proximity indicators.

Request	Boolean Search
Within the same paragraph	wife /p assault
Within the same sentence	Wife /s assault
Within one word of another word	wife /1 assault
Within a certain number of words (*e.g.*, five) of another word	wife /5 assault
Within a certain number of words and in a particular order (*e.g.*, appears within the following three words)	wife +3 assault
A phrase	"wife assault" or
(remember that some systems automatically retrieve two adjacent words as a phrase, without using "quotation marks")	wife assault

Field Search

Searches can also be narrowed down to a specific location with a document. For example, by using either Boolean logic or a dedicated search box within a template, researchers can direct a computer to restrict a search to a particular part of a case such as the names of one or more parties or the name of the court. This saves time.

Cases are stored in databases in much the same format as they appear in the published hard copy in the case reports. Each segment of the reported case is searchable in Boolean logic or in a dedicated search box, and each field is coded for purposes of searching. One field may contain the "style of cause". So if a researcher is searching for a case by the names of the parties in the action, it would be most efficient to search only that particular field or template search box for this information, rather than to search the entire text of all decisions.

Ranking

Computers allow you to ask that your results be displayed in a particular order. A "rank method" determines the order in which your retrieved information will appear. Most information systems automatically call up the most relevant documents first. These are those documents that contain the most occurrences of your search term. This ranking is based on the assumption that those documents with the most occurrences of the search term will be most useful. You can choose chronological rank (in order by date) or statistical rank (with the most occurrences of the term searched). The four choices are essentially as follows:

- Chronological: Oldest document first
- Reverse Chronological: Most recent document first
- Statistical: Most occurrences of term first, oldest documents first if equal occurrences
- Statistical: Most occurrences of term first, most recent documents first if equal occurrences

Many systems default to the last method for cases: most occurrences and most recent cases first.

Save, Print, or e-Mail Results

After completing the search, a researcher may wish to save the results. Most databases have commands that enable you to print the results of your search or save them by downloading them.

The specific procedure or commands for downloading information will vary with each company and the capabilities of your computer printer. Be careful when printing, since often what you see is not exactly what will appear in print. It is best to use a print preview function if available. Virtually all research systems allow you to e-mail your results, either a listing of them or the full text of all or selected documents.

SELF TEST

The following is a self test based on the information provided in this chapter. The answers to these questions are found at the end of the book in the "Answers to Self Tests" section.

1. Describe the "four doors" to the law library.
2. List two benefits and three limitations of using computers to assist research.
3. Name two or more online legal research service providers in Canada.
4. Describe the steps of electronic legal research.
5. Describe what is meant by a "literal" search.

Appendix 5A: Summary of Steps in Electronic Legal Research

There are four stages to any electronic research. Here are the questions you will want to ask at each stage:

1. **Plan your research.**

   - What kind of information do you need?
   - Is the information available in electronic form?
   - Could the information be found more efficiently in a library?
   - What are the legal topics or concepts to be researched?
   - How much time and money do you have?

2. **Select a data source (either a commercial provider or free public website).**

   - What information are you looking for? (*e.g.*, cases, statutes, *etc.*)
   - Which sources are available for your use? (*e.g.*, online or website)
   - Which source is most effective and most efficient for your situation?

3. **Select a database.**

   - Which database has the information you are looking for?
   - Do the databases provide full text, digests, or indexes?
   - Which databases include headnotes, summaries, or annotations?

4. **Formulate your search.**

   - What words or phrases do you want the computer to locate?
   - How should the words be grouped?
   - Do you want to limit the search by dates?
   - Do you want to limit your search by other factors such as judge's name, jurisdiction, or level of court?

Appendix 5B: Helpful Sources for Foreign Law

Although this book does not address foreign law, it is sometimes helpful for researchers to have online links to basic foreign resources, in the event that Canadian law does not address a legal subject adequately. This is especially true in certain emerging areas of the law that foreign jurisdictions may already have begun to examine.

Here are some respected free websites that will give you starting points. These will lead you to other useful sites — mostly official but some from commercial providers — in the countries and regions listed.

Website Name and Jurisdiction	
AsianLII – Asia excluding Australia and New Zealand	<http://www.asianlii.org/>
AustLII – Australia and New Zealand	<http://www.austlii.edu.au/>
BaiLII – Great Britain and Ireland	<http://www.bailii.org/>
CommonLII – a combination of a number of Commonwealth countries including African nations	<http://www.commonlii.org/>
CyLaw – Cyprus	<http://www.cylaw.org/>
Droit francophone – a combination of French-speaking countries	<http://droit.francophonie.org/>df-web/>
HKLII – Hong Kong	<http://www.hklii.org/>
ITTIG – Italy	<http://www.ittig.cnr.it/>
JuriBurkina – Burkina Faso	<http://www.juriburkina.org/>
LII – United States	<http://www.law.cornell.edu/>
NZLII – New Zealand	<http://www.nzlii.org/>
	<http://www.paclii.org/>

PacLII – Pacific Islands	<http://www.saflii.org/>
SafLII – Southern Africa	<http://www.worldlii.org/>
WorldLII – leads to many sites worldwide that do not fit into the above categories. Links to the laws of many individual countries not covered above are also provided.	

Appendix 5C: A Sample Quicklaw Search

Step 1: To sign in, open your Internet browser and go to the new Quicklaw sign-in page at <http://www.lexisnexis.com/ca/legal>. Enter your user ID and Password, and then click the Sign In button.

Step 2: If you know the name of the case or statute you are looking for, the **Find a Document** feature provides a variety of options, such as finding a case by name or citation, noting up a case, or finding legislation and journal articles. To find a document, select one of the tasks from the drop-down list, enter your information, and then click the Go button.

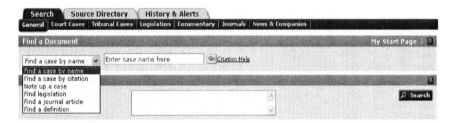

When searching by name, you can enter a single word or phrase, an exact case name, or a Boolean search string.

Step 3: The **General Search** form is useful for general searching across a broad collection, performing a general query, or searching within an unfamiliar area of law or across multiple content types.

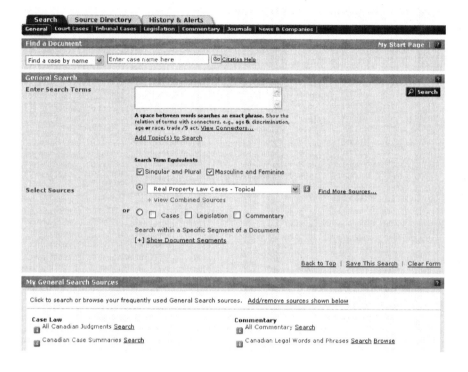

- Enter your search terms in the box provided. Include connectors and other special characters to link terms and phrases, and to search for word variations. Leaving a space between your terms searches an exact phrase.
- Select a source from the drop-down list or check one or more of the broader category boxes below, such as Cases, which retrieves all court and tribunal decisions.
- Click the Search button.

Step 4: Add topics to search within a topical subset of documents. For example, you may enter your search on the **General Search** form, select the **Cases** box, and then click the **Add Topic(s) to Search** link to add index terms to your search. This will restrict your results to a certain area of law such as labour or criminal law. You can also select sub-categories of areas of law.

To improve your results, select LexisNexis® Quicklaw Index Terms to add to your search.

Lookup Options ○ Find ● Hierarchy ○ Alphabet

⊞ ☐ Company Law & Business Entities
⊞ ☐ Competition Law
⊞ ☐ Conflict of Laws
⊞ ☐ Constitutional Law
⊞ ☐ Construction Law
⊞ ☐ Consumer Law
⊞ ☐ Contract & Obligations
⊟ ☐ Criminal Law & Disposition of Offenders
　　☐ Compensation
　　☐ Controlled Drugs & Substances
　　☐ Custodial Institutions & Service of Sentence
　　☐ Financial & Business Offences
　　☐ General Principles of Criminal Liability
　　☑ **Motor Vehicle & Highway Traffic Offences**
　　☐ Offences against Property
　　☐ Offences against the Person
　　☐ Public Order & Administration of Justice Offences
　　☑ **Sentencing Powers & General Principles of Sentencing**
　　☐ Sexual & Public Morals Offences
⊞ ☐ Criminal Procedure
⊞ ☐ Education Law
⊞ ☐ Employment & Labour Law
⊞ ☐ Environmental Law
⊞ ☐ Equity & Trusts

☑ View Selected   → OK - Add to Search   ✕ Cancel

Step 5: You can limit your search by using the category tabs on the **Search** page.

Content-specific search forms are intended for searching within a specific content type. For example, the Court Cases search form searches within common law, civil law, and international court cases only and allows you to search specific segments of a document, such as the Case Name, Judge Name, or Date.

Step 6: Limit your search by date, or select a predefined timeframe. Select a date parameter from the drop-down list provided and enter your date restrictions.

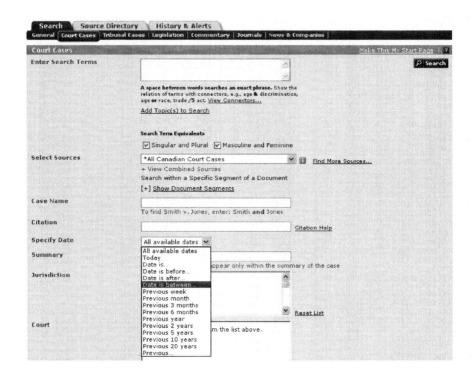

Step 7: Choose the specific sources you would like to search. Click the **Source Directory** tab from any page or click the **Find More Sources** link from the search form to locate sources available to you.

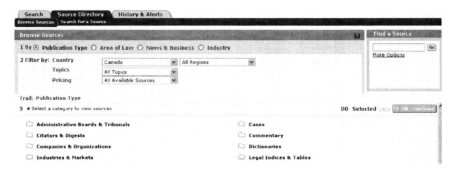

- Use the **Browse Sources** sub-tab to explore the broad **Source Directory**.
- View sources by Publication Type, Area of Law, News & Business, or Industry.
- Filter sources by Country (and Region where applicable), Topics, or Pricing, if desired.

- Click a **folder** icon or an accompanying link to view a category's sources.
- Select a source from the list and click the OK — Continue button, or
- Use the Search for a Source sub-tab when you know the name of the specific source you want to search.

Once you have selected a source, you will be brought to the appropriate search form to search this source. This source will be listed in your drop-down menu as a recently accessed source, and can be saved as a favourite.

Step 8: In addition to searching sources, certain sources such as legislation and secondary material may be browseable. To browse a source, select it from the drop-down menu, then click the **Browse** sub-tab.

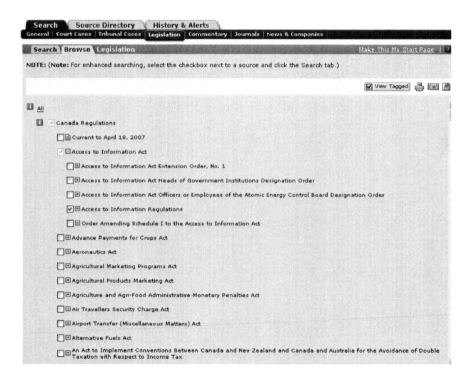

Alternatively, you may click the **Browse** link beside the source name when you find it in the **Source Directory**.

Step 9: The **Results** page displays your search results and includes features that allow you to select viewing options and sort, filter, or narrow your search.

- **View** — view your results in different levels of detail (*e.g.*, List, List with Keywords, and Search Terms in Context).
- **Sort** — change the order in which your results are displayed according to Jurisdiction, Court, and Relevance.
- **Result Groups** — filter displayed results (*e.g.*, view results by Source, Source Type, Court, Jurisdiction, or Topic).
- **Narrow Search** — search within existing results for a word, phrase, or new search string.
- **Next Steps** — modify your search, create a new search, save your search, or create an alert.

Step 10: Click the **Create Alert** icon and complete the form to schedule your search to run automatically. Alerts can be set up to e-mail documents directly to you when the search runs.

Quicklaw automatically saves your recent activity under the **History & Alerts tab**.

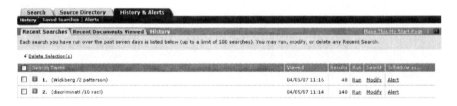

- **History** — displays your recent searches for up to seven days and recently viewed documents for up to 48 hours (up to a maximum of 100 searches/documents), and allows you to redisplay these documents or revisit the search results.
- **Saved Searches** — displays a list of your previously saved search strings.
- **Alerts** — displays a list of your scheduled searches or legal updates. Legal updates allow you to keep up to date with new case law within an area of law and jurisdiction.

To set up a Legal Update, click the **Legal Update Wizard** link on the **Legal Updates** form and follow the step-by-step process. To set up a scheduled search, click the **Create Alert** link on the **Results** page.

Step 11: A QuickCITE record can be retrieved via **Find a Document** or by clicking the **Note up with QuickCITE** link or citator symbol from the full text of a decision.

The **QuickCITE case citator** contains case information such as parallel citations, case history, lists of subsequent citing cases, and the judicial treatments in those citing cases.

Step 12: To find cases that have considered particular statutes, select a case law source that is likely to contain cases that consider the statute. For example, to search for cases that judicially consider an Ontario statute, select the source Ontario Judgments; to search for cases that judicially consider a federal statute, select a national coverage source such as All Canadian Judgments. Enter the title of the Act. You may wish to include acronyms (*e.g.*, Canada Business Corporations Act OR CBCA). If you use a section number as one of your search terms, use a proximity connector of at least /20 between the title of the Act and the section number (*e.g.*, Canada Business Corporations Act OR CBCA /20 143).

Step 13: Select, or tag, documents in your results for delivery or viewing.

- Select the checkbox at the top of the results list to tag all the documents, or
- Select the checkbox next to a document title to tag individual documents.
- Click the print, e-mail, or download icon to select a delivery method. A new window will open allowing you to modify relevant options.

Appendix 5D: A Sample WestlaweCARSWELL Search

Step 1: Obtain a password from Carswell and then go to the WestlaweCARSWELL webpage (<http://www.westlawecarswell.com>) to access the LawSource service.

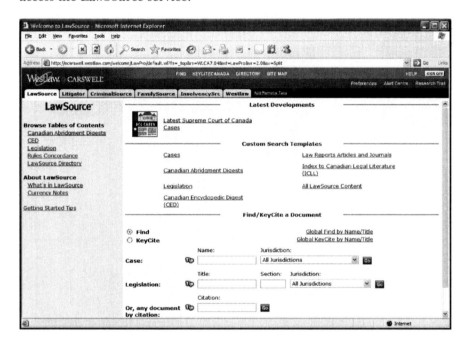

The left-hand column (in grey) allows you to browse various tables of contents (**Browse Tables of Contents**). This is to help those who know very little about a topic and want to find search words. The column also provides information about this LawSource product.

Before conducting a search it is good practice to find out what is contained in LawSource by going to **About LawSource** and clicking on the **What's in LawSource** link on the left frame.

You can click on **Currency Notes** to determine the currency of any information resources contained in LawSource.

Once you have checked these features, close the **What's In** page to return to the home page.

As you can see, the middle section of the home page prompts you to select from the following options:

- **Latest Developments** — If you are looking for recent Supreme Court of Canada Cases
- **Custom Search Templates** — If you wish to search one of the seven databases
- **Find/KeyCite a Document** — If you want to **Find** any case or piece of legislation either by name or by citation OR if you want to **Note up** (**KeyCite**) any case, statute, or rule

Step 2: If you know the name of your case or statute go to the Home Page and select **Find** or **KeyCite** (note-up) at the lower portion of the right-hand side. You can search by name or by citation.

Find/KeyCite a Document

◉ Find   Global Find by Name/Title
○ KeyCite   Global KeyCite by Name/Title

                                Name: Jurisdiction:
Case: 🛈   [   ]   [All Jurisdictions   ▾] GO

                                Title: Section: Jurisdiction:
Legislation: 🛈   [   ]   [   ] [All Jurisdictions ▾] GO

                                Citation:
Or, any document by citation: 🛈 [   ] GO

To search by name:

- Select either **Find** or **KeyCite** as appropriate.
- Enter all or part of the name of the case or statute in the box provided. Note that all statutes and rules of court from all Canadian jurisdictions are included, but only about 1,600 of the most frequently sought regulations are included, again from all jurisdictions.
- For legislation only, you may wish to enter the section number in the box provided, or you can leave that box blank so that the search retrieves all sections of the Act (**FIND**) or retrieves cases that have considered all sections of the Act. Sometimes it is better to get more on the first try and then narrow your search.
- Choose a jurisdiction to help you narrow down your results.
- Click GO.

To search by citation:

- Select either **Find** or **KeyCite** as appropriate.
- Enter the full citation of the case or legislative provision in the box provided.
- Click GO.

Step 3: If you do not know the name of the case or statute you are looking for, go to **Custom Search Templates** and conduct a search of one of the following databases:

- **Cases:** If you want to search full-text cases.
- **Canadian Encyclopedic Digest (CED):** If you want to search statements of the law on any issue.
- **Canadian Abridgment Digests:** If you want to search case digests (summaries).
- **Law Reports Articles and Journals:** If you want to search for case comments in Carswell law reports or for articles in law reviews and journals (in both Carswell journals and law reviews produced by others).
- **Legislation:** If you want to search Canadian statutes, rules of practice and selected frequently consulted regulations.
- **Index to Canadian Legal Literature (ICLL):** If you want to search Carswell's periodical index of Canadian legal literature.
- **All LawSource Content:** If you want to search across all information on the LawSource service.

The following screen appears when you select **Cases**.

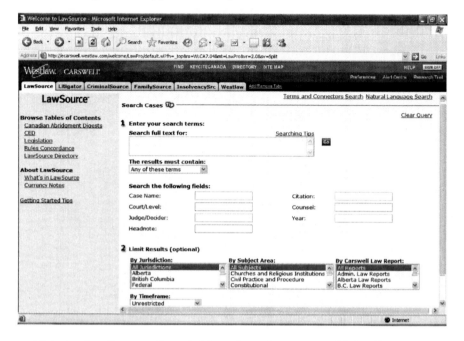

This is the Custom Search Template for cases, which allows you to enter terms to be searched, and fill in boxes or use pulldown menus to search within particular fields. You can also search using Boolean logic and natural language by linking through **Terms and Connectors Search** or **Natural Language Search** at the top right-hand side of the screen. Natural Language searching is helpful when you are having difficulty formulating a precise search. You merely need to frame your search in the form of a question or a statement and the search engine will interpret it.

As you can see above, you simply enter your search terms in the box. The drop-down box allows you to specify whether you want to retrieve documents that contain any of the terms you have entered, contain all of the terms, contain the terms as a phrase, or contain the terms in proximity.

You can then limit your search by field (*e.g.*, Case Name, Court/Level, *etc.*) by placing in the blanks what you know about your case.

By filling in part 2 you can limit your search further by restricting it to one or more Jurisdictions, Subject Areas, or Carswell Law Reports.

Once you have done your search, you can view any document your search has retrieved in the right frame while a list of your search results is shown to the left:

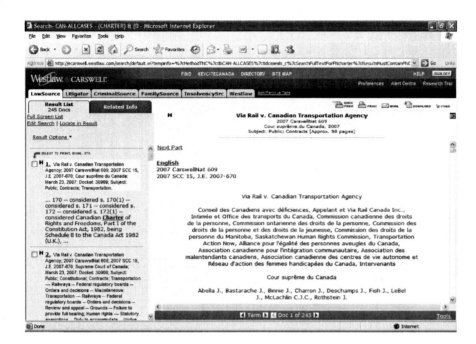

You may also wish to just display a listing of all your results in one frame, for ease of reading or to print out the complete list. To do this, click on **Full Screen List** at the very top of the left-hand panel.

From this page you can do any of the following:

- Modify your search or begin a new one (click the **Edit Search** link).
- Refine your search results (click the **Locate in Result** link).
- Have your search results automatically rerun and receive notification of new results (click on the Result Options pulldown menu, then select the Add Search to **WestClip** option).

From the full-text decision you may also select the Related Info tab in the left pane:

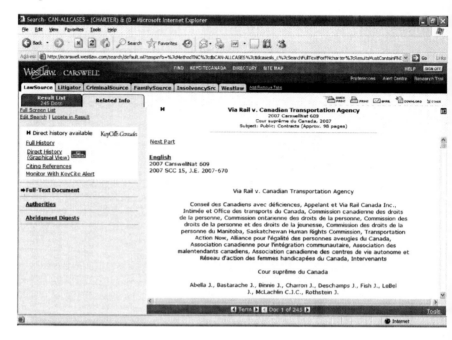

From this page you can do any of the following:

- Access *Canadian Abridgment* digests and classifications for the decision you are viewing (click on the **Abridgment Digests** link).
- Access a list of cases and legislation cited in the decision (click on the **Authorities** tab).
- Note up the decision (click on the **Full History** or **Direct History (Graphical View)** links, or the **Citing References** link for case law and commentary that have cited the decision). By doing this, you get the exact same information that is provided in Carswell's printed case and statute citators that are part of the *Canadian Abridgment* set.

Step 4: For certain databases (*e.g.*, those listed in the left (grey) column, you can either **Browse Table of Contents** or conduct a word search.

For example, if you are searching the **Canadian Abridgment Digests**, you have the following options:

- **Searching:** Perform a search via a template.
- **Browsing:** Select the **Browse** option in the left frame to access the Abridgment Key classification. From there you can access all the

digests under a particular classification, search within any part of the classification, or search for a term within the classification:

The above screen shot is the Table of Contents of **Canadian Abridgment Digests**.

Appendix D material reprinted by permission of Thomson Carswell, a division of Thomson Canada Limited.

How to Find Secondary Materials 6

Secondary materials are books and other sources that assist legal researchers in doing two things: understanding the law and locating the law. They are essential to most research problems and are usually the first sources referred to upon entering a law library. Wise researchers "let the experts begin the work" by finding sound scholarly and practice-oriented materials that explain legal concepts and lead to cases and legislation.

This chapter describes how to locate and use the most popular secondary sources.

The following are sources used to **explain** the law:

- Textbooks
- Journals and Periodicals
- Legal encyclopedias such as the *Canadian Encyclopedic Digest* and *Halsbury's Laws of Canada*
- Legal dictionaries

The following are sources used to **locate** the law:

- Case digests
- Books of words and phrases
- Tables of cases
- Citators

LEARNING OBJECTIVES

At the end of this chapter you will be able to:

- Locate and use textbooks and legal dictionaries
- Use periodical indexes to locate journal articles
- Find and use the two Canadian legal encyclopedias: *Halsbury's Laws of Canada* and the *Canadian Encyclopedic Digest*
- Locate case digests and case indexes
- Explain what a citator is
- Cite secondary sources

The use of secondary sources will be demonstrated with the following fact pattern, which is the same fact pattern used in Chapters 2 and 3.

Fact Pattern

Paul Quint and Melody Jones

Paul Quint and Melody Jones, after ten years of marriage, are getting divorced. They have two children, Lindsay and Wayne, and have agreed that the children will stay with Melody. However, they cannot reach an agreement as to the division of property. They own a house and a boat on Salty Island. In addition, two years ago, Melody was given a $20,000 gift from her grandmother, which she put into a separate bank account in her own name. She wants to know whether the judge will consider the gift to be a family asset when making a decision about the division of property.

SOURCES USED TO EXPLAIN THE LAW

Researchers should look at secondary sources in almost all research situations. Even if you know the name of the particular statute or case you are looking for, secondary sources will put this law into context and explain how the cases and statutes work together to form the law. They are created by editors and experts who know the law well, so it is a good idea to read what they say and refer to the cases that they mention.

Textbooks, Treatises, and Casebooks

Textbooks are books designed to teach a single subject and usually summarize the law on a specific legal topic. Treatises include textbooks and usually cover broader subject areas than textbooks. Textbooks and treatises are extremely useful to those new to a particular area of law. They provide summaries of the law and often include helpful tables of contents and subject indexes.

Every law library has a collection of law textbooks that can be located by using a computer catalogue. Researchers can search the catalogue by subject, keywords, title, author, or call number.

Although textbooks and treatises are not primary sources of law, they have come to be regarded as having a considerable degree of "persuasive" authority because they are often written by academics and scholars. They are sometimes cited as "secondary authority" in Canadian judicial decisions.

Casebooks, unlike textbooks, do not summarize the law. They are collections of excerpts of cases and brief discussions about these cases. They are almost exclusively used in first-year law classes and are designed to help students learn by the case method. These books are used almost exclusively for educational purposes and are rarely referred to after the first year of law school, nor are they cited in decisions.

Journals and Periodicals

Legal journals and periodicals are particularly helpful when researching new or changing areas of the law. If you happen to locate a very recent article on your topic you will save hours of research.

Journals are periodic softcover publications consisting of collections of articles. They can also include other useful information such as advertisements, job postings, legal literature, book reviews, and current news. They tend to include very current information because the time required to produce an article about a new topic is considerably less than that required to produce a book. Many lawyers subscribe to periodicals relevant to their area of practice in order to stay up to date on the law.

The following are a few types of legal journals:

- General interest (*e.g.*, Canadian Lawyer Magazine)
- Special interest (*e.g.*, Canadian Journal of Family Law)
- Bar association (*e.g.*, Canadian Bar Review)
- Scholarly (*e.g.*, Journal of Law & Equality)

Some common features of periodicals include their helpful research tools such as detailed tables of contents, subject indexes, author and title indexes, tables of cases commented on, and book review indexes.

Over the last few years a huge number of published journals have been made available in electronic form so they are accessible on the web pages of various companies. The most well-known legal journal collection is HeinOnline (<http://www.heinonline.org>), which provides access to close to 1,400 legal periodicals. Most university law libraries subscribe to HeinOnline, as well as to collections of other social science electronic journals in law-related areas, since academics need to be able to access the most recent research on their particular topic. Another valuable feature of HeinOnline is that, for virtually all the journals included, coverage goes back to the first volume ever published. HeinOnline also contains volumes of old and rare journals, mostly U.S. and Canadian, that have ceased publication. Both of these features are useful for historical research.

A growing number of journals are now available through commercial online providers. For example, LexisNexis/Quicklaw (LN/QL) provides searchable full-text access to about 30 Canadian academic journals and to a huge number of non-Canadian journals. Some Canadian firms and government agencies purchase this part of LN/QL as an "add-on" to their basic Canadian service. LN/QL also contains many "netletters", which are digital newsletters of great help to practitioners and researchers who are seeking the very newest information on emerging topics. Likewise, Westlaw*e*Carswell (WL*e*C) contains many searchable full-text Canadian journals, including those published by Carswell Thomson, as well as articles and case comments printed within Carswell's many topical reporters, such as Reports of Family Law. There is an "add-on" service to WL*e*C, offering many non-Canadian journals, that some researchers choose to purchase in addition to the basic Canadian coverage.

Some electronic articles are available on free public access websites. Authors simply post their articles for universal accessibility. Keep in mind that these articles are not screened, or "peer reviewed", by editors.

When searching for articles in electronic journals it is best to narrow your search down as much as possible before beginning. You can do this in three ways:

- Select a specific database that only contains certain journals (*e.g.*, only Canadian journals);
- Select a specific field search so that your search will be limited to such fields as author or subject (*e.g.*, environmental law journals); or
- Construct a keyword search in a general journals database that uses connectors such as and/or, not, or adjacent words.

Sometimes this last way is best, because you might miss a useful, subject-specific article that happens to have been selected for publication in a general-interest journal.

Periodical Indexes

Periodical indexes are research aids designed to assist researchers in locating periodicals. In times past, the printed versions of these indexes were critical to locating print journal articles. Almost all of the printed indexes have now been replaced by online versions of them which make searching by keywords or legal topics much easier. And now that many electronic journals are online, in many cases every word of every article can be searched electronically, obviating the need to use an index.

The few remaining indexes that are only available in print are usually published a few times throughout the year (*e.g.*, quarterly), and a cumulative volume is usually published annually. Print versions of periodical indexes list periodicals by subject, author, and title so that researchers can approach the periodical indexes in any of the following ways:

(1) **By title of journal**. If you know the title of a journal that is like to be helpful to your area of research, such as the Canadian Journal of Family Law, but do not know the title or author of any articles, it is often easier to go directly to that periodical on a library shelf and leaf through its index rather than using the periodical indexes.

(2) **By author or title**. If you do not know the title of the journal but know the *author or the title* of the article, look in the author or title index in a printed index or do an electronic word search of either a periodical index or a full-text journal database.

(3) **By subject**. If you know only the subject, it is best to start by looking in the subject indexes in one of the many periodical indexes, either in print or online. The subject categories are different for each journal.

The print versions of indexes are particularly helpful when trying to find out how a legal subject is categorized or to narrow down a subject area. This is because you can scan back and forth quickly searching for key words that can ultimately be used for your electronic search. Each legal publisher describes subjects differently and there are usually a number of topics that are relevant to any research problem.

Printed periodical indexes are hardbound and thus are updated by supplements, so you must look in both. Occasionally, the supplements are consolidated into cumulative volumes, so it is always important to read the spine of the volume to determine whether the index is a consolidation or a supplement. It is usually necessary to search through several hardbound volumes and several softcover supplements to do a thorough search. Often the indexes provide instructions at the front of the volumes to assist researchers in using them. Most indexes include a list of all of the periodicals referred to in that index.

Many periodical indexes are published by geographical region. For example, the *Index to Canadian Legal Periodical Literature* includes only Canadian periodicals.

There are three main legal periodical indexes with Canadian coverage. They are as follows:

Index to Canadian Legal Literature **(ICLL):** Since its inception in 1981, it has indexed Canadian journal articles, books, book reviews, and other legal literature such as continuing legal education (CLE) papers and speeches. It attempts to include all Canadian journal articles and as many of the other types of materials as possible. Hence, it is the closest thing to a complete bibliography of Canadian legal writing. It is available in print by subscription from Thomson Carswell online through LN/QL and WL*e*C.

Illustration 6.1
Excerpt from the *Index to Canadian Legal Literature*

INDEX ANALYTIQUE

MARINE RESOURCES CONSERVATION

– Australia

Oceans law and policy in the post-UNCED era: Australian and Canadian perspectives. ed. by Lorne K. Kriwoken ... [et al.]. (International environmental law and policy series). London; Boston; Cambridge, MA. USA: Kluwer Law International. 1996. xvii, 453 p.: maps.

– International cooperation

Towards regional ocean management in the Arctic: from co-existence to cooperation. by David Vanderzwaag, John Donihee and Mads Faegteborg. (1988) 37 U.N.B. L.J. 1-33.

– Law and legislation

Bill C-98: Oceans Act. by Daniel Dupras. (Legislative summary ; LS-225E). Ottawa: Library of Parliament, Research Branch, 1995. 19 p. Issued also in French.

Canadian ocean law and policy. by David L. VanderZwaag. Markham, Ont.: Butterworths, 1991.

Canadian ocean law and policy. ed. by David L. Vanderzwaag. Toronto: Butterworths. 1992. xxxiv, 546 p.

Implementation of the new law of the sea in West Africa: prospects for the development and management of marine resources. by Peter C. Underwood and Phillip M. Saunders. Halifax: Dalhousie Ocean Studies Programme, 1985.

Implementing international environmental agreements: advocating a functional analysis of hard law and soft law documents. by Sari Graben. (Spring 2000) 15 Inter. Insights 29-52.

Marine structures *see*
     Offshore structures

MARINE TERMINALS

Liability equals responsibility: Canadian marine transport terminal operators in the 1990s. by Roger Harris. (Jan. 1993) 21 Can. Bus. L.J. 229-253.

– Safety measures

Performance audits: British Columbia Ferry Corporation. (Report ; 1995/96 ; 2). Victoria: Office of the Auditor General, 1996. 107 p.: ill. Also issued in electronic format on the Internet at http://www.aud.gov.bc.ca.

Marine transportation *see*
     Shipping

Mariners *see*
     Sailors

Marines de guerre
     = Navies

Marins
     = Sailors

Marins (Marine marchande)
     = Merchant seamen

MARIS
     = Husbands

Les Groupes thérapeutiques à l'intention des maris violents: étude d'un programme mis au point à Vancouver. par Andy Wachtel et Bruce Levens. (Rapport pour spécialistes / Direction des programmes ; no 1984-75). Ottawa: Solliciteur général Canada. Secrétariat, 1984. 243 p.

Maris violents *voir*
     Hommes violents

MARITAIN, JACQUES, 1882-1973

Le Droit naturel et le droit des gens d'après J. Maritain. par Léon Charette. (1988) 19 R.G.D. 947-960.

Marital condition *see*
     Marital status

Marital contracts *see*
     Antenuptial contracts

Marital infidelity *see*
     Adultery

MARITAL PROPERTY
     = Biens communs

"Running hard to stand still": the paradox of family law reform. par Mary Jane Mossman. (Spring 1994) 17 Dalhousie L.J. 5-34.

A Critique of the Manitoba matrimonial property regime. by Jim Stoffman and Sharon Kravetsky. (1988) 3 C.F.L.Q. 269-286.

A Matter of difference: domestic contracts and gender equality. by Brenda Cossman. (Summer 1990) 28 Osgoode Hall L.J. 303-380.

A Note on British Columbia's Personal Property Security Act and the Family Relations Act. by Greg Lanning. (Spring 1990) 8 Can. J. Fam. L. 395-399.

Aboriginal women and matrimonial property: feminist responses. by Mary Ellen Turpel. (Feminism and law workshop series ; WS 94-95 (1)). Toronto: Faculty of Law, University of Toronto. 1994. 40 p. Not for commercial sale.

Advising the family business: impact of the Family Law Act. by Robert Halpern. (April 1995) 10 Money & Fam. L. 25-32.

Advising the family business: impact of the Family Law Act. by Robert Halpern. (May 1995) 10 Money & Fam. L. 39-44.

Alberta introduces changes to pension legislation. by J.M. Norton. (June 1999) 14 Money & Fam. L. 46.

All things come to he (she) who waits: Da Costa v. Da Costa in the Court of Appeal. by Stephen M. Grant. (June 1992) 7 Money & Fam. L. 41-43.

An Overview of pension sharing under the Family Law Act. by Julie A. Colden. Ottawa: [s.n.]. 1993. 26, xxxviii p.

Are gifts and constructive trusts inconsistent? (Mar. 1991) 6 Money & Fam. L. 18-22.

Are gifts and constructive trusts inconsistent? by Lorne H. Wolfson. (1992) 9 C.F.L.Q. 119-131.

Asset hide & seek. by James D. McAuley and Valerie Steele. (June 1993) 8 Money & Fam. L. 45-47.

Bankruptcy and family law problems and solutions. by Robert A. Klotz. (1993) Spec. Lect. L.S.U.C. 253-280.

Bankruptcy and family law. by Anne-France Goldwater. (Jan. 1998) 15 C.F.L.Q. 139-186.

Bankruptcy and family law. by Anne-France Goldwater. dans: Développements récents en droit familial (1997) (Cowansville, Qué.: Éditions Y. Blais. 1997). p. 1-52.

Bankruptcy issues in family law. by Robert A. Klotz. (July 1992) 14 Advocates' Q. 18-69.

Belman v. Belman: a corporate divorce. by A. Scott Davidson. (July 1996) 11 Money & Fam. L. 49-50.

Business agreements and the Family Law Act. by Wolfe D. Goodman. (1986/87) 8 Est. & Tr. Q. 193-203.

Business assets and family law: valuation and income determination workshops. Toronto: Osgoode Hall Law School of York University, Professional Development Programme. Continuing Legal Education. 1998. 1 v. "January 8, 1998".

Business interests and family law. by Stephen M. Grant. (June 1999) 17 C.F.L.Q. 67-85.

CPP [Canada Pension Plan] credit system can work against divorced couples. by Bruce Cohen. (June 1999) 14 Money & Fam. L. 43-44.

Can a trustee in bankruptcy elect under the FLA [Ontario Family Law Act]? (Nov. 1991) 6 Money & Fam. L. 86-88.

Canada Pension Plan credit splitting. (Dec. 1991) 6 Money & Fam. L. 91-93.

The above example is an excerpt from the *Index to Canadian Legal Literature*. As you can see, the section that relates to the Paul and Melody situation is the heading "Marital Property".

LegalTrac: The most comprehensive, widely purchased online index to legal journals indexes approximately 1,400 journals from most of the common-law countries, including French-language journals from Canada. Indexing begins in the mid-1980s for most of the included titles. For some 200 of its journals, there is a direct link to the full text of some or all articles. (See Illustration 6.2.) The print equivalent, ***Current Law Index***, is almost never consulted due to its huge size and difficulty of use. Both the online and print versions are available from Thomson Gale (<http://www.galegroup.com/pdf/facts/legal.pdf>).

Illustration 6.2
Excerpt from LegalTrac

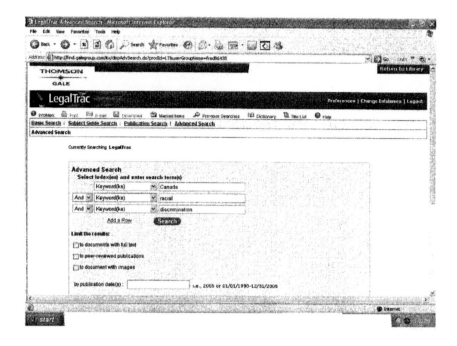

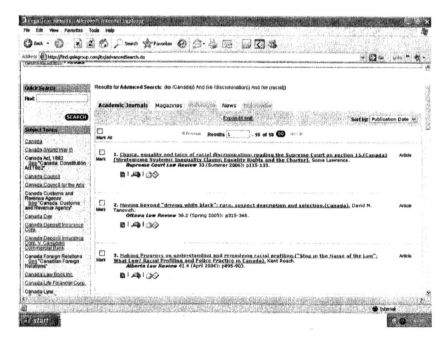

From LegalTrac by Thomson Gale. Reprinted with the permission of Thomson Gale, a division of Thomson Learning: www.thomsonrights.com. Fax 800 730-2215.

Index to Legal Periodicals and Books (ILPB): Indexes about 1,100 journals from the U.S., Canada, the U.K., Ireland, Australia, and New Zealand. The indexing begins in approximately 1982 for most of the included titles, but a separately priced database offers online indexing back to the inception of most of the journals, sometimes as far back as 1926. For approximately 270 of the current journals, a link to full-text articles is provided. In addition,

ILPB indexes approximately 1,400 legal books per year and displays the contents online. A printed version of ILPB, beginning in 1926, is also available, and both online and print versions may be purchased from H.W. Wilson Co. (<http://www.hwwilson.com/default.cfm>).

One additional periodical index with Canadian coverage was published from 1961 through 2002 in print format only. It is the Index to Canadian Legal Periodical Literature and is available in most Canadian academic and larger bar society law libraries. For the period 1961-1981, it was the only tool that covered Canadian journals exclusively, and it is still critical to research for that period of time. With the advent of online indexes in the 1980s, most with Canadian content, it became less useful, although it remained the only source for the majority of Canadian legal newsletter indexing until its cessation in 2002.

Encyclopedias

There are only two Canadian legal encyclopedias, the *Canadian Encyclopedic Digest* and *Halsbury's Laws of Canada*.

Legal encyclopedias are similar to other encyclopedias in that they summarize large amounts of information. They are heavily footnoted with references to both statutes and cases.

These summaries are not the law. They include only an editor's opinion about what the law is, what the cases stand for, or what statutes mean. All cases and statutes referred to should be checked to ensure that the editors of the encyclopedia have interpreted their meaning correctly.

Encyclopedias consist of volumes covering legal subjects organized alphabetically by topic. Because the law is categorized into specific legal topics, researchers must have some understanding of the way in which the subjects are categorized before beginning research. This is accomplished by reviewing the indexes and tables of contents in the encyclopedias. Specific steps are recommended below.

Canadian Encyclopedic Digest

The *Canadian Encyclopedic Digest* (CED) is published by Carswell, in two editions, a western version (CED, Western 3rd ed.), which contains the law of the western provinces, and an Ontario version (CED, Ontario 3rd ed.), which contains the law of Ontario. Researchers use one or the other, depending on where they practise in Canada.

The CEDs are a good place to start research if you know very little about the legal topic you are researching. They are available in print in almost all law libraries as well as online through WL*e*C. A word of caution is in order: the past several years have seen of a decline in the frequency of updating of some of the CED subject volumes. Thus, the timeliness of cited cases and the coverage of emerging directions within certain legal topics of law are beginning to be somewhat questionable. The publisher intends to update more regularly in the near future.

The two sets of CEDs consist of about 40 loose-leaf volumes each. Each volume contains a number of legal subjects (called titles). Each title contains a brief overview of the law and refers to specific statutes and cases. The CED uses an indexing system that categorizes all of Canadian law into approximately 160 different subject areas. An index and a research key and guide are included with the multi-volume set.

The Electronic Version

The CED is available online through Westlaw*e*CARSWELL. There are essentially two ways to search the CED electronically: by scanning the table of contents or by using the template to conduct a word search. Although it is best to scan the contents first to get a general sense of what is included, in the electronic CED you will quickly become overwhelmed by the amount of information and the level of detail. It is best to have a fairly good sense of your topic and how it is categorized before conducting an electronic search. Having said that, if you know your specific topic, there is no harm in doing a quick word search to see what you find and then going back to the more systematic approach. More instructions on how to search electronic sources are found in Chapter 5 (Law Libraries and Electronic Collections of Law).

The Print Version

The print version of the CED consists of the following three parts:

- *Research Guide, Index and Keys* (one or two volumes)
- *Main Set* (about 40 volumes)
- *Supplements* (coloured or shaded pages placed in front of each topic)

The way to use the CED is by looking at each of these parts as described below.

Step 1: Go to the first few volumes. Look in either the *Contents Key* or the *Index* for areas of law that might be relevant to your problem. These sources will refer you to specific volumes in the *Main Set*.

The first few volumes in the set include the following research tools:

- Research Guide: Explains how to use the *Canadian Encyclopedic Digest*.

- Index: Lists the subject titles alphabetically with subheadings.
- Contents Key: Lists all the subject areas or titles (about 160).
- Statutes Key: Lists statutes alphabetically.
- Rules Key: Lists rules alphabetically.

The index and each of the keys direct the researcher to the location in the *Main Set* where the topic is covered much like a textbook. A researcher who is unfamiliar with a legal topic will typically go first to the *Index* or *Contents Key* and peruse it for one or two titles that might be relevant.

For example, if you go to the CED (Western) there is a main heading called *Family Law (General)* and several subheadings such as family assets, bank accounts, and property division. You will see that all of these subjects are found in title 63.1 in Volume 14A. A few of these sections could potentially apply to the Paul and Melody situation.

Step 2: Go to the *Main Set* of volumes and look in the volumes that include your topics. Peruse the table of contents in that volume, locate the relevant topic, and read the relevant paragraphs. Record citations of relevant cases and statutes.

The *Main Set* of volumes of the CED contains all the summaries of the law organized alphabetically by subject area. For example, the first volume includes a summary of the law on *Adoption* and the last volume contains a summary of the law on *Wills*. The volumes are loose-leaf and supplements are included at the front of most of the titles on different coloured or shaded pages. These supplements are cumulative.

By reading the text, the researcher can gain an overview of the topic and also record the citation of statutes and cases on point. These statutes and cases provide a springboard for further research.

Illustrations 6.3 and 6.4 are excerpts from the Contents Key and the Index of the Western version that relate to the Paul and Melody situation.

Step 3: Look at the front of the relevant volume for the Supplement pages to see if the law has changed since the white pages were printed.

The CED is updated by supplements on coloured or shaded pages. Researchers should refer to these pages to see whether the law has changed since the white pages were printed. Every page in the CED is dated to indicate the cut-off date of the information. It is important to note this date to ensure that the information is current and search other sources for more current information. Illustrations 6.7 and 6.8 provide examples of this step.

Illustration 6.3
Canadian Encyclopedic Digest: Contents Key

CONTENTS KEY

LIST OF TITLES

The following is a list of the subject titles in C.E.D. (West. 3rd), showing the volumes in which they appear and their respective title numbers.

Subject Title		Volume
1.	Absentees	1
1.1.	Access to Information and Protection of Privacy	1
2.	Actions	1
3.	Administrative Law	1
4.	Agency	1
5.	Agriculture	1
6.	Animals	2
7.	Annuities	2
8.	Arbitration	2
9.	Armed Forces	2
10.	Associations and Non-Profit Corporations	2
11.	Auctions	2
12.	Aviation and Air Law	2
13.	Bailment	2
14.	Banking	3
15.	Bankruptcy and Insolvency	3
16.	Barristers and Solicitors	4
17.	Bills of Exchange	4
18.	Bills of Sale and Chattel Mortgages	4
19.	Boundaries and Surveys	4
19.1.	Builders' Liens	4
20.	Building Contracts	5
22.	Burial and Cremation	5
23.	Carriers	5
24.	Charities	5
26.	Churches and Religious Institutions	5
28.	Conditional Sales	6
29.	Condominiums	6
30.	Conflict of Laws	6
31.	Conspiracy	6
32.	Constitutional Law	6
33.	Contempt of Court	7
34.	Contracts	7
34.1.	Co-operatives	8
35.	Copyright	8
36.	Coroners and Medical Examiners	8
37.	Corporations	8
38.	Costs	9
39.	Courts	9
40.	Criminal Law (Offences)	10

Illustration 6.4
Canadian Encyclopedic Digest: Index

INDEX

This Index covers all titles published up to and including **Release 2003-1**.

References are to volumes, titles and paragraphs within those titles, except for references to the title "Employment Law", which include a part number. For example, 1-5§44 refers to Volume 1, Title 5, paragraph 44, and 11D-54.1-VI§1050 refers to Volume 11D, Title 54.1, Part VI, paragraph 1050. "(Supp.)" in the reference indicates material found in a supplement to the title.

ABANDONMENT. *See* CONTRACTS; EASEMENTS; INFANTS AND CHILDREN; INSURANCE; LANDLORD AND TENANT; MINES AND MINERALS; OIL AND GAS; PATENTS OF INVENTION; PERSONAL PROPERTY; SALE OF LAND.

ABATEMENT. *See* ACTIONS; NUISANCE; SALE OF LAND; SPECIFIC PERFORMANCE; WILLS.

ABDUCTION. *See* CRIMINAL LAW (OFFENCES); DIVORCE; INFANTS AND CHILDREN.

ABORIGINAL PEOPLE. *See* BURIAL AND CREMATION; CONSTITUTIONAL LAW; EXECUTION; EXECUTORS AND ADMINISTRATORS; FAMILY LAW (GENERAL); FEDERAL AND PROVINCIAL TAXATION; FISH AND GAME; INCOME TAX; INFANTS AND CHILDREN; LIQUOR CONTROL; PREROGATIVE REMEDIES.

ABORTION. *See* CRIMINAL LAW (OFFENCES).

ABSCONDING DEBTOR. *See* DEBTOR AND CREDITOR; EXECUTION; INJUNCTIONS.

ABSENTEES. *See also* DEBTOR AND CREDITOR; DEVOLUTION OF ESTATES; EVIDENCE; EXECUTORS AND ADMINISTRATORS; INSURANCE; JUDGMENTS AND ORDERS; MENTAL INCOMPETENCY; PRACTICE; REAL PROPERTY; TRUSTS.
   absentee. *See also* **missing person.**
     actions by and against 1-1§27 (Supp.)
     declaration of absentee, appeal 1-1§§38, 42

declaration of absentee, generally 1-1§§8, 10, 15, 24, 38, 40
   definition 1-1§§6-8
   legislation dealing with, scope of 1-1§§1, 2
administration, grant of. *See* **probate, grant of.**
committee
   actions against 1-1§28
   appointment 1-1§§13, 15, 23, 24, 30
   guardian of property, as 1-1§25 (Supp.)
   powers 1-1§§25, 26, 29, 31
courts, powers of
   Alberta 1-1§10
   British Columbia 1-1§§5, 11, 12
   Northwest Territories 1-1§16
   Ontario 1-1§§13, 14
   Saskatchewan 1-1§15
curator
   appointment 1-1§§5, 12, 20, 35
   powers 1-1§§21, 22
   removal of 1-1§12
custodian. *See* **Public Trustee.**
declaration of absence. *See* **absentee; missing person.**
interests in land 1-1§§7, 8, 11, 24
missing person. *See also* **absentee.**
   declaration of missing person 1-1§§10 (Supp.), 16, 19 (Supp.), 36
   definition 1-1§§3, 4, 9
   legislation dealing with, generally 1-1§§1, 2
notice, requirements of
   Alberta 1-1§34
   British Columbia 1-1§35
   Northwest Territories 1-1§43
   Ontario 1-1§39
   Saskatchewan 1-1§40

THE KEY TO C.E.D.

V.522

Canadian Encyclopedic Digest

Third Edition

Western Volume 14A   Title 63.1

FAMILY LAW (GENERAL)

This 176-page supplement contains material drawn from:

Cases up to and including:
[2002] C.C.L. Case Law Digests, No. 4

Legislation up to and including:
Canada Gazette No. 136-11, 2002/05/22
Alberta Gazette No. 98-9, 2002/05/15
British Columbia Gazette No. 45-5, 2002/03/26
Manitoba Gazette No. 131-31, 2002/05/25
Ontario Gazette No. 135-21, 2002/05/25
Saskatchewan Gazette No. 98-20, 2002/05/17

CARSWELL
A THOMSON COMPANY

Illustration 6.6
Canadian Encyclopedic Digest: Title 63.1 Family Law (General)

Title 63.1

FAMILY LAW (GENERAL)

prepared by

D.D. PETERSON, B.A., LL.B.
of the Alberta Bar

and updated by

NANCY A. FLATTERS, B.A., LL.B.
of the Alberta Bar

April 1992

Illustration 6.7
Canadian Encyclopedic Digest: Title 63.1 Family Law (General), paragraph 428.

PART VIII – DIVISION OF MATRIMONIAL PROPERTY   §429

D. INHERITANCES AND GIFTS

§428   Where property has been acquired by inheritance or gift, it may be excluded from division as the property does not form part of the product of the marriage.[93]

93. See s. 51(d); *Bateman v. Bateman* (1979), 10 R.F.L. (2d) 63 (B.C.S.C.) (R.R.S.P. purchased with gift from mother); *Bandiera v. Bandiera* (1979), 13 B.C.L.R. 327 (S.C.) (inter vivos gift); *Caskey v. Caskey* (1979), 14 B.C.L.R. 193 (S.C.) (gift in form of loan at low interest rate taken into account); *Richardson v. Richardson* (1982), 32 R.F.L. (2d) 82; reversed on other grounds 43 R.F.L. (2d) 312 (B.C.C.A.) (husband's participation in litigation involving wife's inheritance not a "venture" within meaning of s. 45(3)(e) since no element of risk present; inheritance not family asset); *Barnard v. Barnard* (1987), 7 R.F.L. (3d) 163 (B.C.C.A.) (husband's use of inheritance as part of purchase price of property justifying unequal division); *Jasich v. Jasich* (1984), 40 R.F.L. (2d) 441 (B.C.S.C.) (inheritance kept intact and separate from family assets not constituting family asset); *Rushton v. Rushton* (1984), 38 R.F.L. (2d) 308 (B.C.S.C.) (term deposit held by wife and originating from sale of wife's mother's cottage not family asset); *Gullickson v. Gullickson* (1990), 26 R.F.L. (3d) 220 (bonds purchased by wife's mother and held by mother with wife having no access not family asset); *Maclean v. Maclean* (1990), 28 R.F.L. (3d) 103 (B.C.S.C.) (husband's trust divided 60% to husband and 40% to wife); *Gifford v. Gifford*, [1991] W.D.F.L. 914 (B.C.S.C.) (wife's inheritance a family asset as parties intending it to be basis of secure future; inheritance divisible with exception of inheritance in specie or yet to be paid).

Canadian Encyclopedic Digest (Western) Third Edition. Reprinted by permission of Thomson Carswell, a division of Thomson Canada Limited.

Illustration 6.8
Canadian Encyclopedic Digest:
Amendments to paragraph 428 of Title 63.1

§428 *Add to the end of the paragraph*: Where parents have advanced moneys to their married children, the onus of proving that the moneys were loans rather than gifts is on the person making that allegation.[93.1]

93.1. *Malinowski v. Malinowski*, 2000 BCSC 703 (B.C.S.C.).

§428 note 93

Family Relations Act, R.S.B.C. 1979, c. 121, s. 51(d): see now s. 56(1)(d) of R.S.B.C. 1996, c. 128; *Halpin v. Halpin* (1996), 26 R.F.L. (4th) 30 (B.C. C.A.), varying (August 29, 1994), Prince George 18704 (B.C. S.C.) (significance of gifts over time); *Anderson v. Anderson*, 1996 CarswellBC 2271 (B.C. S.C.); supplemented 1997 CarswellBC 1127 (B.C. S.C.) (inheritance being family asset since used for family); *Brown v. Brown*, 1996 CarswellBC 1538 (B.C. S.C.) (wife inheriting and gifted interest in lots; lots family assets considering use of land and contributions to lots); *Grav v. Grav*, 1996 CarswellBC 1569 (B.C. S.C.) (lake lot inherited by husband and a family asset as confirmed by conveyance of title in wife's name); *Rettie v. Rettie*, 1997 CarswellBC 245 (B.C. S.C.) (inheritance invested in stocks; dividends from stocks used for family purposes; wife making no contributions to stock portfolio; reapportioned in husband's favour); *Hefti v. Hefti* (1998), 40 R.F.L.. (4th) 1 (B.C. C.A.) (husband's inheritance not constituting family asset merely because parties talking about inheritance as possible source of future retirement income); *Borrill v. Borrill*, 1999 CarswellBC 1061 (B.C. S.C.) (gift acquired by husband near end of marriage; husband entitled to three-quarters of value of asset); *Caldwell v. Caldwell* (1999); 126 B.C.A.C. 73 (B.C. C.A.) (husband's interest in land crystallizing on mother's death; estate litigation only postponing husband's possession of land; land a family asset as used to graze family cattle and produce hay).

Canadian Encyclopedic Digest (Western) Third Edition. Reprinted by permission of Thomson Carswell, a division of Thomson Canada Limited.

Halsbury's Laws of Canada

The other Canadian legal encyclopedia is *Halsbury's Laws of Canada*. It is based on the widely used legal encyclopedia, *Halsbury's Laws of England*, and is a comprehensive new Canadian legal encyclopedia that was introduced in 2006 by LexisNexis Canada. Upon completion, the set will comprise 57 hardbound topical volumes presenting current commentary on the full range of Canadian law.

Each volume is authored by a Canadian expert on the topic and is divided into logical divisions and then more detailed subheadings about the particular topic. Each topic is shown on the back of the particular volume.

Generally speaking, *Halsbury's Laws of Canada* will be easier than the CED for the beginning researcher to use because it closely resembles a general encyclopedia. You simply select the appropriate volume based on the legal topic you are researching. However, for additional help, each volume contains a detailed subject index, a recommended list of additional secondary sources for further research, and a glossary of relevant terms.

The printed volumes are being sold by subscription and issued as they are completed. (See Illustration 6.9 for sample pages.) Each volume will be updated by an annual paper supplement.

At this time, there is no online equivalent to *Halsbury's Laws of Canada*, but it is likely that there will be an online version in the near future, since the model on which it is based, that is, *Halsbury's Laws of England*, is now fully available online.

Illustration 6.9
Excerpt from Halsbury's Laws of Canada

Halsbury's
Laws of Canada
First Edition

Immigration and Citizenship

Contributed by

Lorne Waldman
LL.B., LL.M.
of the Ontario Bar

Waldman & Associates
Barrister and Solicitors

Contributing Editor
Mary K. McLean, B.A., LL.B.

LexisNexis·

General Table of Contents

Secondary Materials

A description of secondary legal materials would not be complete without mentioning the following.

News Sources

Often lawyers research news and other media. Criminal and civil issues are covered extensively by news media long before such matters enter the courts, if indeed they ever do. Also, since jury trials do not result in written decisions (because a jury is not required to give reasons for finding guilt or innocence), researchers and lawyers often turn to news sources to provide information before, during and after trials.

Many newspapers provide current and some archival news files on their websites, but using them generally requires that the researcher subscribe to the print version of the paper or purchase access on a "pay-per-view" basis. Also, news is often "embargoed" for days or weeks after an incident happens. As an alternative to such newspaper websites, researchers may subscribe to collections of Canadian and world news sold by commercial online providers.

One news service is **FPInfomart**, available through the CanWest Global group of companies (<http://www.fpinfomart.ca>), which provides same-day and archival access to over 1,100 full-text newspapers, magazines, newswires, broadcast transcripts, and web newsblogs. Both subscription and pay-per-view options are sold.

Another news source is **LexisNexis Canada** which, on the "Nexis" side", sells full-text retrieval of articles and news stories from over 12,000 different sources worldwide, via subscription (<www.lexisnexis.com>). Most of this news is from English-language sources including newspapers, magazines, wire services, company news and profiles, and trade and industry journals.

Newscan (<www.library.newscan.com/Biblio/intro.asp>) is a Canadian-based Virtual News Library, specially designed for public libraries and the education sector, that offers access to an impressive database of current and archival Canadian and European news sources, including French-language sources. Users can subscribe to selected media sources or to the entire service.

Legal Dictionaries

Legal dictionaries define legal terms and common words with special legal meanings. Like standard dictionaries, they list words alphabetically. The most frequently used dictionary is *Black's Law Dictionary*, an American publication (Thomson West). The two main Canadian dictionaries are the popular *Dictionary of Canadian Law*, 3d ed., by Dukelow (Thomson Carswell) and the *Canadian Law Dictionary* by Yogis (Barron's Educational Services), now out of date. Dictionaries are typically located in the reference sections of libraries.

Books of Words and Phrases

In some situations legal research is conducted on the basis of particular words or phrases. To assist researchers in this search there are secondary materials called "books of words and phrases". These sources list and define words and phrases that have been interpreted by courts and administrative tribunals. They also provide citations to cases and statutes that contain certain words or phrases. Here are three Canadian words and phrases sources:

(1) *Words and Phrases Judicially defined in Canadian Courts* (part of the *Canadian Abridgment*). This source consists of eight bound volumes that are updated by supplements. It includes over 50,000 considerations of words and phrases from Canadian judicial and tribunal decisions and provides citations for the cases referenced.

(2) *Sanagan's Encyclopedia of Words and Phrases, Legal Maxims, Canada* (Thomson Carswell). This is a four-volume loose-leaf source. For each word or phrase listed, the authors provide summaries of the judicial comments and/or relevant quotations relating to each word or phrase and also provide ratios of the cases which have spoken most recently and most distinctly to the meanings of the words or phrases in question. Largely continues the product below.

(3) *Words and Phrases, Legal Maxims.* This source consists of three loose-leaf volumes and defines words and phrases interpreted by Canadian courts. It was originally published by DeBoo and is now largely being continued by Sanagan's Encyclopedia (see above).

Abbreviations Lists

Researchers may encounter hundreds of legal abbreviations every day. Interpreting these quickly and correctly is crucial to finding the cited sources, whether they be secondary materials, cases, or legislation. One excellent, free online source for interpreting abbreviations is the Cardiff Index (<http://www.legalabbrevs.cardiff.ac.uk/>) produced by the Cardiff University Law Library. Another free website for this purpose is the Monash University Library Abbreviations List (<http://www.lib.monash. edu.au/legal-abbreviations/>). The best printed resource is *Index to Legal Citations and Abbreviations*, 2d ed., compiled by Donald Raistrick (London: Bowker-Saur, 1993). All three of these sources cover abbreviations to case reports, statutes, journals, and other secondary sources from the common law countries.

Loose-leaf Services

The loose-leaf format is quite common in legal publishing. Loose-leaf services, usually purchased by ongoing subscription, consist of one or more volumes of very current material about a fairly narrow area of the law, such as family law or environmental law. Updates are sent to lawyers periodically, so that they can insert the pages in order to stay up to date with changes to the law.

Loose-leaf services usually contain commentary by experts, including citations to leading cases and relevant statutes pertaining to the topic at hand. Some may provide the full text of relevant statutes and regulations, along with legislative histories of Acts. Some also include practitioner aids such as research checklists, sample forms, tables of costs and damages, *etc.* Check the holdings of your local academic or law society library to determine what loose-leaf services are available, or check the websites of prominent Canadian publishers such as Thomson Carswell, LexisNexis Canada/Butterworths, Canada Law Book, CCH Canadian, *etc.*

Government Documents

Numerous government bodies produce studies or publications on different areas of the law. For example, federal and provincial law reform commissions investigate problems in the law and recommend changes. These commission reports are very useful summaries and critiques of the law. Often parliamentary committees or royal commissions produce reports on investigations or controversial areas of law. In law libraries these are often treated like textbooks and categorized by subject and call number. Often they are listed in periodical indexes and, more recently, they can be located on government websites.

In addition, ministries, departments and agencies of the federal, provincial and territorial governments produce annual reports as well as unique, "one of a kind" documents that have both legal and policy implications. Again, law libraries treat these either as serial publications, arranging them by jurisdiction and year, or as books with call numbers. They can be highly persuasive and may be cited as secondary authority in judicial decisions. Frequently they appear on government websites, but there are no guarantees that they will remain permanently archived for public access, so many libraries download and process the most important ones for permanency.

Other government documents consulted by researchers include the debates of the House of Commons and Senate of Canada and those of the provincial and territorial legislatures, often referred to as the "Hansard". Most large law libraries will have these in print format, and some recent years are on legislative websites. Debates can inform about the reasons for passing or amending legislation but they are almost never cited as authority in judicial decisions.

Directories

There are literally hundreds of legal directories. Some list lawyers and firms, or legal services such as title searching, or addresses, phone numbers and e-mail information for government officials, corporations, or non-governmental organizations. Two particularly helpful directories for

locating Canadian practitioners and firms by practice area are the
Canadian Law List (Canada Law Book) in print and online
(<http://www.canadianlawlist.com/>) and the Martindale-Hubbell Canadian
Law Directory (LexisNexis Martindale-Hubbell) in print and online
(<http://www.martindale.com/>).

Case Digests

Case digests are summaries of reported and unreported cases. They are
written by editors and compiled in periodic publications and newsletters.
They are prepared primarily for use by lawyers so that they can quickly
read about current cases in their area of practice. A lawyer who wants the
full text can order it from the publisher or the courts or go online to one
of several commercial online providers. The digests are arranged
according to subject matter. Unlike the CED, digests are simply abstracts
and rarely used by beginning researchers.

The main Canadian case digest collection is the *Canadian Abridgment:
Case Digests*. It is organized in a fashion similar to the CED; cases are
filed according to a similar classification scheme. Each topic is assigned a
multi-level number. These same digests can also be found online in
WL*e*C. Likewise, LN/QL has several databases containing case summaries
written by legal editors. The case digests are explained in more detail in
Chapter 9 (How to Find and Update Cases).

Citators

Citators are very useful annotations of the law. They typically identify the
law and all of its updates and judicial considerations. There are both
statute and case citators. Statute citators consist of lists of statutes,
including revisions, and cases that refer to statutes. Case citators consist of
alphabetical lists of decided cases, each followed by a list of cases that have
judicially considered the original case. The two most comprehensive
paper-based citators are published as part of the *Canadian Abridgment:
Canadian Case Citations* and *Canadian Statute Citations*. Citators are
explained in more detail in Chapters 7 (How to Find and Update Statutes)
and 9 (How to Find and Update Cases).

Continuing Legal Education Materials

Other useful sources are materials published by continuing legal
educators, law societies, and bar associations. Often materials are
published as part of a course or workshop for practising lawyers or
articling students seeking bar admission and are written by experts.
Similar materials include proceedings of bar society conferences and
symposia. These materials can be found at law libraries or through the
originating organization. Sometimes they can be purchased online
through the organization's website.

Forms and Precedents

There are a few publications of forms and precedents. These are used primarily by lawyers in practice as examples or templates of commonly used forms. Examples include: *O'Brien's Encyclopedia of Forms* (Canada Law Book), in print and online (<http://www.clbonline.ca>), and *Canadian Forms and Precedents* (LexisNexis Butterworths), currently in print only. They include reusable forms related to commercial law, corporate law, banking, real estate, and wills.

CITATION OF SECONDARY MATERIALS

The authoritative book on Canadian legal citation is the *Canadian Guide to Uniform Legal Citation* (the "McGill Guide" published by Thomson Carswell). Be sure to use the current edition, since this guide often changes when it is reissued. The main rule of citation of any source is to remain consistent. Each part of a citation has a purpose with the ultimate goal of enabling the reader of the citation to locate the source. The following is an example of a proper citation:

Author	Title	Edition	Publication Info.	Page
↓	↘	↘	↓	↓

Peter W. Hogg, *Constitutional Law of Canada*, 2d ed. (Toronto: Carswell, 1985) at 73.

The following are some tips about textbook citation:

Author:	List the author's exactly as he/she used it in the work being cited, followed by a comma
Title of textbook:	Italicize or underline, followed by comma
Volume:	If there is one
Edition:	Use abbreviations, *e.g.*, 3d
Place of publication:	Name of city followed by a colon
Publisher:	Full name of publisher
Year of publication:	Of that particular edition
Page reference:	Only if referring to a specific passage (this is known as a "pinpoint" citation)

The following are the parts of a journal article citation and some tips:

L. Edward Weinrib, "Learning to Live with the Override" (1990) 35 McGill L.J. 541 at 562.

Author:	List the author's exactly as he/she used it in the work being cited, followed by a comma
Title of article:	Put in quotation marks
Year of publication:	Place in round brackets
Volume number:	If there is one
Name of journal:	Use proper abbreviations
First page of article:	Always included in citation
Page reference:	Only if referring to a specific passage (this is known as a "pinpoint" citation)

Electronic Citation

If your secondary material is taken from an electronic source, it is helpful to your readers if you add that information to the citation so that the material can be found easily. After the citation (above) add a comma and then the word "online" followed by a colon. If a commercial online system was used, add the abbreviation for the provider (*e.g.*, WL*e*C, LN/QL). If a website was used, add the name of the website followed by the name of the specific part of the site, then the URL (Uniform Resource Locater) in angled brackets. This information is necessary so that your reader can locate the information but also to prove the prior existence of the information should the website be taken offline in the future.

SELF TEST

The answers to these questions are found at the end of the book in the "Answers to Self Tests" section.

1. How do you locate a textbook?
2. How do you locate journal articles by subject?
3. What is the *Canadian Encyclopedic Digest*?
4. What is a book of words and phrases?
5. What is a case digest?
6. What is a citator?

SAMPLE EXERCISES —
FINDING SECONDARY MATERIALS

Objectives

At the end of this exercise you should be able to:
- Locate and use relevant books and treatises

- Through periodical indexes, locate and use relevant journal articles
- Locate and use the *Canadian Encyclopedic Digest* (CED)
- Properly cite a journal article and a book

Instructions

- Do background reading on secondary materials.
- Keep a record of all the steps and the time taken to complete the exercise.

Canadian Encyclopedic Digest

Read the following fact pattern and answer the following questions.

Fact Pattern

Mr. Bark

Your client, Mr. Bark, has just been visited by the police. He apparently has been charged with both causing unnecessary pain and suffering to and unlawfully killing his dog, Wolff. Last week Wolff attacked the four-year-old girl next door. Mr. Bark fought off Wolff with a hockey stick and in the process killed him. He can't understand why he is now being charged with an offence, when he actually saved the little girl's life. What are his rights?

1. Brainstorm and list five words that you might look for in the library. Before looking at the law, list the facts you think are relevant.

    Words:

    Relevant facts:

2. Go to the *Canadian Encyclopedic Digest* (West 3rd) and look in the first few volumes for the *Contents Key* and *Index*. List those subject titles and volumes that appear to be relevant to the fact pattern. Or look in the WL*e*C online version in the Table of Contents.

    Subject titles/volumes:

3. Go to the specific *Canadian Encyclopedic Digest* volume that contains the most relevant subject title (from Question 2). Look in

the *Index* to that volume and find the most relevant sections. List the most relevant heading, subheading(s), and paragraph(s) that appear to be relevant to the fact pattern.

Number:

Heading:

Subheading(s):

Paragraph Numbers:

4. Read the other relevant titles *briefly*. List any new paragraphs you find that may be relevant to the fact pattern. Look in the Supplement pages (if any) and list those paragraphs you selected above which have been updated. *Do not solve the problem.*

New paragraphs:

Paragraphs that have been updated:

Books

Use the library computer catalogue to locate a treatise/book on the subject of criminal law by D. Stuart. Provide the proper citation and record the call number.

1. Citation:

2. Call number:

Periodicals

Go to the legal periodical indexes (paper or electronic). Give the proper citation for one periodical that addresses the following:

1. By subject. Use the *Index to Canadian Legal Literature (Canadian Abridgment)*:

    Naskapi Indians (Innu) of Labrador and an environmental impact assessment.

    Citation:

2. By author (use the *Index to Canadian Legal Periodical Literature*):

    A 2000 article by Randall Echlin on labour law.

    Citation:

3. By a keyword search in *LegalTrac* online:

A 1999 article by Penny about municipal solid waste

Citation:

Dictionaries

Give a complete clear and succinct legal explanation in your own words for the following term. Name the source you used.

Res judicata

Source:

ANSWERS TO EXERCISES

Canadian Encyclopedic Digest

1. Animal; dog; self defence; neighbour; children.

   Relevant Facts: A man killed his dog with a hockey stick during an attack on a four-year-old girl. He has been charged with causing unnecessary pain and suffering to the dog and unlawfully killing it.

2. | Title Numbers | Subject Titles | Volumes |
   |---|---|---|
   | 6 | Animals | 2 |
   | 40 and 40.1 | Criminal Law | 10 and 10A |

3. Volume 2, title 6, section XII: Offences Relating to Animals, part 1: Causing Unnecessary Suffering at par. 558. And section IX: Dogs, part 5: Liability for Injuries Inflicted by Dogs at par. 330.

4. Paragraph 558 has a new note listing new cases. March 2003 update.

Books and Treatises

1. Don Stuart, *Canadian Criminal Law: A Treatise*, 4th ed. (Toronto: Carswell, 2001).

2. Call Number: KM520.S8849 2001 (The call number may be different in different libraries.)

Periodicals

1. Patricia Fry, "A Social Biosphere: Environmental Impact Assessment, the Innu, and their Environment" (1998) 56 U.T. Fac. L. Rev. 177.

2. Randall Scott Echlin, "Developments in Labour and Employment Law: The 1999-2000 Term" (2000) 13 S.C.L.R. (2d) 247-267.

3. William L. Penny, "The Municipal Solid Waste Landfill Presumptive Remedy" (1999) 13 Natural Resources & Env't 471.

Dictionaries

Res judicata: An issue that has been definitively settled by judicial decision.

Source: *Black's Law Dictionary*, 8th ed. (St. Paul, Minn.: West Publishing Co., 2004).

Appendix 6A: Checklist: How to Find Secondary Materials

Locating and reading secondary materials to gain an overview of the law is the best way to start your research. Generally, start with books or a legal encyclopedia, then move on to legal journals and periodicals. If your topic is "emerging" or recent, start with legal journals and periodicals.

Many law library catalogues are accessible online, allowing you to check holdings elsewhere — for a possible interlibrary loan, which you can arrange through the library staff at your local university, law society, or firm library.

As you read the materials, look for particular **keywords** describing your topic, make notes of relevant **subject headings** and **descriptors** assigned to your topic, and record references to specific cases, statutes, and other sources.

TEXTBOOKS

❑ *In the library*: Search a law library's electronic catalogue using **keywords** to generate a list of book titles. Examine the full records of relevant book titles and note and search the **subject headings** assigned for this topic. Record the books' titles and call numbers.

- Locate these books in the library and browse adjacent shelves for similar, relevant books. Check for similar call numbers in the library's "Reserve" area where the most current, highly used materials are kept.
- Scan each book's *Table of Contents* to get an overview of its arrangement and check its *Index* for your subject headings or keywords. Read generally at first. Record relevant cases, statutes, articles, and books mentioned in the text and footnotes.
- Some researchers photocopy important pages with specific citations for cases and statutes or key quotations. Photocopying the book's title page too will save you time later, and make a note of its call number in case you have to find it again. For loose-leaf texts, note the date of the last release filed, since this indicates the currency of the information.

❑ *Electronically*: Some books are in electronic format (known as e-books) on LN/QL, although they are generally only sold to practitioners and not included in the complimentary passwords given to Canadian law students and law teachers. At this time, there are no "e-books" within the Canadian content on WL*e*C. Other publishers also distribute some books in electronic format. Check with publishers and online service providers or search their catalogues or lists on their websites. Note the title, author, publisher, and date of publication so that you can easily find the resource(s).

LEGAL ENCYCLOPEDIAS

❑ *In the library*: Locate and review the first few volumes of CED (Western) or CED (Ontario). Use the *Contents Key* or the *Index* to locate relevant subject titles in CED. Alternatively, select relevant volumes from *Halsbury's Laws of Canada*.

In the CED, find the volumes containing these subject titles and note the currency date of the information. Each title has its own Table of Contents — showing the subject headings and subheadings used — and an Index. Read generally at first. Update the information you read by referring to the title's supplement. After you have focused your research, record relevant cases and statutes referred to. In each *Halsbury's* volume, use the table of contents to locate the appropriate subheadings of the subject and read those sections, again, recording relevant cases and statutes.

❑ *Electronically*: The CED is also available through WL*e*C. You can browse its *Table of Contents,* or search the full text using keywords and the search template provided.

LEGAL JOURNALS AND PERIODICALS

❑ *In the library*: Most law libraries have huge collections of journals. To locate articles, go to the legal periodical indexes — in print or electronic format. Search by subject (from your prior research), keywords, author, case name, or statute title. In electronic indexes, read the search tips and use the advanced search template to construct a more defined search.

As you find relevant journal articles on your subject, note the **subject headings** or **descriptors** assigned to them and follow these leads to find more relevant articles. The main legal periodical indexes are:

- *Index to Canadian Legal Literature* (ICLL) (online and in print as part of the *Canadian Abridgment*)
- *LegalTrac* (online)
- *Index to Legal Periodicals and Books* (ILPB) (online and in print)

If you locate a particularly relevant journal (*e.g.*, Canadian Journal of Women and the Law), either through indexes or just by browsing library shelves, it is a good idea to scan the Tables of Contents of recent issues of that journal for more articles.

❑ Electronically: LN/QL and WL*e*C have databases containing different types of secondary materials: periodical indexes, newsletters, topical report series with commentary or small articles included, and full-text journals. Browse their database lists. A very comprehensive collection of full-text legal journals is <http://www.HeinOnline.org>. Some law libraries subscribe to this service, which may be searched by author, title, or keyword.

How to Find and Update Statutes 7

Statute research involves locating and updating statutes and also locating cases that have interpreted or applied statutes. For example, a researcher confronted with a situation involving the dismissal of an employee would look for labour and employment statutes, determine whether they have been repealed or revised, and then search for cases that have considered or interpreted those statutes. Often cases that apply statutes add a new interpretation to a statute, so a researcher should always look for the most recent cases even if a statute is new.

The most important concept to keep in mind when applying statutes to situations is **when** the client did the action, or **when** someone else did the action to the client. The researcher must always determine **when** things happened, because the law that was in force on that date is the law that must be applied or used or argued, not an earlier or later version of that law.

The other very important concept to remember is that legislation has mandatory authority **only** in its own jurisdiction. A person living or working in British Columbia cannot be held to the requirements of a Manitoba statute, although the Manitoba statute might have some persuasive authority if B.C. had no statute that addressed the particular legal issue in Manitoba. Legislation in its own jurisdiction has "binding" ·or mandatory authority. Thus, legal researchers must be familiar with the laws of their own province or territory, along with any federal statutes that have a bearing on the issue at hand.

The following also should be kept in mind when conducting statute research:

- Statutes work in combination with cases;
- There may be more than one applicable statute;
- There may be overlap between provincial and federal statutes;
- Statutes are revised regularly, so research must always be current; and
- Cases interpret statutes and can affect the meaning of statutes.

This chapter describes two basic ways to find statutes and provides a step-by-step technique. It explains how statutes are published, provides instruction on how to find cases that have considered statutes, and demonstrates how cite a statute. It also explains how to determine when a statute "came into force" or became a statute that is enforceable in its jurisdiction.

LEARNING OBJECTIVES

At the end of this chapter you will be able to:

- Describe how statutes are created and published
- Locate a statute by title in the library and electronically
- Locate a statute by subject in the library and electronically
- Update a statute (*i.e.*, find revisions)
- Find out when a statute came into force
- Locate cases that have considered statutes (*i.e.*, note up a statute)
- Write a citation for a statute

HOW STATUTES ARE CREATED AND PUBLISHED

In order to research statutes properly you must understand the stages through which a statute passes and the way in which statutes are published.

As explained in Chapter 4 (Introduction to Law and Legal Materials), governments are constantly introducing or repealing statutes and thereby creating new law. Proposed legislation goes through a lengthy legislative process before becoming law. To determine whether a bill has become law, a researcher must trace the progress of a bill through each of its versions. Statutes are published by the federal government and by each provincial and territorial government. These governments also publish research aids such as tables and indexes of statutes, although many of the tools researchers use to locate statutes are published by commercial publishers.

Provincial parliaments consist of single legislatures, whereas the Canadian Parliament consists of the Senate and the House of Commons. A provincial bill must be read three times in the legislature. A federal bill must be read three times in each house as well as receive the consent of both houses before legislation can be effective.

The five basic stages of the creation of statutes are as follows:

Bill/First Reading	➔ Second Reading	➔ Third Reading
➔ Royal Assent	➔ Coming into Force (by Proclamation or Delayed Effective Date)	

There is one set of federal statutes published by the federal government and one set of statutes for each of the provinces and territories, published by their respective governments. Some of the provinces and territories have devolved the responsibility for publishing their statutes to private sector publishers.

Within each of set of statutes (provincial and federal) there are the following four main components:

Format	Stage
Bills/First Reading	Merely proposed but not yet approved
Gazettes/First Printing	First publication of statutes once they are passed (usually as individual paper Acts or several paper Acts softbound together)
Annual or Sessional Volumes	Formal bound set, usually published annually
Revised Statutes	Consolidation of statutes at a point in time

Each of these is described in detail here. It is important to note that, at least for the time being, there is only one official version of statutes. These are the government published versions. The federal and some provincial governments have now stated that the electronic versions of their laws, available on government websites, are acceptable for public consultation, but all government websites have a disclaimer that the printed statutes issued by provincial Queen's Printers are the only actual "official" versions and should always be consulted.

All commercially published versions are unofficial versions but, because they usually come out quicker than government versions, many researchers use them as starting points.

Bills/First Reading

A statute is first introduced in a provincial legislature or the federal Parliament as a bill. At first reading, bills are assigned a number and then are usually sent to a committee to be debated. This first reading is merely a formality. A bill may be either a public bill, which deals with public policy, or a private bill, which affects individuals or institutions.

The Parliament of Canada consists of two houses — the House of Commons and the Senate. Federal laws must be passed by each house. A statute is introduced in the House of Commons as a commons bill or in the Senate as a senate bill. The bills are assigned alpha-numeric numbers indicating where they were introduced (C = Commons; S = Senate) and when they were introduced in a particular session.

Explanatory Notes

A bill at first reading contains explanatory notes that can be helpful to researchers when determining the intent of a statute. However, these notes are never cited in judicial decisions because they are not actually part of the law. A bill may be debated and/or sent to a committee for further deliberations. The federal government has established an online Index to the Debates of the Senate, which currently goes back to 1991 (<http://dsp-psd.pwgsc.gc.ca/Collection-R/Senate/index-e.html>). This is handy for finding debates by subject alphabetically.

The statute is read three times in the House of Commons and three times in the Senate. At the third reading, the statute is voted on and passed and then receives royal assent by the Queen's federal representative, the Governor General. The Royal Assent date is printed on the front of every bill that is passed (see further discussion of assent below).

How a Statute Comes into Force

Just because an Act receives Royal Assent does not mean it automatically has enforceability. There are several ways by which an Act may "come into force" (CIF):

Immediately: The Act may be entirely silent on the coming into force. In this case the Act is deemed to be in force "on assent", that is, on the exact day it received Royal Assent.

Retrospectively: Very occasionally, legislators make an Act come in force retrospectively, meaning it is deemed to have come into force at an earlier date than it actually received Royal Assent. An example of this would be a taxation Act that was enforced retroactively to allow a government to collect "back taxes". To locate this date you look at the last (or nearly last) section of the Act where it states a specified day of coming into force (a commencement clause). It is almost always a future date.

Delayed: If the last section of the Act states that the Act (or specific sections of the Act) shall come into force on "a day or days to be proclaimed by the Governor General, acting on behalf of the federal cabinet" this means the Act has a "delayed effective date". This is usually because a date could not be determined at the time of assent and usually occurs when complicated administrative arrangements must be carried out before it is possible for the government to actually enforce the Act. The effective date is postponed until such preparations are in place.

Each of the provincial and territorial parliaments consists of one house. The legislation-making process is similar for all provinces. A statute is introduced as a bill and must receive three readings and Royal

Assent by the Queen's provincial representative, the Lieutenant Governor, before becoming law. The CIF procedure for provincial and territorial Acts is very similar to that of the federal Parliament, with most Acts coming into force by one of the ways mentioned above.

Bills are made only when Parliament is in session, so laws are categorized by session — usually one or two years in length. Any bills that do not become law in a session die "on the order table" and must be reintroduced in the next session. Each sitting of Parliament is numbered after each election. For example, the 36th Parliament since Confederation in 1867 began in June 1997 after that federal election.

The first reading of the bill is particularly important to researchers because it contains explanatory notes that help determine the intent of the statute.

A bill is debated at its second reading. At the third reading, the bill is reviewed in final form, with any changes that have been made in committee or as a result of debates. This is the version that usually becomes law. The third reading of a bill is also published, but is only important because it is the final written version of the statute until the statute is formally published a few months later, in the *Canada Gazette, Part III*, and then at the end of the year in the annual statutory volume(s) for that year.

Royal Assent

Royal Assent is the symbolic acceptance by the sovereign and simply involves signing the statute by the Governor General (for federal statutes) or Lieutenant Governor (for provincial and territorial statutes). Royal Assent occurs after the bill goes through the procedure described above and is approved by both houses (federal) or the legislature (provincial or territorial). However, not all statutes become law upon Royal Assent. As mentioned above, the effective date of some statutes may be delayed. This results in the statute coming into effect later, upon proclamation, or on a specified date. (See above discussion of "coming into force".)

For an example of the first page of a federal Act, see Appendix 7B. An example of the first page of a typical provincial Act appears in Appendix 7C.

RESEARCH TOOLS FOR BILLS

Most law libraries have print copies of federal and provincial bills (from their jurisdiction, at least) or research aids that explain what stage the bill is at. Bills may also be obtained directly from the federal and provincial governments by subscription, although this type of service is beginning to be discontinued in favour of online versions of bills from current legislative sessions.

There are several publications that list the progress of a bill. The most current information can be found on most government websites (*e.g.*, in a "legislative digest" or a "progress of bills" table) or by phoning the relevant legislature's library or clerk's office. LN/QL and WL*e*C also have federal and provincial statute and regulation databases from all Canadian jurisdictions, but only some bills appear in LN/QL at this time, and historical versions vary.

The following are examples of some of the research aids that can assist researchers in locating bills and determining their status:

Federal Bills

Ottawa Letter: A newsletter that contains information entitled "Progress of Legislation", which describes the progress of federal bills through Parliament. This is a useful source for determining the status of a bill in the House of Commons or the Senate.

Legislation: Legislation is part of the *Canadian Abridgment* that may be bought on subscription. Each monthly issue shows the progress of new federal, provincial, and territorial legislation, amendments to existing legislation, and regulations that have been promulgated. This information cumulates into the *Legislation Annual*, which is a complete snapshot of all legislative and regulatory action for all Canadian jurisdictions. (Note: no full text of legislation is provided.) It is an excellent current and historical reference, especially for identifying bills that never went past first reading. It is not currently online in WL*e*C, but there is some indication that it may be forthcoming.

Canadian Legislative Pulse: A recently created web-based service from CCH Canadian, one of the commercial online providers in Canada, allows researchers to check the current status and recent progress of legislation for all Canadian jurisdictions from one consolidated source. It includes online full-text versions of bills, customized e-mail updates on selected legislation changes on selected bills (based on the client's profile), and e-mail updates summarizing all legislative changes from all across Canada. Having links to full text obviates the need for the researcher to obtain bills elsewhere.

Order Paper and Notices: Parliament's agenda, outlining what will happen to a bill that day. This is rarely used for research but is handy for tracking legislation.

Provincial Bills

Each provincial legislature publishes similar lists that can be used by researchers to determine the status of a bill. Each of these publications contains similar information from province to province. Current-session versions of many of these are now online and available to the public through the websites of provincial and territorial legislatures, although they may disappear at the end of a legislative session. (See Appendix 7E for a list of these websites.) The following are some of the titles used:

Orders of the Day (sometimes called "Progress of Bills" or "Progress of Legislation"): A daily agenda of a provincial legislative assembly. It contains information on bills and the stage they are at.

Legislation and Legislation Annual, part of the *Canadian Abridgment* (see above).

Canadian Legislative Pulse (see above).

Legislative Digest or *Legislative Record*: Both resources list bills and what stage they are at. This is the most up-to-date tool and reasonably easy to use.

Votes and Proceedings: A program of what happened on a particular day during a legislative sitting.

First Printing of Statutes

After bills receive Royal Assent and thus become statutes, each one is assigned a chapter number. Then all the statutes from that year are collected together and printed. The chapter numbers assigned to federal statutes are consecutive numbers beginning with Chapter 1 in each new year. Thus, a federal statute about genetically modified foods might be Chapter 3 of a given year's statutes, and a statute about human rights might be Chapter 4 of that same year's statutes. The subject matter of the statutes has no logical relationship to the chapter number assigned.

Some provinces number their statutes in slightly different ways. For example, for brand new legislation, some use an alpha-numeric system, so that a new Act about farm animal health might be Chapter F-2. For amendments to existing Acts, they usually use the simple numeric designation. For example, an Act to amend an existing law about employment standards might be simply Chapter 45. Researchers will soon become familiar with the numbering system in place in their jurisdictions of interest.

Federal statutes are printed in the *Canada Gazette, Part III* (see Illustration 7.1) and provincial statutes are published in various ways, including what is typically called the *Third Reading Bills*. These softbound publications fill the gap between the printing of the individual original statute and the publication of the hardbound volume of statutes. Because they are softbound, libraries receive them within a few months of Royal Assent. Presently, the federal *Canada Gazette, Part III* and most of the provincial and territorial gazettes are on public websites.

Illustration 7.1
Canada Gazette, Part III

Vol. 26, No. 3

Vol. 26, n° 3

Canada Gazette
Part III

Gazette du Canada
Partie III

OTTAWA, TUESDAY, JANUARY 20, 2004

Statutes of Canada, 2003

Chapters 20 to 28

Acts assented to from 20 June, 2003
to 7 November, 2003

OTTAWA, LE MARDI 20 JANVIER 2004

Lois du Canada (2003)

Chapitres 20 à 28

Lois sanctionnées du 20 juin 2003
au 7 novembre 2003

NOTICE TO READERS

The *Canada Gazette* Part III is published under the authority of the *Statutory Instruments Act*. The purpose of Part III is to publish public Acts as soon as is reasonably practicable after they have received Royal Assent in order to expedite their distribution.

Part III of the *Canada Gazette* contains the public Acts of Canada and certain other ancillary publications, including a list of Proclamations of Canada and Orders in Council relating to the coming into force of Acts, from the date of the previous number to the date shown above.

AVIS AU LECTEUR

La Partie III de la *Gazette du Canada*, dont la publication est régie par la *Loi sur les textes réglementaires*, a pour objet d'assurer, dans les meilleurs délais suivant la sanction royale, la diffusion des lois d'intérêt public.

La Partie III de la *Gazette du Canada* présente en outre certains textes complémentaires, comme la liste des décrets d'entrée en vigueur et des proclamations du Canada ultérieurs au numéro précédent.

Illustration 7.1: This illustration gives the "look" of an opening page of the *Canada Gazette, Part III*.

The following describes the contents of the publications that accompany the hardbound federal statutes:

- *Canada Gazette, Part I*: Contains formal notices required by statute to be published.
- *Canada Gazette, Part II*: Contains new regulations (see Chapter 8).
- *Canada Gazette, Part III*: Contains new statutes and a table of proclamations.
- *Table of Public Statutes and Responsible Ministers*: A cumulative list showing the history of all federal public statutes, both those that are in force and those that have been repealed since the last printed revised set (see below).

Because it is difficult to recall all of the detailed steps involved in statute research, it is better to understand these fundamental parts. If you understand the *framework* of statutes, you will be able to do research in any jurisdiction.

Just remember that the release of provincial and territorial Acts to the public follows virtually the same procedure as at the federal level: the "assented to" version is published in paper form and then cumulated into annual volumes (see below) and various government websites offer both versions online, at least for the past several years (see Appendix 7E).

Annual or Sessional Volumes

At the end of each year or legislative session, all of the statutes from that year or session are collected and published in hardbound volumes called the "annual" or "sessional" volumes. Provincial sets of annual statutes are fairly similar to the federal set, although they go by slightly different titles. These volumes are received by libraries within a year after the end of the year or session. Often, they appear on the public websites of the various governments at the same time that they are distributed in print (see Appendix 7E). Until the annual volume(s) is released, one can always refer back to the official versions published in the gazette of the jurisdiction (see previous sections).

Annual or sessional volumes also typically include helpful research tools such as tables of contents, tables of statutes, and tables of proclamations. Each volume is identified by the year or session on its spine. Some sessions may span more than one year or there may be more than one session in a single year, although at the provincial and territorial levels, the modern trend is to stick strictly to publication by year. There may be one or several volumes per year, depending on the amount of legislation passed in that year.

Revised Statutes

The federal government and most provincial governments periodically consolidate their statutes into a "revised" set of statutes in force. This involves reprinting all statutes that are still in force, that is, not repealed, and incorporating all amendments up to that time. The revisions effectively repeal and replace all prior legislation. They are essentially consolidations of all public statutes in effect at the time of publication.

The federal government did this in 1886, 1906, 1927, 1952, 1970, and 1985. The most recent federal consolidation is the *Revised Statutes of Canada, 1985*, which consists of about 15 large volumes.

The old annual volumes that contain statutes from before the consolidation are rarely used and remain in the library mainly for historical purposes (*e.g.*, to see a statute in its original form). Researchers should rarely have to consult the pre-consolidated version of a statute, although this does occur.

Illustration 7.2

Arrangement of Statutes in a Library

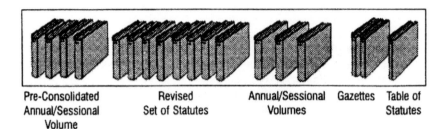

| Pre-Consolidated Annual/Sessional Volume | Revised Set of Statutes | Annual/Sessional Volumes | Gazettes | Table of Statutes |

For federal research, it is important to note that it took so long (four years) to produce the 1985 revision that the statutes that were amended or introduced between 1984 and 1988 were placed in supplements to the revised set. Therefore, the *Revised Statutes of Canada, 1985* consists of eight main volumes plus five supplements: one for each of the years from 1985 to 1988 and an Appendix volume. The main volumes and four supplements include all statutes enacted up to December 12, 1988. A researcher should always keep this problem in mind since this situation is true for most provinces also; many statutes continue to be passed while the revised set is being compiled.

Unofficial and Office Consolidations of Statutes

In a law library, you will find not only the official version of the consolidated statutes, but unofficial versions as well. These are usually published by commercial publishers and are edited in a way that makes them useful to researchers.

A few of the more popular statutes are published individually, with all current amendments incorporated into them. They often include the regulations and are in softcover. Examples include the Company Acts from various provinces and the *Criminal Code*. Some of these "desktop consolidations" include commentary from experts, citations to cases that have interpreted the statute, historical information on sections, *etc.*

Loose-leaf Editions of Statutes and Citators

There are several sets of commercially published loose-leaf editions of statutes. These are extremely useful tools because they are updated regularly by inserts so that you can avoid having to go through several volumes of statutes to determine which sections have been revised. As well, they are often annotated with lists of any cases that have considered a statute. These are called "annotations" or "statute citators". They are in both print and electronic form, although they are becoming less popular with the increasing number of statutes being made available by commercial online providers. The print and online versions are discussed further below, under noting up statutes.

Electronic Versions of Statutes

Computers have revolutionized statute research in three key ways:

- Statute databases can be searched by a simple keyword command;
- The electronic form can be kept fairly current because no time is needed to print, publish, and distribute the statutes; and
- The electronic version may be consolidated on a continuing basis — meaning that changes can be incorporated right into the statute so you do not have to search through several supplements and revisions to locate amendments.

However, the electronic versions are still not viewed by all courts as official, so print-based research is still necessary. Keep in mind that some of the statute databases are organized much like statute volumes on the shelves of a library. For example, one database may contain a consolidated set of statutes, while another may contain a year's worth of annual statutes. If this is so, then you must look in each of these databases for information relating to your statute.

There are some convenient places to locate electronic versions of statutes: public websites and commercial online providers.

Public websites: The federal government and most provinces maintain websites that include statutes and regulations (see Illustration 7.3 for a typical provincial website containing statutes). A list of these websites is appended to this chapter. CanLII and some other non-governmental websites, as well as several university and courthouse law libraries, provide access to federal and most provincial statutes, often through links to the originating website. See Chapter 5 (Law Libraries and Electronic Collections of Law) for recommended free websites.

Illustration 7.3
Government of British Columbia Website
Statutes and Regulations of British Columbia

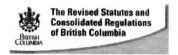

The Revised Statutes and
Consolidated Regulations
of British Columbia

QUEEN'S PRINTER
Ministry of Management Services

Home   Search

Complete Alphabetical Listing of Statutes
with Associated Regulations

[A |B|C|D|E|F|G|H|I|J|L|M|N|O|P|Q|R|S|T|U|V|W|Y]

Access to Abortion Services Act
[RSBC 1996] Chapter 1
    Historical Table
    Abortion Services Access Zone Regulation (B.C. Reg. 337/95)

Access to Education Act - [Repealed]
[SBC 2001] Chapter 1
    Table of Legislative Changes

Accountants (Certified General) Act
[RSBC 1996] Chapter 2
    Historical Table

Accountants (Chartered) Act
[RSBC 1996] Chapter 3
    Historical Table

Accountants (Management) Act
[RSBC 1996] Chapter 4
    Historical Table

Adoption Act
[RSBC 1996] Chapter 5
    Historical Table
    Table of Legislative Changes
    Adoption Agency Regulation (B.C. Reg. 292/96)
    Adoption Fees Regulation (B.C. Reg. 293/96)
    Adoption Regulation (B.C. Reg. 291/96)

Adult Guardianship Act
[RSBC 1996] Chapter 6
    Supplement
    Table of Legislative Changes
    Adult Guardianship (Abuse and Neglect) Regulation (B.C. Reg. 13/2000)
    Designated Agencies Regulation (B.C. Reg. 19/2002)

Age of Majority Act
[RSBC 1996] Chapter 7
    Historical Table

Agricultural and Rural Development (BC) Act - [Repealed]

As you can see, each statute, in its consolidated form, is listed and is available in electronic form. The currency date, that is, the date of the most recent consolidation, is usually shown at the top of the text of each Act. It is important to the researcher to know how recently the text has been consolidated (also referred to as "revised"). The historical tables or legislative changes may be listed below each statute, as in the above illustration, or changes may be in a separate table (see discussions below).

Illustration 7.4
Government of British Columbia Website

Name Act

HISTORICAL TABLE   Page 1 of 2

Copyright © 2004: Queen's Printer,
Victoria, British Columbia, Canada   IMPORTANT INFORMATION

Legislative History
NAME ACT
RSBC 1996, chapter 328

Section	History
1	RS1979-295-1; 1987-55-36.
2	RS1979-295-2; 1985-68-94(a),(c); 1985-68-94(b); 1985-86-23; 1992-62-4.
3	RS1979-295-3; 1992-62-5.
4	RS1979-295-3; 1984-19-5; 1985-68-95; 1987-55-37; 1988-38-9; 1992-62-6.
5	RS1979-295-4; 1985-68-96; 1987-55-38.
6	RS1979-295-5; 1987-55-39.
7	RS1979-295-6.
8	RS1979-295-6.1; 1987-55-40.
9	RS1979-295-7; 1982-7-88; 1987-55-41; 1993-38-28.
10	RS1979-295-8; 1984-19-6; 1985-68-97; 1987-55-42.
11	RS1979-295-9.
12	RS1979-295-10; 1987-55-43.
13	RS1979-295-11; 1987-55-44.
14	RS1979-295-12; 1985-68-98.
15	RS1979-295-15 (2), (3)(part).
16	RS1979-295-15 (1), (3)(part), (4).
17	RS1979-295-13; 1987-55-45.
18	RS1979-295-14; 1987-55-46.

Copyright © 2007 Province of British Columbia. All rights reserved. Reprinted with permission of the Province of British Columbia. www.ipp.gov.bc.ca

Commercial online service providers: LN/QL and WL*e*C have databases of statutes and regulations including all federal, provincial, and territorial statutes. The two services are almost identical in terms of content although they have different types of interface and varying search tools and updater features. Always use their tools (often a hyperlink) to check the coverage and currency of the database before you do a search.

As with other electronic sources, it is critical that you find out exactly what is in the database and how current the information is. Note whether the statutes are consolidated, and, if not, which other databases update these databases. For example, you may have to look in three databases: the revised statutes, gazettes (for very recent legislation), and bills (for legislation not yet passed). You will need to search in print sources or phone the legislature to locate changes, if any, since the latest update.

THE FIVE STEPS TO LOCATING AND UPDATING STATUTES

There are essentially two ways to find statutes: by title or by subject. If you know the name of a particular statute, you can do an electronic search or search by title in various print indexes (called tables of statutes). If you know only the subject area, other research tools must be used.

Statutes are generally much easier to find than cases because the federal, and provincial, and territorial governments, usually through the jurisdictional Queen's Printer, edit and maintain the statutes and publish consolidated lists of statutes.

There are five steps to finding, updating and noting up statutes. They are as follows:

Step 1: Find a statute by name or citation.
Step 2: Find a statute by subject.
Step 3: Find out whether the statute is in force.
Step 4: Find out if the statute has been amended (*i.e.*, update it).
Step 5: Find cases that considered it (*i.e.*, note it up).

A summary of these steps is appended to this chapter. Each section below discusses how to access both the library and electronic collections for each step.

Step 1: Find a Statute by Name or Citation

It is fairly easy to locate a statute if you have the name of the statute or its citation. The easiest way is by an electronic search, keeping in mind that you may also need an official print version statute for a court. For the official version, you may find some from recent years online, but for older Acts you will have to go to a law library with an historical collection.

The quickest way to locate the statute in its consolidated form is to go to <http://www.CanLII.org> or the relevant government website and conduct a word search by entering your statute title in the template provided. This search could also be conducted through LN/QL or WL*e*C.

If you decide to use print sources, the quickest way to locate a statute is by looking in a commercially published loose-leaf statute set, sometimes known as a "statute" citator. Although citators are not the official version of statutes, they will give you the proper title of the statute, any revisions to that statute, and, in some citators, cases that have considered the statute. Commercially published sets of statutes are excellent research tools but you should confirm the information in the official set of statutes in print form. There are no longer any loose-leaf sets of statutes published by the governments of any Canadian jurisdictions except Québec and Prince Edward Island. And, given the convenience, speed and economy of online consolidation, it is doubtful that most commercially produced loose-leaf sets will be continued much longer.

The other most direct way to locate print statutes is by looking in the relevant federal or provincial table of statutes. This way works regardless of jurisdiction and is freely available to anyone without having to purchase expensive commercial products. Most provincial governments and the federal governments publish comprehensive consolidated tables of public statutes. The tables are cumulative, alphabetical lists of all statutes in force and are constantly updated. Other important information is usually included in the tables, such as the date the statute came into effect and the way it was brought into effect (*e.g.*, by proclamation and on what date).

The table also lists amendments to the statute. These tables are a researcher's most important tool for finding statutes. By locating the title of your statute in the table (by year and chapter number) you can easily locate it in the main set of statutes, whether it is in the consolidated ("revised") set or in an annual volume. Instructions on how to read tables of statutes are at the end of this chapter.

The federal table is called the *Table of Public Statutes and Responsible Ministers* and is published in the final annual volume for each year. It is published in English (gold pages) and French (blue pages), making it easy to located in the hardcover volume. It is also published in paperback format up to three times annually. For the past several decades, the minister responsible for enforcing each Act has been shown. An online version of this table can be found at <http://laws.justice.gc.ca/en/publaw/index.html>.

Provincial and territorial tables of statutes have various titles and various frequencies of publication. Some are published on coloured paper for ease of locating. Some tables give coming into force (CIF) information on the same page as the history of the Act, while others give this important information in separate "proclamation" tables or schedules. Researchers need to become familiar with the layout and contents of the tables of their jurisdictions of interest. Some provinces no longer publish these tables but publish a list of legislative changes instead. In these situations it is best to use electronic sources. These tables of statutes and proclamations are usually linked from government websites that display provincial consolidated statutes. See Appendix 7E for a list of such sites.

The example below shows how (in this case, federal) statutes are listed alphabetically and how their location is indicated by the year, volume, and chapter number of the statute. This is called the citation. The table also lists amendments to each section. At the bottom is convenient CIF information for the original act itself and each change to each section. Researchers must get in the habit of noting not only the changes to sections of interest, but also the CIF information.

Illustration 7.5
Statutes of Canada: Table of Public Statutes
and Responsible Ministers

Citizenship Act — R.S., 1985, c. C-29
    (Citoyenneté, Loi sur la)

Minister of Citizenship and Immigration (SI/94-86)

s. 2, R.S., c. 28 (4th Supp.), s. 36(2) (Sch., item 2); 1992, c. 21, s. 6; 2000, c. 12, s. 74; 2001, c. 26, s. 286, c. 27, s. 227.1; 2002, c. 8, par. 183(1)(*d*)
s. 3, 1995, c. 5, s. 25(1)(*e*)
s. 5, R.S., c. 44 (3rd Supp.), s. 1; 1992, c. 21, s. 7; 2000, c. 12, s. 75; 2001, c. 27, s. 228
s. 9, 1992, c. 21, s. 8
s. 11, 2001, c. 27, s. 229
s. 14, 1995, c. 15, s. 23; 2001, c. 27, s. 230
s. 16, 2002, c. 8, par. 182(1)(*j*)
s. 19, 1992, c. 1, s. 144 (Sch. VII, item 22)(F); 1997, c. 22, s. 1
s. 19.1, added, 1997, c. 22, s. 2
s. 19.2, added, 1997, c. 22, s. 2
s. 19.3, added, 1997, c. 22, s. 2
s. 20, 1997, c. 22, s. 3
s. 22, R.S., c. 30 (3rd Supp.), s. 11; 1992, c. 47, s. 67, c. 49, s. 124; 1999, c. 31, s. 42; 2000, c. 24, s. 33; 2001, c. 27, s. 231
s. 35, R.S., c. 28 (1st Supp.), s. 49; 2001, c. 27, s. 232
s. 37, 1993, c. 28, s. 78 (Sch. III, item 18); 2002, c. 7, s. 131
Conditional amendments, 2000, c. 12, ss. 76, 77
General, 1995, c. 5, s. 25(2)
Transitional, 1997, c. 22, s. 10
CIF, R.S., c. 28 (1st Supp.), s. 49 proclaimed in force 30.06.85 *see* SI/85-128
CIF, R.S., c. 30 (3rd Supp.), s. 11 proclaimed in force 30.10.87 *see* SI/87-251
CIF, R.S., c. 44 (3rd Supp.), s. 1 proclaimed in force 15.02.88 *see* SI/88-32

CIF, R.S., c. 28 (4th Supp.), s. 36(2) proclaimed in force 01.01.89 *see* SI/88-231

CIF, 1992, c. 1, s. 144 (Sch. VII, item 22)(F) in force on assent 28.02.92

CIF, 1992, c. 21, ss. 6 to 8 in force 30.06.92 *see* SI/92-126

CIF, 1992, c. 47, s. 67 in force 01.08.96 *see* SI/96-56

CIF, 1992, c. 49, s. 124 in force 01.02.93 *see* SI/93-16

CIF, 1993, c. 28, s. 78 (Sch. III, item 18) in force 01.04.99 *see* s. 79

CIF, 1995, c. 5, s. 25 in force 13.05.95 *see* SI/95-65

CIF, 1995, c. 15, s. 23 in force 10.07.95 *see* SI/95-76

CIF, 1997, c. 22, ss. 1 to 3 and 10 in force 20.05.97 *see* SI/97-64

CIF, 1999, c. 31, s. 42 in force on assent 17.06.99

CIF, 2000, c. 12, ss. 76 and 77 in force on assent 29.06.2000; ss. 74 and 75 in force 01.07.2003 *see* SI/2003-118

CIF, 2000, c. 24, s. 33 in force 23.10.2000 *see* SI/2000-95

CIF, 2001, c. 26, s. 286 comes into force on a day to be fixed by order of the Governor in Council *see* s. 334. Not in force 31.08.2003

CIF, 2001, c. 27, ss. 227.1 to 232 in force 28.06.2002 *see* SI/2002-97

CIF, 2002, c. 7, s. 131 in force 01.04.2003 *see* SI/2003-48

CIF, 2002, c. 8, ss. 182 and 183 in force 02.07.2003 *see* SI/2003-109

A citation is simply an abbreviated reference used to help locate statutes. If the abbreviation starts with an "R" then you know that the statute you are looking for is part of a revised (consolidated) set of statutes. If it starts with an "S" then you know the statute was published *after* the most recent printed revised set and can be found only in its original, as-passed version in the sessional or annual volume(s) for the year of passage. The remaining few first letters represent the jurisdiction:

Examples of Statute Abbreviations	
Abbreviation	**Full Title**
R.S.C.	*Revised Statutes of Canada*
S.C.	*Statutes of Canada*
R.S.O.	*Revised Statutes of Ontario*
S.O.	*Statutes of Ontario*

Step 2: Find a Statute by Subject

If you do not know the name of the statute you are looking for, then it is best to narrow your search before going to electronic versions of statutes. Although search engines enable you to drill through significant information, you can spend substantial time on your computer searching for a statute if you do not know its proper name, because keyword searching will find *every* instance of a word in *every* statute within the database, whether or not it is the exact statute you want (see below). Having said that, if you know there is relevant statute, but do not know the name, you might want to start with a word search on CanLII. Its search engine is so powerful that it will pull up several statutes and you can get a sense of what you are dealing with. However, always follow this up with other research.

There are several reasons why you might not want to start with an electronic search. First, there are possibly thousands of statutes that contain the words that you are searching for. More important is the fact that you might find one statute that is relevant and overlook another that is also relevant. For example, you might find a statute that deals with matrimonial property on death and miss a statute that deals with matrimonial property on divorce. The other problem with electronic searches is that they search by word. This means that unless you know the specific word or words that define the concepts you are looking for, you will have a difficult time locating the statute.

The best way to begin a subject search for a statute is by refining your search: read about your topic generally in secondary sources and then conduct an electronic search for the statute by title.

The most helpful secondary materials are the *Canadian Encyclopedic Digest* (CED), *Halsbury's Laws of Canada,* and textbooks. The CED is available through WL*e*C. *Halsbury's* is only in print format at this time. Textbooks are available from law libraries, although a growing assortment are being published online. These secondary materials are essentially explanations and commentary about the law and are described in detail in Chapter 6 (How to Find Secondary Materials). They provide an overview of the law and direct the researcher to specific cases and statutes.

You may be wondering why there are no statute subject indexes. They are rare because indexing every significant word in every statute is a huge, formidable job. A few provincial governments publish subject indexes as part of their set of statutes. These indexes list statutes by subject and provide citations. These subject indexes are usually bound volumes and are typically included with the latest set of revised statutes. They list statutes by subject and provide citations (*i.e.,* year and chapter numbers). These subject indexes are slowly disappearing with the introduction of electronic sources. Many are out of date, since they are often only prepared as part of a consolidation. For example, the last subject indexes for federal statutes were published in 1985, called the *Revised Statutes of Canada, 1985 English Index.* Provincial indexes go by various titles. Another index entitled *Index to Federal and Ontario Statutes* is on the Captus Press website (<http:www.captus.com>).

As mentioned above, there are many electronic versions of statutes. These include CanLII, government websites, LN/QL and WL*e*C. Most allow you to use their templates and conduct a word search for statutes. Thus, every significant keyword can be found much easier than using a printed index.

Step 3: Find Out Whether the Statute Is in Force

Some statutes are not in force immediately. All statutes need Royal Assent but many have delayed effective dates. This date may be stated in the statute itself or may have been proclaimed on a later date, as discussed previously in this chapter.

The delayed effective date, almost always a future date, is usually mentioned in the last section of the statute. If no date is stated, then the Act is deemed to have come into force on assent. If the last section mentions a proclamation, then the Act has to be proclaimed.

It is important to understand that the official way of proclaiming an Act in force is for the representative of the Crown (Governor General or Lieutenant Governor) to publish a written proclamation in the *Gazette*. This proclamation is known as a "statutory instrument" or a "regulation" but it is really just the proclamation of the Act. It must be published so that the general public knows that the Act is in force, but researchers rarely look at proclamations. Instead, they rely on CIF information as displayed in the federal *Table of Public Statutes and Responsible Ministers* (see above) or in tables or separate schedules published in the annual statutes of provinces and territories. Since these tables are official publications of the Queen's Printer, they can be deemed to be correct for CIF purposes. Again, researchers must always verify through these tables that the statute (or a section thereof) that they intend to apply or argue was actually "in force" on the day the client's legal issue commenced.

Step 4: Find Out if the Statute Has Been Amended (Update It)

It is very important to determine whether and how a statute has been amended. And, there is always the possibility that a statute has been repealed or replaced with a new statute. There are two ways to find out how a statute has been amended: the official way and the unofficial way.

The Official Way

To find out if a statute has been amended (or repealed) it is easy to look in the relevant federal or provincial table of statutes, either online or in print. The tables list each statute and the sections of the statute that have been amended, in numerical order. They also provide a citation for the amending statute and indicate when the amendment came into effect.

This way always works, regardless of jurisdiction, because *all* Canadian jurisdictions have some kind of tables and thus researchers do not have to purchase costly commercial alternatives (see below). The drawback is that some government-produced tables may not be quite as up to date as commercial counterparts. But for some research, timeliness is not necessarily that critical, especially if your research involves some issue that happened in the relatively distant past.

The Unofficial Way

The unofficial way to locate amendments to a statute is by using a commercially published statute citator (print or electronic). Citators, which are discussed in more detail below, are used primarily for locating cases that consider statutes, but they often list all statutes and their amendments. They are a wonderful starting point but all of the information must be confirmed because they are not considered official and may have errors. Researchers should note that there are almost no surviving printed citators for the smaller provinces and the territories because of lack of sufficient numbers of purchasers. Also, citators are not free, as are government-produced tables. With the advent of online citators (see below), all jurisdictions now have electronic statute citators. CanLII recently introduced a new release which provides a citator function for each jurisdiction to the public at no cost.

Illustration 7.6
Cover Page of a Federal Table of Public Statutes and Responsible Ministers

**TABLE OF PUBLIC STATUTES AND RESPONSIBLE MINISTERS
(UPDATED TO DECEMBER 31, 2002)***

SHOWING ALL THE CHAPTERS OF THE REVISED STATUTES, 1985, WITH
AMENDMENTS THERETO, AND CERTAIN OTHER PUBLIC ACTS AND
AMENDMENTS THERETO
(UPDATED TO DECEMBER 31, 2002)*

NOTE TO USERS:

Acts in the following categories are listed alphabetically thereunder:
Agreements — Income Tax, Estate Tax, Succession Duty, and related tax matters
Agreements — Trade, Commerce and related matters
Bridges, Electoral Districts, Provincial Boundaries, and Treaties of Peace.

Immediately beneath the title of each Act is the equivalent title, printed in italics, of the Act in the other official language. This will assist users of this Table in finding the Act in the French version of this Table.

References in bold face beneath an Act indicate the provisions of that Act that have been amended or added. The reader should refer to the coming into force (CIF) entry for each amendment at the end of the listing of amendments to an Act. CIF dates are by day, month and year (e.g. 05.01.89 is 5 January, 1989).

The term SOR or SI is a reference to Statutory Orders and Regulations or Statutory Instruments as published in the *Canada Gazette* Part II. CIF refers to the date of coming into force. (E) indicates the English version only is amended and (F) indicates the French version only is amended.

To subscribe to this publication, to change the address of your current subscription, or for information about your subscription, please contact: **Canadian Government Publishing, PWGSC, Ottawa, Ontario, Canada, K1A 0S9. Tel: 1-800-635-7943; Fax: 819-994-1498.**

Any comments or inquiries concerning the contents of the Table of Public Statutes should be directed, preferably in writing, to:

Robert DuPerron
Chief Legislative Editor
Department of Justice
St-Andrew's Tower
284 Wellington Street, Room 3115
Ottawa, Ontario
Canada   Tel: 613-957-0026
K1A 0H8   Fax: 613-957-7866

---

*There are a certain number of public Acts, passed before January 1, 1985, that were not consolidated in the Revised Statutes of Canada, 1927, 1952, 1970 or 1985. As those Acts are still in force, they are included in this Table. There are also a number of sections (or parts thereof) in Acts passed before January 1, 1985, that were not consolidated in the Revised Statutes of Canada, 1927, 1952, 1970 or 1985. Those provisions may be found in Schedule A to the Revised Statutes of Canada, 1927 (p. 4283 of Volume IV), Schedule A to the Revised Statutes of Canada, 1952 (p. 5967 of Volume V (Supplement)). Schedule A (Reprinted) to the Revised Statutes of Canada, 1970 (p. 397 of the 2nd Supplement, replacing what was Schedule A in the 1st Supplement). Schedule A (Continued) to the Revised Statutes of Canada, 1970 (p. 435 of the 2nd Supplement) and the Schedules to the Revised Statutes of Canada, 1985 (Appendix I in the "Appendices" volume and the Schedules at the end of the 1st to 4th Supplements). In each Schedule the sections (or parts thereof) that were not consolidated are shown as exceptions in the third column entitled "Extent of Repeal."

Illustration 7.7
Excerpt from a Federal Table of Public Statutes
and Responsible Ministers

Citizenship Act — R.S., 1985, c. C-29
(Citoyenneté, Loi sur la)

Minister of Citizenship and Immigration (SI/94-86)

s. 2, R.S., c. 28 (4th Supp.), s. 36(2) (Sch., item 2); 1992, c. 21, s. 6; 2000, c. 12, s. 74; 2001, c. 26, s. 286, c. 27, s. 227.1; 2002, c. 8, par. 183(1)(*d*)

s. 3, 1995, c. 5, s. 25(1)(*e*)

s. 5, R.S., c. 44 (3rd Supp.), s. 1; 1992, c. 21, s. 7; 2000, c. 12, s. 75; 2001, c. 27, s. 228; 2003, c. 22, s. 149(E)

s. 9, 1992, c. 21, s. 8

s. 11, 2001, c. 27, s. 229; 2005, c. 17, s. 1

s. 14, 1995, c. 15, s. 23; 2001, c. 27, s. 230

s. 16, 2002, c. 8, par. 182(1)(*j*)

s. 19, 1992, c. 1, s. 144 (Sch. VII, item 22)(F); 1997, c. 22, s. 1

s. 19.1, added, 1997, c. 22, s. 2

s. 19.2, added, 1997, c. 22, s. 2

s. 19.3, added, 1997, c. 22, s. 2; 2005, c. 10, s. 14

s. 20, 1997, c. 22, s. 3

s. 22, R.S., c. 30 (3rd Supp.), s. 11; 1992, c. 47, s. 67, c. 49, s. 124; 1999, c. 31, s. 42; 2000, c. 24, s. 33; 2001, c. 27, s. 231

s. 35, R.S., c. 28 (1st Supp.), s. 49; 2001, c. 27, s. 232

s. 37, 1993, c. 28, s. 78 (Sch. III, item 18); 2002, c. 7, s. 131

Conditional amendments, 2000, c. 12, ss. 76, 77

General, 1995, c. 5, s. 25(2)

Transitional, 1997, c. 22, s. 10

CIF, R.S., c. 28 (1st Supp.), s. 49 proclaimed in force 30.06.85 *see* SI/85-128

CIF, R.S., c. 30 (3rd Supp.), s. 11 proclaimed in force 30.10.87 *see* SI/87-251

CIF, R.S., c. 44 (3rd Supp.), s. 1 proclaimed in force 15.02.88 *see* SI/88-32

CIF, R.S., c. 28 (4th Supp.), s. 36(2) proclaimed in force 01.01.89 *see* SI/88-231

CIF, 1992, c. 1, s. 144 (Sch. VII, item 22)(F) in force on assent 28.02.92

CIF, 1992, c. 21, ss. 6 to 8 in force 30.06.92 *see* SI/92-126

CIF, 1992, c. 47, s. 67 in force 01.08.96 *see* SI/96-56

CIF, 1992, c. 49, s. 124 in force 01.02.93 *see* SI/93-16

CIF, 1993, c. 28, s. 78 (Sch. III, item 18) in force 01.04.99 *see* s. 79

CIF, 1995, c. 5, s. 25 in force 13.05.95 *see* SI/95-65

CIF, 1995, c. 15, s. 23 in force 10.07.95 *see* SI/95-76

CIF, 1997, c. 22, ss. 1 to 3 and 10 in force 20.05.97 *see* SI/97-64

CIF, 1999, c. 31, s. 42 in force on assent 17.06.99

CIF, 2000, c. 12, ss. 76 and 77 in force on assent 29.06.2000; ss. 74 and 75 in force 01.07.2003 *see* SI/2003-118

CIF, 2000, c. 24, s. 33 in force 23.10.2000 *see* SI/2000-95

CIF, 2001, c. 26, s. 286 comes into force on a day to be fixed by order of the Governor in Council *see* s. 334. Not in force 31.08.2003

CIF, 2001, c. 27, ss. 227.1 to 232 in force 28.06.2002 *see* SI/2002-97

CIF, 2002, c. 7, s. 131 in force 01.04.2003 *see* SI/2003-48

CIF, 2002, c. 8, ss. 182 and 183 in force 02.07.2003 *see* SI/2003-109

CIF, 2003, c. 22, s. 149 in force 01.04.2005 *see* SI/2005-24

CIF, 2005, c. 10, s. 14 in force 04.04.2005 *see* SI/2005-29

CIF, 2005, c. 17, in force on assent 05.05.2005

In the illustration, s. 5 of the *Citizenship Act* was amended in the *Revised Statutes of Canada, 1985*, Chapter 44 (3rd supplement), by s. 1, in 1992 in the *Statutes of Canada*, Chapter 21, by s. 7, in 2000 in the *Statutes of Canada*, Chapter 12, by s. 75, and in 2001 in the *Statutes of Canada*, Chapter 27, by s. 228. If you look at the CIF (coming into force) references, you can see that these amendments came into effect on 15.02.88, 30.06.92, 01.07.2003, and 28.06.2002, respectively.

Each of the provincial legislatures keeps track of bills and statutes and records any amendments. These records are maintained by the government office that oversees the proceedings of the legislature. Indeed, expert researchers will simply call the legislative library to find out the most recent revisions to particular statutes, since they can be changed daily.

For the most recent amendments to statutes (*i.e.*, those published after the date of publication of the most recent table of statutes), you can look in the various publications from the various legislatures. These were mentioned previously in this chapter, under the heading **RESEARCH TOOLS FOR BILLS**.

Typically the most current versions of statutes are either on government websites or available through academic law libraries, legislative libraries, and the libraries in courthouses or operated by bar societies. Look very closely for the date that the information was updated. If it is a few days old, it is best to update even further by speaking to a law librarian, who can usually provide you with contact information for the clerk of the appropriate legislature.

Locate the Amending Statute

Armed with the citation of the amending statute, a researcher can locate the amending statute(s). The amending statute may amend more than one statute. If so, you must locate the specific sections that amend your particular statute. For example, if you look up the first amendment to s. 5 of the *Citizenship Act* (in c. 44 (3rd supplement) of the *Revised Statutes of Canada, 1985*), you will see that the title of the statute is *An Act to amend the Citizenship Act (period of residence)*. Section 1 of that Act amends the *Citizenship Act*.

You can ensure that the amendment is effective by looking up the regulation that brought the amendment into effect. For example, you can see from the *Table of Public Statutes and Responsible Ministers* above that the first amendment to s. 5 of the *Citizenship Act* came into effect on 15.02.88 (that is, February 15, 1988) by proclamation (published as a statutory instrument numbered SI/88-32). Again, researchers rarely need to look at the actual written proclamation since it is verifiable by consulting various government-produced tables.

Step 5: Find Cases that Considered It (Note It Up)

The way in which a court interprets a statute is as important to statutory research as locating the statute itself. Cases tell a researcher how a statute has been interpreted by the courts and whether it is consistent with the Constitution and other statutes. Therefore, locating cases that have considered statutes is a vital part of statute research. This step is called noting up a statute.

Statute citators are the most useful tools for noting up statutes. They are specific research aids designed specifically to locate cases that have considered statutes. Many citators also list amendments to statutes. Statute citators are essentially annotated statutes. They are books that list statutes and amendments to the statutes, and often they include summaries or lists of cases that have considered the statutes.

Citators are particularly useful because they are usually in electronic or loose-leaf form and are continually updated. However, they are secondary sources and should not be relied on as a final version of the law. Information in the citators should be confirmed in the official statute and specific cases.

In a law library you will typically find the following statute citators:

All Canada: *Canadian Statute Citations* (*Canadian Abridgment*, Thomson Carswell), and through WL*e*C. This citator consists of a set of volumes listing federal, provincial, and territorial statutes by title as well as those cases that have considered each statute. Statutes are listed alphabetically by jurisdiction (see Illustration 7.9).

Federal Statutes: *Canada Statute Service* (Canada Law Book) in loose-leaf format (see Illustration 7.8).

Provincial Statutes: There are also numerous provincial citators, since each province has its own set of statutes. The main legal publishers each have their own versions. However, at present there are no separate citators for the smaller provinces and the territories because of a lack of purchasers. There are commercially produced statute citators for the larger provinces, such as Alberta, British Columbia, and Ontario. The following are examples of a few British Columbia statute citators:

- *British Columbia Statute Service* (Canada Law Book), also on CD-ROM
- *Statutes of British Columbia Judicially Considered* (Carswell), also on CD-ROM and through Westlaw*e*CARSWELL
- *British Columbia Decisions: Statute Citator* (Canada Law Book)

Because there are often several statute citators, an easy way to distinguish them is by publisher.

WL*e*C has a powerful electronic citator, *KeyCite Canada*, that is easily identified on the home page. You can enter a statute's name and jurisdiction, plus a relevant section number, and hyperlinks will appear to the full text of cases that have interpreted that statute and section. At this time, LN/QL does not have an equivalent statute citator feature, although the company has indicated that one is forthcoming. In the meantime, researchers who have LN/QL can construct Boolean searches combining a statute name and section number to find cases that have those search terms present.

The new release of CanLII does have a statute citator feature covering all Canadian jurisdictions. A drawback is that the case law files in CanLII do not go all the way back in time. Thus you will only retrieve recent cases, but not all cases, that have interpreted your statute of interest. Individual government sites do not have citators, so it is best to use CanLII, which links to many government case law sites, if you do not purchase a commercial online service.

Illustration 7.8
Canada Statute Citator (Canada Law Book)

CANADA

STATUTE

CITATOR

R.S.C. 1985

VOLUME 2

Canada Post Corporation Act to Energy Supplies Emergency Act

Legal Editor
Rebecca Y. Tobe, B.A., LL.B.

Production Editor
Lilly Della Posta, B.Sc.

CANADA LAW BOOK INC.
240 EDWARD STREET, AURORA, ONTARIO, L4G 3S9

JUNE 2000

Reprinted by permission of Canada Law Book.

CITIZENSHIP ACT

R.S.C. 1985, Chap. C-29

Administered by the Department of Citizenship and Immigration

Amended R.S.C. 1985, c. 28 (1st Supp.), s. 49
Amended R.S.C. 1985, c. 30 (3rd Supp.), s. 11
Amended R.S.C. 1985, c. 44 (3rd Supp.)
Amended R.S.C. 1985, c. 28 (4th Supp.), s. 36
Amended 1992, c. 21, ss. 6 to 8; brought into force June 30, 1992 by SI/92-126, *Can. Gaz.*, *Part II*, July 15, 1992
Amended 1992, c. 47, s. 67; brought into force August 1, 1996 by SI/96-56
Amended 1992, c. 49, s. 124; brought into force February 1, 1993
Amended 1993, c. 28, Sch. III, s. 18; in force April 1, 1999
Amended 1995, c. 5, s. 25(1)(e); brought into force May 13, 1995 by SI/95-65, *Can. Gaz.*, *Part II*, May 31, 1995
Amended 1995, c. 15, s. 23; brought into force July 10, 1995 by SI/95-76, *Can. Gaz.*, *Part II*, July 12, 1995
Amended 1997, c. 22, ss. 1 to 3; brought into force May 20, 1997 by SI/97-64, *Can. Gaz.*, *Part II*, June 11, 1997
Amended 1999, c. 31, s. 42; in force June 17, 1999
Amended 2000, c. 12, ss. 74 to 77; ss. 74, 75 brought into force July1, 2003 by SI/2003-118, *Can. Gaz.*, *Part II*, June 18, 2003; ss. 76, 77 to come into force as provided by these sections
Amended 2000, c. 24, s. 33; brought into force October 23, 2000 by SI/2000-95, *Can. Gaz.*, *Part II*, November 8, 2000
Amended 2001, c. 26, s. 286; to come into force by order of the Governor in Council
Amended 2001, c. 27, ss. 227.1 to 232; brought into force June 28, 2002 by para. (*f*) of SI/2002-97, *Can. Gaz.*, *Part II*, June 14, 2002
Amended 2002, c. 7, s. 131; brought into force April 1, 2003 by SI/2003-48, *Can. Gaz.*, *Part II*, April 9, 2003
Amended 2002, c. 8, ss. 182(1)(*j*), 183(1)(*d*); brought into force July 2, 2003 by SI/2003-109, *Can. Gaz.*, *Part II*, June 4, 2003
Amended 2003, c. 22, s. 149; to come into force by order of the Governor in Council

Generally

NOTE: SI/94-86 (P.C. 1994-1122, June 30, 1994), *Can. Gaz.*, *Part II*, July 27, 1994, designates the Minister of Citizenship and Immigration as Minister of this Act.

NOTE: 1997, c. 22, s. 10 provides as follows:

10. If, before section 1 of this Act comes into force, a legal proceeding has been commenced with respect to an investigation under subsection 19(4) of the *Citizenship Act*, a final decision in that proceeding that the Review Committee must cease its investigation is deemed to be a decision of the Review Committee under subsection 19(4.1) of that Act, as enacted by subsection 1(2) of this Act.

Section 2

Subsec. (1) definition "common-law partner" new 2000, c. 12, s. 74:

"common-law partner", in relation to an individual, means a person who is cohabiting with the individual in a conjugal relationship, having so cohabited for a period of at least one year;

Reprinted by permission of Canada Law Book.

Illustration 7.9
Canadian Statute Citations (*Canadian Abridgment*, Carswell)

ILLUSTRATION

Statutes
This sample is taken from the Canada section of the statutes:

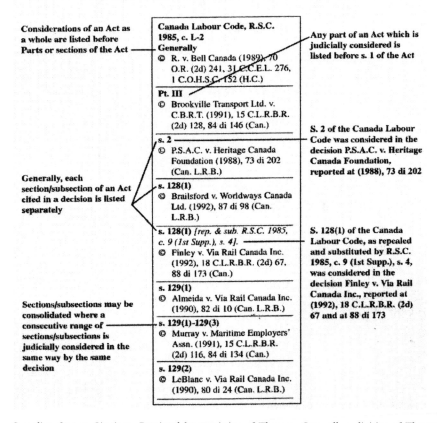

Considerations of an Act as a whole are listed before Parts or sections of the Act —

Canada Labour Code, R.S.C. 1985, c. L-2
Generally
© R. v. Bell Canada (1989), 70 O.R. (2d) 241, 31 C.C.E.L. 276, 1 C.O.H.S.C. 152 (H.C.)

Any part of an Act which is judicially considered is listed before s. 1 of the Act

Pt. III
© Brookville Transport Ltd. v. C.B.R.T. (1991), 15 C.L.R.B.R. (2d) 128, 84 di 146 (Can.)

s. 2
© P.S.A.C. v. Heritage Canada Foundation (1988), 73 di 202 (Can. L.R.B.)

S. 2 of the Canada Labour Code was considered in the decision P.S.A.C. v. Heritage Canada Foundation, reported at (1988), 73 di 202

Generally, each section/subsection of an Act cited in a decision is listed separately

s. 128(1)
© Brailsford v. Worldways Canada Ltd. (1992), 87 di 98 (Can. L.R.B.)

s. 128(1) *[rep. & sub. R.S.C. 1985, c. 9 (1st Supp.), s. 4].*
© Finley v. Via Rail Canada Inc. (1992), 18 C.L.R.B.R. (2d) 67, 88 di 173 (Can.)

S. 128(1) of the Canada Labour Code, as repealed and substituted by R.S.C. 1985, c. 9 (1st Supp.), s. 4, was considered in the decision Finley v. Via Rail Canada Inc., reported at (1992), 18 C.L.R.B.R. (2d) 67 and at 88 di 173

s. 129(1)
© Almeida v. Via Rail Canada Inc. (1990), 82 di 10 (Can. L.R.B.)

Sections/subsections may be consolidated where a consecutive range of sections/subsections is judicially considered in the same way by the same decision

s. 129(1)-129(3)
© Murray v. Maritime Employers' Assn. (1991), 15 C.L.R.B.R. (2d) 116, 84 di 134 (Can.)

s. 129(2)
© LeBlanc v. Via Rail Canada Inc. (1990), 80 di 24 (Can. L.R.B.)

Canadian Statute Citations. Reprinted by permission of Thomson Carswell, a division of Thomson Canada Limited.

How to Write a Citation for a Statute

A citation provides information about where to locate a source. Therefore, the fundamental rule in all citation is to include enough information in the citation to enable a reader to locate the material referred to. There is a reason why citations take the form they do, and researchers should be aware of the logic underlying citation, as well as the precise rules of citation itself.

There are three parts to the citation of a statute:

1. Title
2. Location
3. Section Number

Example:

> *Powers of Attorney Act*, R.S.O. 1990, c. P.20, as am. by S.O. 1992, c. 32, s. 24; 1993, c. 27, Sched.

Title

The title of the statute is obviously a critical part of a statute citation. Several statutes have very similar titles, so precision is important. It is acceptable to refer to a short title if there is one. This short title is often stated in the first section of a statute.

The title must be *italicized* and any quotations or references to years in the title must appear in the citation exactly as they do in the title. For example, statutes may have a date in the title that distinguishes them from other statutes with the same name. The title must be italicized or underlined. In the above example, this is *not* the case.

Location

Statutes are labelled by the year they were brought into effect (or revised) and a specific chapter number. Each statute is published in an annual or sessional volume. The following abbreviations describe the volumes and chapter designation:

- Statutes = S. (*i.e.*, annual or sessional volumes)
- Revised Statutes = R.S. (*i.e.*, consolidated volumes)
- R.S.B.C. = *Revised Statutes of British Columbia*
- R.S.C. = *Revised Statutes of Canada*
- c. = chapter

Section Number

If you refer to a specific section in a statute, you must refer to that section in the citation. The following abbreviations are used to describe section numbers:

- s. = one section
- ss. = several sections

Amendments

Although statutes are usually assumed to undergo amending over time, and likewise are often are repealed over time, you may choose to specify a specific statute that amended or repealed another one, particularly if the amendment or repeal is crucial to your presentation or argument. If you chose to identify the repealing or amending Act, add its citation to the end of the primary citation, as shown below. Otherwise, the title of the amending statute is simply omitted in the citation. Use these abbreviations:

- as amended = as am.; *or* as am. by citation to amending Act
- repealed by = as rep.; *or* as rep. by citation to repealing Act
- an Act that amends an earlier Act = amending
- an Act that repeals an earlier Act = repealing

Punctuation

Some basic rules of punctuation in statute citation are as follows:

- Use periods after abbreviations.
- Use commas after the title and the year.
- Use commas before notations (*i.e.*, as am. by).

Electronic Citations

If the statute is taken from an electronic a source it is recommended that you add that information to the citation, for the ease of readers trying to locate that statute. After the citation (above), add a comma and then the word "online" followed by a colon. If a commercial online system was used, add the abbreviation for the provider (*e.g.*, LN/QL or WL*e*C). If an Internet site was used, add the name of the website followed by the name of the specific part of the site, then the URL (Uniform Resource Locater) in angled brackets. For example:

Strata Property Act, S.B.C. 1998, c. 43, online: LN/QL

Labour Relations Regulation, B.C. Reg. 7/93, online: Queen's Printer (Revised Statutes and Consolidated Regulations) <http://www.qp.gov.bc.ca/statreg>

SELF TEST

The answers to these questions are found at the back of the book in the "Answers to Self Tests" section.

1. Where on the Internet could you locate a statute?
2. How are statutes arranged in a library?
3. What is a table of statutes?

4. Name two commercial providers that provide access to electronic statutes.
5. What is a statute citator?

SAMPLE EXERCISES —
FINDING AND UPDATING STATUTES

Objectives

At the end of this exercise you should to be able to:

- Locate a statute and its amendments
- Determine the effective date of a statute
- Locate cases that have considered a statute
- Properly cite a statute

Instructions

- Do background reading on how to locate, update, and cite statutes.
- Keep a record of all of the steps and time taken to complete the exercise.

Statutes

Provincial Statutes

Read the following fact pattern and answer the following questions. Assume the research situation occurred in your province.

Fact Pattern

Mr. Chapps

Mr. Chapps has recently acquired the property of his dreams. After years of saving he finally was able to purchase an old farmhouse on a piece of property overlooking a lake. He moved into the farmhouse last month and has just begun to renovate.

Two days ago, he received a letter from the Minister of Municipal Affairs. The letter stated, "This letter will serve as notice of expropriation." It went on to explain that Mr. Chapp's property was going to be expropriated so that the city could build a sewage treatment plant on it. Mr. Chapp is very upset and wants to know what he can do to fight the expropriation.

1. Before entering the library, brainstorm for possible legal subject areas. List about five words relating to the above research situation that you might search for in the library.

   Words:

2. Using either a provincial subject index or a table of statutes, find a statute relevant to your research situation. Give the proper citation to the most recent consolidation of that statute.

   Citation:

Amendments

3. Use the most recent table of statutes or table of legislative changes to determine whether the consolidated statute you found in Q. 2 above has ever been amended. Locate one amendment to s. 2 of that Act and give the full citation of the amending statute. Locate that statute and record the name.

   Citation:

   Coming into Force:

4. Look at the table of legislative changes from Q. 3 above. Does it provide effective dates of legislation? If yes, what was the effective date (CIF) of s. 1 of the amending statute you found in Q. 3 above?

   Date of CIF:

Statutes Judicially Considered

5. Using the *Canadian Abridgment, Canadian Statute Citations,* locate your statute and record:
   a. A case name that considered the statute:
   b. Section number of the statute that was considered:
   c. Volume and date of the citator:

Federal Statutes

1. Give the proper citation for the following federal statute: S.C. 1990, c. 22.

   Citation:

Amendments

2. Using the most recent federal *Table of Public Statutes and Responsible Ministers,* determine whether the statute from Q. 1 above was amended. Note the amendment to s. 46 and record the citation. Locate the amending statute and give the full citation, including the name of the statute and explain how and when it came into effect.

Citation:

Statutes Judicially Considered

3. Locate the *Canada Statute Citator* (Canada Law Book) and the *Canadian Abridgment, Canadian Statute Citations* (Carswell). Find your statute in both sources and record the name of a case that has considered the statute. Record the section number of the statute that has been considered by the case. If the statute has not been judicially considered, state this.

   a. Case name:
   b. Section number:
   c. Name of citator:

ANSWERS TO EXERCISES

Note: Amendments occurring after the publication of this text will not be shown in these answers.

Provincial Statutes

(British Columbia was used to answer this question.)

1. Municipal affairs; property; expropriation; sewage treatment.
2. *Expropriation Act*, R.S.B.C. 1996, c. 125.

Amendments

3. The most recent *Table of Legislative Changes* (changes in force) dated Jan. 1, 2005-Dec. 31, 2005 states that amendments were made to s. 1 (and other sections) of the *Expropriation Act*. The first amendment to s. 1 was made by 2004-61-1. If you look up this statute in the annual volume for 1994, c. 61, s. 1, you find the *Expropriation Amendment Act, 2004*, S.B.C, c. 61. Section 1 of that act amends the *Expropriation Act*.

COMING INTO FORCE

4. Yes, it does give effective dates. CIF March 18, 2005

Statutes Judicially Considered

5. a. *TFL Forest Ltd. v. British Columbia*, 2002 BCSC 180, 202 CarswellBC 270, 48 R.P.R. (3d) 132, 44 C.E.L.R. (N.S.) 263, 7 L.C.R. 187

   b. Generally

   c. *Canadian Abridgment, Canadian Statute Citator* — BC Volume A-E (July 1994-Sept. 2003)

Federal Statutes

1. *Plant Protection Act,* S.C. 1990, c. 22.

Amendments

2. Yes, the statute has been amended. For example, s. 46 was amended by S.C. 1993, c. 34, s. 102 (which is the *Miscellaneous Statute Law Amendment Act, 1993*). The *Table of Public Statutes* shows that S.C. 1993, c. 34, ss. 102 and 103 came in force on assent, which occurred 23-06-93. (You could confirm this by merely going to the statute, but that is not necessary. The table is official.)

Statutes Judicially Considered

3. *Canadian Statute Citations* (Carswell)

   a. *BC Landscape & Nursery Assn. v. Canada (Attorney General)* (2000), 2000 CarswellNat 1535, 35 C.E.L.R. (N.S.) 169, 186 F.T.R. 62

   b. Generally

   c. *Canadian Abridgment, Canadian Statute Citations* (Sept. 2006) Vol. Canada Ind to Pro.

Canada Statute Citator (Canada Law Book):

   a. *Rodd v. Canada (Minister of Agriculture)* (2005), 2005 FC 1625

   b. S. 58

   c. *Canada Statute Citator,* Vol. 7 (March 2007)

Appendix 7A: How to Read Tables of Statutes

The following is an example of how to read the federal *Table of Public Statutes and Responsible Ministers*. If you look up the *Citizenship Act* in the *Table of Public Statutes and Responsible Ministers*, you will find the following information:

Citizenship Act — R.S., 1985, c. C-29
(Citoyenneté, Loi sur la)

Minister of Citizenship and Immigration (SI/94-86)

s. 2, R.S., c. 28 (4th Supp.), s. 36(2) (Sch., item 2); 1992, c. 21, s. 6; 2000, c. 12, s. 74; 2001, c. 26, s. 286, c. 27, s. 227.1; 2002, c. 8, par. 183(1)(*d*)
s. 3, 1995, c. 5, s. 25(1)(*e*)
s. 5, R.S., c. 44 (3rd Supp.), s. 1; 1992, c. 21, s. 7; 2000, c. 12, s. 75; 2001, c. 27, s. 228; 2003, c. 22, s. 149(E)
s. 9, 1992, c. 21, s. 8
s. 11, 2001, c. 27, s. 229; 2005, c. 17, s. 1
s. 14, 1995, c. 15, s. 23; 2001, c. 27, s. 230
s. 16, 2002, c. 8, par. 182(1)(*j*)
s. 19, 1992, c. 1, s. 144 (Sch. VII, item 22)(F); 1997, c. 22, s. 1
s. 19.1, added, 1997, c. 22, s. 2
s. 19.2, added, 1997, c. 22, s. 2
s. 19.3, added, 1997, c. 22, s. 2; 2005, c. 10, s. 14
s. 20, 1997, c. 22, s. 3
s. 22, R.S., c. 30 (3rd Supp.), s. 11; 1992, c. 47, s. 67, c. 49, s. 124; 1999, c. 31, s. 42; 2000, c. 24, s. 33; 2001, c. 27, s. 231
s. 35, R.S., c. 28 (1st Supp.), s. 49; 2001, c. 27, s. 232
s. 37, 1993, c. 28, s. 78 (Sch. III, item 18); 2002, c. 7, s. 131
Conditional amendments, 2000, c. 12, ss. 76, 77
General, 1995, c. 5, s. 25(2)
Transitional, 1997, c. 22, s. 10
CIF, R.S., c. 28 (1st Supp.), s. 49 proclaimed in force 30.06.85 *see* SI/85-128
CIF, R.S., c. 30 (3rd Supp.), s. 11 proclaimed in force 30.10.87 *see* SI/87-251
CIF, R.S., c. 44 (3rd Supp.), s. 1 proclaimed in force 15.02.88 *see* SI/88-32
CIF, R.S., c. 28 (4th Supp.), s. 36(2) proclaimed in force 01.01.89 *see* SI/88-231
CIF, 1992, c. 1, s. 144 (Sch. VII, item 22)(F) in force on assent 28.02.92
CIF, 1992, c. 21, ss. 6 to 8 in force 30.06.92 *see* SI/92-126
CIF, 1992, c. 47, s. 67 in force 01.08.96 *see* SI/96-56
CIF, 1992, c. 49, s. 124 in force 01.02.93 *see* SI/93-16
CIF, 1993, c. 28, s. 78 (Sch. III, item 18) in force 01.04.99 *see* s. 79
CIF, 1995, c. 5, s. 25 in force 13.05.95 *see* SI/95-65

CIF, 1995, c. 15, s. 23 in force 10.07.95 *see* SI/95-76
CIF, 1997, c. 22, ss. 1 to 3 and 10 in force 20.05.97 *see* SI/97-64
CIF, 1999, c. 31, s. 42 in force on assent 17.06.99
CIF, 2000, c. 12, ss. 76 and 77 in force on assent 29.06.2000; ss. 74 and 75 in force 01.07.2003 *see* SI/2003-118
CIF, 2000, c. 24, s. 33 in force 23.10.2000 *see* SI/2000-95
CIF, 2001, c. 26, s. 286 comes into force on a day to be fixed by order of the Governor in Council *see* s. 334. Not in force 31.08.2003
CIF, 2001, c. 27, ss. 227.1 to 232 in force 28.06.2002 *see* SI/2002-97
CIF, 2002, c. 7, s. 131 in force 01.04.2003 *see* SI/2003-48
CIF, 2002, c. 8, ss. 182 and 183 in force 02.07.2003 *see* SI/2003-109
CIF, 2003, c. 22, s. 149 in force 01.04.2005 *see* SI/2005-24
CIF, 2005, c. 10, s. 14 in force 04.04.2005 *see* SI/2005-29
CIF, 2005, c. 17 in force on assent 05.05.2005

This information reads as follows:

Top Line — The *Citizenship Act* (Canada) can be found in the *Revised Statutes of Canada, 1985* in c. C-29.

Line 1 — Section 2 was amended in the *Revised Statutes of Canada, 1985* in c. 28 (4th Supp.) by s. 36(2) of the Schedule, item 2. (If you look up c. 28, you will see that the title of the statute is *An Act to amend the Immigration Act and to amend other Acts in consequence thereof*) and s. 36(2), Schedule, item 2 specifically amends the *Citizenship Act*). Section 2 was amended again in the *Statutes of Canada*, 1992 in c. 21, by s. 6, in 2000, in c. 12, by s. 74, in 2001, in c. 26, by s. 286 and in c. 27, by s. 227.1, and in 2002, c. 8, by par. 183(1)(*d*).

Line 24 — Section 2 came into force (CIF) in c. 28 of the *Revised Statutes of Canada, 1985* (4th Supp.) on January 1, 1989 (see SI/88-231 for confirmation). Note: this confirmation is rarely done by researchers. Since the *Table of Public Statutes and Responsible Ministers* is an official document produced by the federal Queen's Printer, the CIF information displayed therein is deemed to be correct. Note that each revision has corresponding CIF information.

The proper citation for this statute is: *Citizenship Act*, R.S.C. 1985, c. C-29.

Note: Provinces and territories have similar tables of public statutes and are generally read the same way as shown above. For the CIF of provincial statutes, "O.C." means the statute came into effect by an order-in-council and "Proc." means the statute came into effect by a proclamation. Statutes brought into effect by either order-in-council or proclamation require, officially, that a regulation be introduced, but in reality, these regulations are almost never examined. Since such tables are official documents produced by the jurisdictional Queen's Printer, the CIF information displayed therein is deemed to be correct.

Appendix 7B: Sample Federal Statute and Legislative History

The following is an example of the first page of a typical federal statute.

55 ELIZABETH II

55 ELIZABETH II

CHAPTER 13

An Act to impose a charge on the export of certain softwood lumber products to the United States and a charge on refunds of certain duty deposits paid to the United States, to authorize certain payments, to amend the Export and Import Permits Act and to amend other Acts as a consequence

[Assented to 14th December, 2006]

Her Majesty, by and with the advice and consent of the Senate and House of Commons of Canada, enacts as follows:

SHORT TITLE

Short title

1. This Act may be cited as the *Softwood Lumber Products Export Charge Act, 2006*

INTERPRETATION

Definitions

2 The following definitions apply in this Act

Agency
«Agence»

"Agency" means the Canada Revenue Agency continued by subsection 4(1) of the *Canada Revenue Agency Act*

assessment
«cotisation»

"assessment" means an assessment or a reassessment under this Act

bank
«banque»

"bank" means a bank as defined in section 2 of the *Bank Act* or an authorized foreign bank, as defined in that section, that is not subject to the restrictions and requirements referred to in subsection 524(2) of that Act.

board foot
«pied-planche»

"board foot" means a unit of measurement of lumber equal to 12 inches × 12 inches × 1 inch, and one thousand board feet is equal to 2 35974 cubic metres or 92 90227 square metres of lumber

CHAPITRE 13

Loi imposant des droits sur l'exportation aux États-Unis de certains produits de bois d'oeuvre et des droits sur les remboursements de certains dépôts douaniers faits aux États-Unis, autorisant certains paiements et modifiant la Loi sur les licences d'exportation et d'importation et d'autres lois en conséquence

[Sanctionnée le 14 décembre 2006]

Sa Majesté, sur l'avis et avec le consentement du Sénat et de la Chambre des communes du Canada, édicte :

TITRE ABRÉGÉ

Titre abrégé

1. *Loi de 2006 sur les droits d'exportation de produits de bois d'oeuvre.*

DÉFINITIONS ET INTERPRÉTATION

Définitions

2. Les définitions qui suivent s'appliquent à la présente loi

«Agence»
"Agency"

«Agence» L'Agence du revenu du Canada, prorogée par le paragraphe 4(1) de la *Loi sur l'Agence du revenu du Canada*

«banque»
"bank"

«banque» S'entend au sens de l'article 2 de la *Loi sur les banques* Est également visée la banque étrangère autorisée, au sens de cet article, qui n'est pas assujettie aux restrictions et exigences visées au paragraphe 524(2) de cette loi

«commissaire»
"Commissioner"

«commissaire» Le commissaire du revenu, nommé au titre de l'article 25 de la *Loi sur l'Agence du revenu du Canada*

«cotisation»
"assessment"

«cotisation» Cotisation ou nouvelle cotisation établie en vertu de la présente loi.

Since 2003, the federal Queen's Printer has been supplying a legislative history that is bound adjacent to each statute in the annual statutory volumes. This history gives the original bill number and all of the steps through which the bill went, in both the House of Commons and the Senate. Thus, the researcher has all the necessary background information pertaining to the progress and passage of the legislation.

The following is an example of page from the Legislative History describing the various readings of this statute.

LEGISLATIVE HISTORY / HISTORIQUE

An Act to impose a charge on the export of certain softwood lumber products to the United States and a charge on refunds of certain duty deposits paid to the United States, to authorize certain payments, to amend the Export and Import Permits Act and to amend other Acts as a consequence – Bill C-24
(Introduced by: Minister of International Trade)
Loi imposant des droits sur l'exportation aux États-Unis de certains produits de bois d'œuvre et des droits sur les remboursements de certains dépôts douaniers faits aux États-Unis, autorisant certains paiements et modifiant la Loi sur les licences d'exportation et d'importation et d'autres lois en conséquence – Projet de loi C-24
(Déposé par : Le ministre du Commerce international)

House of Commons / Chambre des communes		Senate / Sénat	
Bill Stage / Étape du projet de loi	Date	Bill Stage / Étape du projet de loi	Date
First Reading / Première lecture	2006-09-20	First Reading / Première lecture	2006-12-06
Debate(s) at Second Reading / Débat(s) à la deuxième lecture	2006-09-25 2006-09-26 2006-09-27 2006-09-29 2006-10-03 2006-10-06 2006-10-16 2006-10-17 2006-10-18	Debate(s) at Second Reading / Débat(s) à la deuxième lecture	2006-12-07 2006-12-12
Second Reading / Deuxième lecture	2006-10-28	Second Reading / Deuxième lecture	2006-12-12
Committee / Comité	International Trade / Commerce international	Committee / Comité	National Finance / Finances nationales
Committee Meeting(s) / Réunion(s) du comité	2006-10-24 2006-10-26 2006-10-31 2006-11-02 2006-11-07	Committee Meeting(s) / Réunion(s) du comité	2006-12-13
Committee Report / Rapport du comité	2006-11-09	Committee Report / Rapport du comité	2006-12-14
Debate(s) at Report Stage / Débat(s) à l'étape du rapport	2006-11-21 2006-11-22 2006-11-29	Debate(s) at Report Stage / Débat(s) à l'étape du rapport	
Report Stage / Étape du rapport	2006-12-04	Report Stage / Étape du rapport	2006-12-14
Debate(s) at Third Reading / Débat(s) à la troisième lecture	2006-12-05	Debate(s) at Third Reading / Débat(s) à la troisième lecture	
Third Reading / Troisième lecture	2006-12-06	Third Reading / Troisième lecture	2006-12-14
Royal Assent : December 14, 2006, Statutes of Canada, 2006, chapter 13 Sanction royale : Le 14 décembre 2006, Lois du Canada (2006), chapitre 13			

Appendix 7C: Sample Provincial Statute

The following is an example of the first page of a typical provincial statute.

CHAPTER 42

Health Services Act

(Assented to June 7, 2005)

BE IT ENACTED by the Lieutenant Governor and the Legislative Assembly of the Province of Prince Edward Island as follows:

Definitions

1. In this Act

(a) "community hospital" means a community hospital as defined in the *Community Hospital Authorities Act* R.S.P.E.I. 1988, Cap C-13.1; community hospital

(b) "community hospital authority" means a community hospital authority as defined in the *Community Hospital Authorities Act*; community hospital authority

(c) "Department" means the Department of Health; Department

(d) "facility" means any institution, residence or building, including a community hospital, under the administration of a community hospital authority, to which persons are admitted or in which they receive treatment; facility

(e) "health services" means hospital, health, and such other services as the Lieutenant Governor in Council may determine; health services

(f) "Minister" means the Minister of Health; Minister

(g) "provincial hospital" means the
(i) Queen Elizabeth Hospital,
(ii) Prince County Hospital, and
(iii) Hillsborough Hospital. provincial hospital

2. (1) The Minister is responsible for the administration of this Act. Administration

(2) The Minister shall Duties
(a) ensure the provision of essential health services in the province; and
(b) promote and maintain the good health of the residents of the province.

(3) The Minister may Powers
(a) establish the goals, objectives, and strategic guidelines for the delivery of health services;
(b) plan the overall provincial system of health services;

Source: *Statutes of Prince Edward Island* 2005, c. 42.

Appendix 7D: Checklist: How to Find, Update, and Note Up a Statute and Ensure It Is in Force

STEP 1: LOCATE A STATUTE BY NAME OR CITATION

To locate a statute by name or citation, use any of the following sources:

In the Library

❏ If you know the title of a statute, look in the most recent federal or relevant provincial table of statutes (often called *Table of Public Statutes*), which list all statutes alphabetically.

❏ Find your statute title in the *Table* and note the location of the statute (*i.e.*, its year and chapter number). This is its citation. Make notes of any amendments listed in the Table. You will need this information for Step 5.

❏ Knowing the citation of the statute, you can find its original version in the jurisdictional statute volumes which are arranged by year, volume and chapter number.

❏ Note that statutes can also be located by referring to commercially produced printed statute citators. These include the statute citation and may also provide the text of the original Act plus any amendments These almost always include citations to cases providing judicial consideration. Citators are not official sources, so confirm the wording of amendments by checking the official version in the statute(s).

Electronically

❏ **Internet:** Most government websites include electronic full-text statutes. A list of such websites is appended to this chapter. CanLII (<http://www.CanLII.org>) and several university and courthouse law library websites provide links to many Canadian statutes. To locate a statute you can either browse the alphabetical list or do a keyword search in the templates provided. Update by checking legislative updates in Step 5.

❑ **LN/QL and WL*e*C** have collections of all federal, provincial, and territorial consolidated statutes. Since statutes are updated regularly, always determine when these commercial online consolidations were last updated. Both of these services now have some "point-in-time" consolidations that display how a statute looked at a specific date in the past, to aid researchers who need to know exactly what the statute said at that time. Consult the online help functions within these services for more information. Not all jurisdictions have point-in-time statutes as yet. Locate statutes either by browsing the list of statutes provided or by conducting a keyword search in the templates provided.

STEP 2: SEARCH FOR STATUTES BY SUBJECT

❑ If you do not know the title of the statute, read secondary sources to find out more about your topic. Secondary sources often provide the exact title and citation for relevant statutes either within the text, in footnotes or in tables of statutes. Excellent secondary sources include textbooks, *Halsbury's Laws of Canada* in print, and the *Canadian Encyclopedic Digest* (CED) available in print or electronically via WL*e*C. Always check the currency of the information and be sure to update it with later sources.

❑ Another option is to locate federal, provincial, or territorial statute subject indexes. Scan the topics for relevant statutes. Remember that such indexes are becoming rare as more researchers turn to electronic keyword searching. But older printed indexes are still helpful for historical research.

❑ Once you have learned more about your topic, scan the tables of statutes (print or electronic) or conduct a keyword search in any of the electronic sources, including LN/QL, WL*e*C, CanLII or government websites.

❑ It is best **not** to search by subject or keyword in electronic statutes until you have refined your topic using secondary sources. Although electronic searches are powerful, they are not the best way to begin your research unless you know the exact name of your statute or the specific keywords relating to it. Doing an electronic search too early can retrieve too many irrelevant statutes or none at all. Ideally, you should know the exact title of the statute.

STEP 3: FIND THE STATUTE

❑ Once you know the citation of the statute, you can find the original print version in the library or print it from an electronic source. Print statutes are organized by year, volume, and chapter number. Remember that the only official source is the one found in print statute volumes. Neither commercial consolidations nor Internet versions of statutes are considered official.

STEP 4: FIND OUT WHEN THE STATUTE CAME INTO FORCE

❑ A statute or section of a statute can be used as authority in judicial decisions or enforced by the government **only** if it is force. You can determine whether a statute has come into force ("CIF") by finding its commencement provision(s). The commencement section, if one exists, is usually at the end of the statute. Commencement or "coming into force" may be on a specified date — usually this is a future date, but occasionally it is a past date, meaning that the legislature wanted it to come into force retrospectively for some reason.

❑ If there is no commencement section, the statute comes into force on the date of Royal Assent. Note that later consolidations of a statute within the revised statute volumes will **not** contain a commencement clause if the statute is already in effect.

❑ If the commencement clause does not name a specific date but rather refers to coming into force by proclamation or order, that means that you will have to consult proclamation information in various places:

• For federal CIF information, look up the Act in the *Table of Public Statutes and Responsible Ministers* in the back of the annual statutory volume for the same year that the Act received assent; the CIF will be stated on the same page. Alternatively, consult the table online at <http://laws.justice.gc.ca/en/publaw/index.html>.

• For provincial or territorial CIF information, there are usually "proclamation tables" or "schedules of proclamations" in the back of each annual statutory volume. Consult these to determine the CIF date. Note: if the proclamation did not occur during the same year that the Act received Royal Assent, you will have to look at proclamation tables in the next several years until you see the CIF. Some provinces and territories publish separate "Indexes of Proclamations" or similar free-standing tools; check with a law librarian or contact the jurisdictional legislative library for guidance.

STEP 5: FIND OUT IF THE STATUTE BEEN AMENDED (UPDATE THE STATUTE)

In the Library

❑ To determine whether a statute has been amended, go to the relevant federal, provincial, or territorial tables of statutes (see Step 4). Look in the alphabetical listing for your statute. If there is no table of statutes, look in a table of separately published legislative changes.

❑ In the table, each statute is listed with all its amendments. Information about when and how the amendment came into force may also be there, but in some cases, you must consult a "proclamation" table, either in annual statutory volumes or in a separately published volume. Check with a law librarian if you are unsure.

❑ Note the date of the table of statutes and check for more recent amendments from that date forward — *i.e.* look for recent amending statutes affecting your statute. If you find any amendments, you will need to ascertain whether they are in force. To further update the statute and its amendments, look in the most recent publications from the various legislatures, such as legislative indexes.

❑ Knowing the citation of the amending statute, you can locate that statute in the printed statute volumes. Statutes are arranged by year, volume, and chapter number. To verify that an amendment is in effect, follow the same method that you used in Step 4 of this appendix (see above) to find the CIF information.

❑ Statutes may also be updated by referring to commercial loose-leaf statute citators, which may include amendments to statutes as well as judicial considerations. If you use these statute citators, you must confirm the wording of the statutory amendment by checking the official version as published by the government of the jurisdiction.

Electronically

❑ Select the electronic source you wish to use, such as WL*e*C, LN/QL, or Can LII (<http://www.CanLii.org>), or government websites.

❑ Search for your statute by exact title. Once you find your statute, note when the information was consolidated. Consolidation means that all statutory revisions have been inserted into the text of the statute up to a certain date. The consolidation date is usually near the title of the statute. Then, you will need to locate any revisions since the consolidation date of your statute.

❑ If the electronic version is not consolidated then you must look in other databases that contain the revisions, such as databases of gazettes. Note that, at present, there are very few unconsolidated statutes online as yet. The demand for statutes in their "as passed", unconsolidated form is fairly low, because most practitioners and researchers want to see current consolidations — *the law today*. Historical annual volumes are online only for the larger provinces and the federal government in both LN/QL and WL*e*C. The federal Department of Justice has annual statutes back to 2003 (see <http://laws.justice.gc.ca/en/BrowseAnnual>); check provincial and territorial government websites for coverage of annual volumes.

❑ If you are using WL*e*C, you can use the electronic citators. While viewing your statute, you can hyperlink to the electronic citator function that lists amendments and cases that have considered the statute. At this time, LN/QL does not have an online statute citator, although one may be forthcoming soon.

❑ Alternatively, in WL*e*C, you can select the electronic citator known as **KeyCite Canada** and search for your statute. It lists all cases that have considered your statute.

STEP 6: FIND OUT WHETHER THE STATUTE HAS BEEN CONSIDERED IN CASES (NOTE UP THE STATUTE)

In the Library

❑ The best place to look for cases that have considered statutes is in statute citators. Some examples of statute citators are: *Canada Statute Citator* (Canada Law Book) and *Canadian Statute Citations* (part of *Canadian Abridgment*, Carswell).

❑ A prudent researcher will use all available statute citators for the jurisdiction to ensure that all relevant cases are found.

Electronically

❑ Use the appropriate template in WL*e*C to search for your statute. Once you are looking at your statute you can use **KeyCite Canada** to see amendments and also cases that have considered the statute.

❑ Alternatively, select **KeyCite Canada** and search for your statute. It lists all cases that have considered your statute.

❑ Government websites do not have statute citators or hyperlinks from statutes to relevant cases, nor does QL/LN at this time.

❑ CanLII (<www.canlii.org>) has recently released a new version that permits noting up of statutes in order to find cases that have interpreted statutes from all Canadian jurisdictions. However, since the cases in CanLII usually go back only to the late 1990s or early 2000s, you will not get each and every case, but only those from recent years.

Appendix 7E: Legislation on Government Websites

Although much legislation can be linked through CanLII (<www.canlii.org>), not all bills and gazettes are available through that site. Sometimes you may want to go directly to the original government website, especially if you are looking for progress of bills, and names, e-mail addresses, and telephone numbers of government officials and members of the legislature.

Jurisdiction	Government Site
Federal	<http://laws.justice.gc.ca/en/index.html>
	Bills: www.parl.gc.ca
	Gazettes: <http://canadagazette.gc.ca/index-e.html>
British Columbia	<http://www.qp.gov.bc.ca/statreg/default.htm>
	Bills: <http://www.qplegaleze.ca/default.htm>
	Gazette: <http://pss.gov.bc.ca/pubs/bc-gazette.html>
Alberta	<http://qpsource.gov.ab.ca/>
	Bills: <http://qpsource.gov.ab.ca/>
	Gazette: <http://qpsource.gov.ab.ca/>
Saskatchewan	<http://www.qp.gov.sk.ca/>
	Bills: <www.legassembly.sk.ca>
	Gazette: <http://www.qp.gov.sk.ca/>
Manitoba	<http://web2.gov.mb.ca/laws/statutes/index.php>
	Bills: <http://www.gov.mb.ca/legislature/homepage.html>
	Gazette: <http://www.gov.mb.ca/chc/statpub/gazette/index.html>
New Brunswick	<www.gnb.ca/acts>
	Bills: <http://www.gnb.ca/legis>
	Gazette: <http://www.gnb.ca/0062/gazette/index-e.asp>
Ontario	<www.e-laws.gov.on.ca>
	Bills: <http://www.ontla.on.ca/documents/bills/index.htm>
	Gazette: <http://www.gov.on.ca/>
Quebec	<http://www2.publicationsduquebec.gouv.qc.ca/home.php>
	Bills: <http://www.gouv.qc.ca/portail/quebec/pgs?lang=en>
	Gazette: <http://www2.publicationsduquebec.gouv.qc.ca/home.php>

Jurisdiction	Government Site
Prince Edward Island	<http://www.gov.pe.ca/law/statutes/index.php3> Bills: <www.assembly.pe.ca> Gazette: <http://www.gov.pe.ca/royalgazette/index.php3>
Nova Scotia	<www.gov.ns.ca/legislature/legc/> Bills: <http://www.gov.ns.ca/legislature/legc/> Gazette: <http://www.gov.ns.ca/legislature/legc/>
Yukon	<http://www.gov.yk.ca/legislation/> Bills: <http://www.legassembly.gov.yk.ca/> Gazette: <http://gazette.gov.yk.ca/pdf_index.html>
Northwest Territories	<http://www.justice.gov.nt.ca/Legislation/SearchLeg&Reg.htm> Bills: <http://www.assembly.gov.nt.ca/housebusiness/index.html> Gazette: no link
Nunavut	<http://www.justice.gov.nu.ca/english/leg/statreg.html> <Bills: www.assembly.nu.ca> Gazette: <http://www.justice.gov.nu.ca/english/gazette/?year=2007>

How to Find and Update Regulations

8

Regulations, rules, and municipal bylaws are similar to statutes in that they are laws created by a particular authority. Unlike statutes, they are not created by the legislature, but are created by a delegated authority. They are sometimes called delegated or subordinate legislation.

This chapter describes a step-by-step technique for finding regulations. It also explains how regulations are published.

LEARNING OBJECTIVES

At the end of this chapter you will be able to:

- Describe how regulations are made
- Locate and update a regulation
- Provide a proper citation for a regulation
- Describe what a municipal bylaw is
- Explain how to locate bylaws

HOW REGULATIONS ARE MADE AND PUBLISHED

Legislatures are continually making subordinate legislation or regulations. These regulations provide the "flesh on the bones" of statutes. People come into contact with regulations daily; for example, a regulation may state how many metres one must stay back from an emergency vehicle while driving on a highway, or how many litres of waste may be legally disposed of in a waterway. Regulations spell out the details of subject matter covered in their "enabling" statute.

There are three types of subordinate legislation: regulations, rules, and proclamations. Unlike statutes, in order for regulations to become law they need only be "passed" by the authority described (and usually specifically named) in the statute (a government ministry, board, agency, or department), "filed or deposited", and published.

Passed: Regulations are passed by the executive arm of governments. For example, they are usually prepared by a department or agency of government and then passed by the Lieutenant Governor in Council (provincial or territorial cabinet) or the Governor in Council (federal cabinet) without the need for approval in the House of Commons.

Filed: Federal regulations are effective when filed with the clerk of the Privy Council. Provincial regulations are effective on the date deposited with a government office such as the registrar of regulations. These effective dates are specified in the regulation.

Published: Because regulations do not go through the House of Commons or the Senate, or through provincial or territorial legislatures, and do not go through readings like bills, they are only published once — in the official gazettes (provincial, territorial, or federal).

Rules, regulations, and proclamations are published in sets called regulations. They can be found in law libraries, usually right beside the statutes for each particular jurisdiction. When first published, regulations appear in the federal or provincial softbound gazettes. Federal regulations are published in the *Canada Gazette, Part II*. After a number of gazettes have accumulated, they are usually hardbound. Provincial and territorial gazettes usually follow this same pattern; the issues come out periodically — usually weekly — and then the issues are gathered and bound.

Periodically, governments consolidate their regulations. The federal government and some provinces have consolidated their regulations into "revised" sets, much like the revised versions of statutes. An example of a consolidation is the 1978 federal government consolidation of all federal regulations: the *Consolidated Regulations of Canada, 1978 (C.R.C. 1978)*. The *C.R.C. 1978* incorporates all regulations and amendments to the regulations up to the date of publication.

Thus, on the library shelves there are usually four parts to each set of federal regulations:

- A consolidated set of regulations. The federal set is called the *Consolidated Regulations of Canada, 1978* (18 volumes).
- Annual or sessional regulations. The federal set consists of the *Canada Gazette, Part II*, hardbound for each year.
- Current regulations. The federal version is the *Canada Gazette, Part II*, which includes the most recent regulations, in paper form.
- An index. The federal *Canada Gazette, Part II* includes the most recent *Consolidated Index of Statutory Instruments*. This index can be found online at: <http://laws.justice.gc.ca/en/StatutoryInstrument>.

Provincial regulations usually follow a similar pattern to the above. Some have consolidated their regulations from time to time. Others simply have bound their gazette (often called the *Royal Gazette*) into annual volumes. They may or may not have indexes, and some of the indexes are cumulative while others are not.

A few provinces and territories have loose-leaf sets of consolidated regulations. These are very useful because amendments to the regulations are inserted directly into the set and you avoid looking in several volumes for amendments to the regulations. Some of the more popular regulations (for the larger, more populous provinces) are published by commercial publishers and annotated. These annotated sets usually include the relevant statute and revisions to both the statute and the regulations, and refer to cases that considered the statute or the regulations.

A new publication from Thomson Carswell, part of the *Canadian Abridgment*, is entitled *Regulations Judicially Considered*. It does for regulations what the Carswell statute citator does for statutes, that is, it identifies cases from all Canadian jurisdictions that have considered or interpreted regulations. It is available by subscription and is a welcome addition to the legal research field. It is not currently available on WL*e*C (see below for discussion of regulations in electronic form).

Rules of Court

Researchers should be aware of a certain type of regulation know as "a rule" or "rules of court". Rules set out the requirements and policies that must be met in order to present cases to the various courts and tribunals. Rules also give guidance to practitioners about court deadlines, procedures, and various forms.

For provinces and territories, these are enabled under a statute usually called a *Judicature Act* or a *Courts Act*. At the federal level, the enabling Acts are the *Supreme Court Act* and the *Federal Courts Act* as well as the Acts that have established federal administrative tribunals such as the Competition Bureau.

Another new publication from Thomson Carswell, again part of the *Canadian Abridgment*, is entitled *Rules Judicially Considered*. It does for rules what the other Carswell citators do for statutes and regulations (see above) — it identifies cases from all Canadian jurisdictions that have considered or interpreted court or tribunal rules. It is available by subscription and is another welcome tool for legal researchers. It is not available on WL*e*C.

Electronic Publications

As with statutes, there are several sources of electronic regulations, including online providers and government websites. WL*e*C and LN/QL both have electronic collections of federal, provincial and territorial regulations and rules. Both services strive to stay up to date with regulations and rules as soon as they are published. Most provincial governments maintain websites that contain legislation, including regulations. As with statutes, usually the commercial online providers are ahead of government websites in terms of timeliness because, as value-added providers, they actually monitor the government's daily activities more closely than the government itself does.

A list of government websites containing statutes, regulations, and rules is appended to Chapter 7 (How to Find and Update Statutes).

How to Read a Regulation

It is important to be able to read a regulation so you can find out quickly how it impacts the law and when it came into effect. A regulation typically consists of the following five parts:

- Regulation number (*e.g.*, SOR/93-246 (federal), or B.C. Reg 91/80 (provincial or territorial);
- Date of filing or deposit (*e.g.*, 11 May 1993, or March 21, 1980);
- Title (and sometimes the short title);
- Enabling statute (*e.g.*, *Citizenship Act*, s. 27, or *Name Act*, s. 13); and
- How it was brought in (PC: federal Privy Council; OC: provincial or territorial Order in Council).

The parts of regulations can be seen in the following excerpts from a federal and a provincial regulation:

Illustration 8.1
Sample Federal Regulation: Citizenship Regulations (SOR/93-246)

Registration

SOR/93-246 11 May, 1993

CITIZENSHIP ACT

Citizenship Regulations, 1993

P.C. 1993-943 11 May, 1993

His Excellency the Governor General in Council, on the recommendation of the Minister of Multiculturalism and Citizenship, pursuant to section 27 of the Citizenship Act, is pleased hereby to revoke the Citizenship Regulations, C.R.C., c. 400, and to make the annexed Regulations respecting Citizenship, in substitution therefor.

REGULATIONS RESPECTING CITIZENSHIP

Short Title

1. These Regulations may be cited as the *Citizenship Regulations*, 1993

Illustration 8.2
Sample British Columbia Regulation:
Name Act Regulation (B.C. Reg. 91/80)

B.C. Reg. 91/80 Filed March 21, 1980

Effective June 1, 1980

O.C. 617/80

Name Act

NAME ACT REGULATION

[includes amendments up to B.C. Reg. 110/97]

Fees

1 Under the *Name Act* the fee

(a) on filing an application for a Change of Name shall be $137 for the applicant and $27 for each person who is listed in the application as a person whose name will be changed by reason of a change of name of the applicant, which fees include the issuance of one certificate of Change of Name for the applicant and each listed person and the cost of publication of the certificates in the Gazette following approval of the application.

(b) for a search of one registration of Change of Name shall be $27 for each 3 year period or part of a 3 year period covered by the search,

(c) for each certificate of Change of Name shall be

(i) $27 including the fee for a search covering one 3 year period, or

(ii) $60 including, where same day search service is offered and requested, the fee for a search that same day covering one 3 year period, and

(d) for copies of documents supporting an application for Change of Name shall be $50.

[am. B.C. Regs. 326/84; 73/87; 121/88; 111/90; 133/91; 87/92; 79/94; 132/95; 554/95; 110/97.]

[Provisions of the *Name Act*, RSBC 1996, c. 328, relevant to the enactment of this regulation: section 17]

Empowering Statute

All regulations are made under the authority of a statute. Therefore you must know the statute under which the regulation is made. Since law-making power is delegated through statutes, each regulation must have an empowering, or enabling, statute, which authorizes an executive arm of the government to create regulations. This is evidenced by an "enabling section", which describes who has the power to make regulations and the matters about which regulations can be made. One might think of the relationship between a statute and a regulation as that of a parent to a child; the child holds on to the parent and does not function independently of the parent.

The following is an example of such an enabling section.

Illustration 8.3
Sample of an Enabling Section, *Citizenship Act*

Regulations **27.** The Governor in Council may make regulations

    (*a*) prescribing the manner in which and the place at which applications and registrations are to be made and notices are to be given under this Act and the evidence that is to be provided with respect thereto;

    (*b*) fixing fees for

        (i)   the making of any application under this Act,

        (ii) the issuing of any certificate under this Act,

        (iii) the registration of any person as a citizen under this Act,

        (iv) the provision of any certified or uncertified copy of a document from the records kept in the course of the administration of this Act or prior legislation,

        (v) the administration of any oath, solemn affirmation or declaration filed, made, issued, delivered or administered pursuant to this Act or the regulations, or

        (vi) any search of the records referred to in sub-paragraph (iv);

    (*c*) providing for the remission of fees referred to in paragraph (b);

    (*d*) providing for various criteria that may be applied to determine whether a person

        (i)   has an adequate knowledge of one of the official languages of Canada, ...

HOW TO FIND AND UPDATE REGULATIONS

There are three steps to finding and updating regulations:

Step 1:   Find the title of the regulation
Step 2:   Find the regulation
Step 3:   Update the regulation

Step 1: Find the Title of the Regulation

Computers have revolutionized regulation research. Because there are several available full-text electronic versions of both federal and many provincial and territorial regulations, searches are fairly straightforward. Also, because many of the electronic versions are consolidated, you need only look at the consolidated version.

One advantage of electronic regulations is that you do not need to know the related statute. You can simply do a search for a word in the statute or a word in the regulation. However, be aware that these databases are huge and it can be very difficult to isolate the particular regulations that you may be looking for.

You can search by scanning the table of regulations or by conducting a word search using the template provided. Keep in mind, however, that the electronic version is still not viewed by all courts as the official version, so you may need to locate the official print version.

In the Library

In the library, regulations are filed according to their enabling statute. Therefore, researchers must determine the title of the statute before attempting to locate a regulation. Finding the title of the statute is made easy because most jurisdictions publish two tables: one that lists all *regulations* and their corresponding statutes (called a concordance) and one that lists all *statutes* and their corresponding regulations. These tables are usually consolidated and therefore include all regulations in force at the time of publication and all their amendments. They are called different things in each province but federally they are called the *Consolidated Index of Statutory Instruments*, Table I and Table II. This handy index is also online at:<http://laws.justice.gc.ca/en/StatutoryInstrument>.

Carswell also publishes the *Canadian Regulations Index*, which is a very useful research tool if you know the name of the relevant statute. It is in loose-leaf form and lists all regulations made pursuant to each federal statute.

Examples of Regulations Tables

Federal: Consolidated Index of Statutory Instruments (in Canada Gazette, Part II)

1. Table I: *Table of Regulations, Statutory Instruments (other than Regulations) and Other Documents.* All regulations and their corresponding statutes are listed. (The abbreviation SI stands for "Statutory Instrument". The SI number is merely a way of numbering and organizing regulations chronologically for publishing.)
2. Table II: *Table of Regulations, Statutory Instruments (other than Regulations) and Other Documents Arranged by Statute.* (The abbreviation SOR stands for "Statutory Orders". The SOR number is merely a way of numbering and organizing these other types of documents chronologically for publishing.)

The regulations and other documents, that is, the SORs and SIs pertaining to each statute, are listed underneath each statute.

British Columbia: Consolidated Regulations of British Columbia

1. The *Regulation/Act Concordance* is found in the front of the *Consolidated Regulations of British Columbia* (C.R.B.C. Volume I). It lists all regulations and corresponding statutes.
2. *Table of Contents* or *Index* of Current B.C. Regulations. Both list all statutes of British Columbia and their corresponding regulations.

If you know only the title of the regulation, look in the first table. If you know the title of the statute, look in the second table. It is important to note the date on the table to ensure it is current. You must update from that date forward.

Other provinces and territories have similar tools.

Example 1: Federal Regulations

If you know the **name of the statute**, look in Table II: *Table of Regulations, Statutory Instruments (other than Regulations) and Other Documents Arranged by Statute*.

Illustration 8.4
Canada Gazette, Part II: Consolidated
Index of Statutory Instruments

Canada
Gazette
Part II

Gazette
du Canada
Partie II

CONSOLIDATED INDEX

OF STATUTORY

INSTRUMENTS

INDEX CODIFIÉ

DES TEXTES

RÉGLEMENTAIRES

JANUARY 1, 1955 TO DECEMBER 31, 2003

DU 1ᵉʳ JANVIER 1955 AU 31 DÉCEMBRE 2003

(French version after blue sheet at centre of issue)

(Version française à la suite du feuillet bleu au centre de l'édition)

Illustration 8.5
Sample Federal Table of Regulations — Listed by Statute

59

II—TABLE OF REGULATIONS, STATUTORY INSTRUMENTS (OTHER THAN
REGULATIONS) AND OTHER DOCUMENTS ARRANGED BY STATUTE

DECEMBER 31, 2003

. . .

**CANADIAN WHEAT BOARD ACT [RC
1985, c. C-24]—*Cont.***

**Election of Directors of the Canadian
Wheat Board—Regulations
respecting, SOR/98-414—*Cont.***
   s. 20, SOR/2000-302, s. 7
   s. 27, SOR/2002-323, s. 3
   s. 28.01, added, SOR32002-323, s. 4
   s. 28.02, added, SOR32002-323, s. 4
   s. 28.1, added, SOR/2000-302, s. 8
   Sch. 2, repealed, SOR/2000-302, s. 9

**Instructions to the Trade (Not registered
or published)**
   **Place for inspection and sale of
copies:**

   Office of the Secretary to the Canadian
Wheat Board, 423 Main Street,
Winnipeg, Manitoba

**CAPE BRETON DEVELOPMENT
CORPORATIONS ACT [RC 1985, c.
C-25]**
   *(SOCIETÉ DE DÉVELOPPEMENT
DU CAP-BRETON (LOI))*

**Order Designating the Minister of
Natural Resources as Minister for
Purposes of the Act, SI/95-53**
   *(Décret chargeant le ministre des
Ressources naturelles de
l'application de la Loi)*

**CHILDREN'S SPECIAL
ALLOWANCES ACT [SC 1992, c.
48]**
   *(ALLOCATIONS SPÉCIALES POUR
ENFANTS (LOI))*

**Children's Special Allowance
Regulations, SOR/93-12**
   *(Allocations spéciales pour
enfants—Règlement)*
   s. 3, SOR/99-326, s. 1
   s. 4, SOR/97-35, s. 1
   s. 6, SOR/97-35, s. 2(E); SOR/99-
326, s. 2
   s. 6.1, added, SOR/99-326, s. 3 ←
   s. 9, SOR/97-35, s. 3

CITIZENSHIP ACT [RC 1985, c. C-29]
   (CITOYENNETÉ (LOI))

**Citizenship Regulations, 1993, SOR/93-
246**
   (Citoyenneté, 1993—Règlement)
   s. 3, SOR/94-442, s. 1
   s. 11, SOR/94-442, s. 2
   s. 12, SOR/94-442, s. 2
   s. 13, repealed, SOR/94-442, s. 2
   s. 14, SOR/94-442, s. 2
   s. 15, SOR/94-442, s. 3
   s. 22, SOR/94-442, s. 4
   s. 32, added, SOR/95-122, s. 1
   s. 33, added, SOR/95-122, s. 1
   sch., SOR/95-122, s. 2; SOR/97-23,
s. 1

As you can see, the regulations (SOR and SI) pertaining to each statute are listed underneath each statute. If the regulation was made before 1985, it will have a reference to C.R.C. 1978. This table will provide information on the regulations.

At this stage, you should record the number and year of all of the relevant regulations and their citations (*i.e.*, the location in the *Canada Gazette, Part II*). For example, the first regulation under the *Citizenship Act* is the *Citizenship Regulations, 1993*, SOR/93-246.

Other regulations listed often amend prior regulations. For example, regulation SOR/93-246 was amended by SOR/94-442, and again by SOR/95-122 and SOR/97-23. You should look at all of the regulations to ensure you have the most current version.

If you know the **name of the regulation**, look in Table I (Table of Regulations, Statutory Instruments (other than Regulations) and Other Documents. All regulations and their corresponding statutes are listed.

Illustration 8.6
Sample Federal Table of Regulations (Listed by Regulation)

I—TABLE OF REGULATIONS, STATUTORY INSTRUMENTS (OTHER THAN REGULATIONS) AND OTHER DOCUMENTS

DECEMBER 31, 2003

This Table provides a reference to regulations, statutory instruments (other than regulations) and other documents that have been made under statutory or other authority and that were in force at any time during the current calendar year.

The instruments are listed alphabetically according to their title showing the authority under which they were made and are listed in Table II.

For instruments no longer in force, that were published in the *Canada Gazette* Part II, reference should be made to the Consolidated Index of December 31st of the year in question.

ACOA Loan Insurance Regs
Atlantic Canada Opportunities Agency Act

AECB Cost Recovery Fees Regs
Nuclear Energy Act

AECB Cost Recovery Fees Remission Order
Financial Administration Act

AECL Tandem Accelerator Superconducting Cyclotron Complex Remission Order
Customs Tariff

Abandonment of Branch Lines Prohibition Orders
Northwest Territories Act

Accounting for Imported Goods and Payment of Duties Regs
Customs Act

Accrued Interest under Canada Account Loans to Madagascar, Poland, Tanzania and Zambia Remission Order
Financial Administration Act

Acting Customs Excise Enforcement Officers Exclusion Approval Order
Public Service Employment Act

Additional Legislative Powers Designation Order
Northwest Territories Act

Affiliated Persons (Trust and Loan Companies) Regs
Trust and Loan Companies Act

African Development Bank Privileges and Immunities Order
Foreign Missions and International Organizations Act

African Development Fund Privileges and Immunities Order
Foreign Missions and International Organizations Act

Age Guideline
Canadian Human Rights Act

Example 2: Provincial Regulations

If you know the name of the provincial statute, look in the table that lists the statutes and all the corresponding regulations. In British Columbia this is called the Regulation/Act Concordance and is found in the front of the *Consolidated Regulations of British Columbia* (C.R.B.C.). It lists all regulations and corresponding statutes. Other provinces and territories have similar tables.

Illustration 8.7
Sample Consolidated Regulations of
British Columbia; Title page of Volume 8

Province of British Columbia

CONSOLIDATED

REGULATIONS OF

BRITISH COLUMBIA

A consolidation of regulations
of general public interest
published under the authority of
the *Regulations Act*

VOLUME 8

Queen's Printer for British Columbia
Victoria, 1999

Illustration 8.8
Sample British Columbia List of Regulations by Title:
B.C. Regulation Act/Concordance

REGULATION / ACT CONCORDANCE

REGULATION	ACT
Miscellaneous Registrations Regulation	Miscellaneous Registrations, 1992
Mission & District Community Health Council Regulation	Health Authorities
Mortgage Brokers Act Regulations	Mortgage Brokers
Motion Picture Act Regulations	Motion Picture
Motor Carrier Regulations	Motor Carrier
Motor Carrier Regulation No. 2	Motor Carrier
Motor Dealer Act Regulation	Motor Dealer
Motor Dealer Exemption Regulation	Real Estate
Motor Dealer Leasing Regulation	Motor Dealer
Motor Fuel Tax Regulation	Motor Fuel Tax
Motor Fuel Tax Refund and Remission Regulation	Motor Fuel Tax; Financial Administration
Motor Vehicle Act and Commercial Transport Act Retention of Fees Regulation	Financial Administration
Motor Vehicle Act Regulations	Motor Vehicle
Motor Vehicle Fees Regulation	Motor Vehicle
Motor Vehicle Insurance Policy Limits Regulation	Insurance
Motor Vehicle Prohibition Regulation	Wildlife
Motor Vehicle Prohibition (Temporary) Regulation	Wildlife
Mount Pleasant Commission Retention Regulation	Financial Administration
Mount Waddington Health Council Regulation	Health Authorities
Municipal Act Fees Regulation Nos. 1 & 2	Municipal
Municipal Act Tax Regulation	Municipal
Municipal Administration Certification Regulation	Municipal
Municipal Bylaw Enforcement Ticket Regulation	Municipal
Municipal Finance Authority Act Regulation	Municipal Finance Author.
Museum Fee Regulation	Museum Act
Muskwa Kechika Access Management Area Regulation	Wildlife Act
Nakusp Unorganized Territory	Curfew
⇒ Name Act Regulation	Name
Nanaimo Health Council Regulation	Health Authorities
Nanaimo Regional District Regulation	Municipal
Natural Gas Price Act Regulation No. 2	Natural Gas Price
Natural Products Marketing (BC) Act Regulations	Natural Products Marketing (BC)
Nelson and Area Health Council Regulation	Health Authorities
New Westminster Health Council Regulation	Health Authorities
Nicola Valley Health Council Regulation	Health Authorities
Non-Reporting Company Exemption Regulation	Financial Institutions
North Coast Community Health Council Regulation	Health Authorities

If you know the title of the statute, look in the table that lists all of the regulations and the corresponding statutes. In British Columbia this is called the *Index of Current B.C. Regulations*. It lists all regulations in British Columbia and their corresponding statutes. Most other provinces and territories have similar indexes or tables that list their consolidated regulations.

Illustration 8.9
Sample British Columbia Index of Regulations (Listed by Statute)
Index of Current B.C. Regulations

INDEX OF CURRENT B.C. REGULATIONS

These regulations are all technically in effect, but not all are in active use. Most, but not all, have been published in the B.C. Gazette, Part II. Regulations made under a repealed Act but which are still in use are listed under the replacement Act. Some regulations which were previously listed no longer meet the definition of "regulation" under the present *Regulations Act*, R.S.B.C. 1996, c. 402, and so have been deleted from this index. Symbols used are as follows:

　　* = not published
　　# = published in Part I Gazette
Citations such as "1985-55-42" signify the year, chapter and section of the statute cited.

			B.C. Reg.
ACCESS TO ABORTION SERVICES ACT c. 1, R.S.B.C. 1996			
Abortion Services Access Zone Regulation			337/95
amended	*385/98*	*277/2000*	*106/2002*

. . .

MUNICIPALITIES ENABLING and VALIDATING ACT c. 261, R.S.B.C. 1960			
Prescribed Rates – District of Kent			380/2002

MUNICIPALITIES ENABLING and VALIDATING ACT (NO. 2) c. 61, S.B.C. 1990			
Community Airport Bodies Regulation			167/99
Partnering Agreements Regulation			126/2000

MUNICIPALITIES ENABLING and VALIDATING ACT (NO. 3) c. 44, S.B.C. 2001			
Community Port Authorities Regulation			194/2002

MUSEUM ACT c. 12, S.B.C. 2003				
Museum Fees Regulation				286/95
amended	*166/96*	*140/97*	*257/97*	*56/99*
	283/99	*254/2002*		

MUSKWA-KECHIKA MANAGEMENT AREA ACT c. 38, S.B.C. 1998			
Muskwa-Kechika Management Plan Regulation			53/2002

→ **NAME ACT** c. 328, R.S.B.C. 1996			
Name Act Regulation			91/80
amended	*326/84*	*73/87*	*121/88*	*111/90*
	133/91	*87/92*	*79/94*	*132/95*
	554/95	*110/97*		

Note where to find the number and year of the regulation (*e.g.*, B.C. Reg. 91/80) and amendments to the regulation (*e.g.*, B.C. Reg. 326/84).

Step 2: Find The Regulation

You can find the regulation from the information obtained in Step 1. Most regulations are filed by number and date and sometimes by page. Once you have the proper number of the regulation you are looking for, it is most efficient to search for that **number**, rather than search for the title, which can be very long.

Federal regulations are located in either the consolidated set (the *Consolidated Regulations of Canada, 1978*), or in the *Canada Gazette, Part II* issues that have been published since the 1978 consolidation.

Likewise, provincial and territorial regulations receive numbers based on the jurisdiction's preferred numbering scheme. For example, here is an excerpt from British Columbia Regulation 91/80 (made pursuant to the *Name Act*). Note that it repeals a prior regulation.

Illustration 8.10
Sample British Columbia Regulation: B.C. Regulation 91/80
(Change of Name Act Regulation)

B.C. Reg. 91/80   Filed March 21, 1980

CHANGE OF NAME ACT
[Section 14]

Order in Council 617, Approved and Ordered March 20, 1980

On the recommendation of the undersigned, the Lieutenant-Governor, by and with the advice and consent of the Executive Council, orders that, effective June 1, 1980, Order in Council 3437, approved November 7, 1967 (B.C. Reg. 253/67), be repealed and the following regulation be made.

CHANGE OF NAME ACT REGULATIONS

1. Under the *Change of Name Act* the fee

    (a)   on filing an application for a Change of Name shall be $25, which fee includes the issuance of one certificate of Change of Name and cost of publication of the certificate in the Gazette following approval of the application,

    (b)   for a search of one registration of Change of Name shall be $2 for each three-year period or part of a three-year period covered by the search, and

    (c)   for each certificate of Change of Name shall be $5, including the fee for a search covering one three-year period.

K. R. MAIR
Minister of Health

W. R. BENNETT
Presiding Member of the Executive Council

. . .

apl -- 3506

Illustration 8.11
Sample British Columbia Consolidated Regulations:
From Government Website

Name Act -- NAME ACT REGULATION   Page 1 of 1

B.C. Reg. 91/80   Filed March 21, 1980
O.C. 617/80   effective June 1, 1980

Name Act

NAME ACT REGULATION

[includes amendments up to B.C. Reg. 110/97]

Fees

1 Under the *Name Act* the fee

(a) on filing an application for a Change of Name shall be $137 for the applicant and $27 for each person who is listed in the application as a person whose name will be changed by reason of a change of name of the applicant, which fees include the issuance of one certificate of Change of Name for the applicant and each listed person and the cost of publication of the certificates in the Gazette following approval of the application.

(b) for a search of one registration of Change of Name shall be $27 for each 3 year period or part of a 3 year period covered by the search,

(c) for each certificate of Change of Name shall be

(i) $27 including the fee for a search covering one 3 year period, or

(ii) $60 including, where same day search service is offered and requested, the fee for a search that same day covering one 3 year period, and

(d) for copies of documents supporting an application for Change of Name shall be $50.

[am. B.C. Regs. 326/84; 73/87; 121/88, 111/90; 133/91; 67/92; 79/94; 132/95; 554/95; 110/97.]

[Provisions of the *Name Act*, R.S.B.C. 1996, c. 328, relevant to the enactment of this regulation: section 17]

Note that the consolidated regulation includes all of the amendments up to B.C. Reg. 110/97 and is not an official version.

Illustration 8.12
B.C. Regulation 110/97

B.C. Reg. 110/97, deposited March 27, 1997, pursuant to the **NAME ACT** [Section 13 (1)]. Order in Council 359/97, approved and ordered March 26, 1997.

On the recommendation of the undersigned, the Lieutenant Governor, by and with the advice and consent of the Executive Council, orders that, effective April 1, 1997, section 1 (a) of B.C. Reg. 91/80, the Name Act Regulation, is amended by striking out "$125" and substituting "$137". — J. K. MACPHAIL, *Minister of Health and Minister Responsible for Seniors;* G. CLARK, *Presiding Member of the Executive Council.*

Step 3: Update the Regulation

To locate the most recent amendments to regulations, you should consult very recent print publications from the legislative body (usually found in a law library), or consult the appropriate government website, or look in a service of a commercial online provider.

For library research of federal regulations, this means looking in the index of each of the softcover editions of the *Canada Gazette, Part II,* that have come out **after** the most recent *Consolidated Index of Statutory Instruments.* To further update, you must look at the *Canada Legislative Digest* or Thomson Carswell's *Legislation,* a very helpful monthly publication that updates both statutes and regulations from all Canadian jurisdictions (see **Chapter 7** for a full description). You could also speak to a law librarian or call the Library of Parliament.

For provincial amendments to regulations, look at the most current softcover editions of the provincial gazettes (often there is an index included) and the most recent legislative digest from a librarian or the legislature. Or, use Thomson Carswell's *Legislation* (see above).

An excellent new online service for updating regulations (as well as statutes) from all Canadian Jurisdictions is CCH Canadian's *Legislative Pulse* (described in detail in Chapter 7). This commercial online service makes updating very quick and thorough. However, even this service may not be entirely up to date, so be sure to update in the library from the currency date noted in the electronic version.

HOW TO WRITE A CITATION FOR A REGULATION

The citation of regulations is fairly straightforward.

Federal Regulations

The title of a federal regulation is the short title, which is often stated in the regulation. Although it is not necessary to state the title of the regulation in the citation, it is good practice to do so, to confirm for your readers that they are reading the correct regulation. Those published in the *Consolidated Regulations of Canada, 1978* can be cited as follows: *Civil Service Insurance Regulations*, C.R.C., c. 401. Note you do not need to put the date in because the **only** C.R.C. that has ever been published is dated 1978.

Those published after the consolidation (*i.e.*, in the *Canada Gazette, Part II*) include both the SOR or SI number and the page reference. They are cited as follows: *Foreign Ownership of Land Regulations*, SOR/79-416, 2113. This means SOR number 416, published in 1979, at page 2113.

Provincial Regulations

The proper way to cite provincial regulations is by the name of the province (abbreviated) and the regulation number, for example: B.C. Reg. 91/80. This means this was the 91st regulation made in British Columbia in 1980 and it can be located in the 1980 volume of regulations. Note again that the title of the regulation is not necessary, but it is always good to state it, for the sake of clarity.

ELECTRONIC CITATION

If the regulation is taken from an electronic a source it is necessary to add that information to the citation. After the citation (above) add a comma and then the word "online" followed by a colon. If a commercial online system was used, add the abbreviation for the provider (*e.g.*, LN/QL). If an Internet site was used, add the name of the website followed by the name of the specific part of the site, then the URL (Uniform Resource Locator) in angled brackets.

EFFECTIVE DATES OF STATUTES

As mentioned in Chapter 7 (How to Find and Update Statutes), some statutes require proclamation in order to come into force (CIF). Such proclamations officially appear in the form of a regulation from the jurisdiction. In actual fact, a researcher would never need to actually find and read the proclamation because, as stated in Chapter 7, legislatures publish "proclamation tables" either as separate documents or bound into annual statutory volumes.

These tables include information about when statutes were proclaimed and provide citations for the regulations that brought them into effect. One example of such a table is the *Canada Gazette, Part III*, entitled *Proclamations of Canada and Orders in Council Relating to the Coming into Force of Acts.*

Illustration 8.13
Sample Federal Table of Proclamations (*Canada Gazette, Part III*)

PROCLAMATIONS OF CANADA AND ORDERS IN COUNCIL RELATING TO THE COMING INTO FORCE OF ACTS — 1 JANUARY, 2002 TO 31 DECEMBER, 2002	Date in force	Canada Gazette Part II
Accession of the People's Republic of China to the Agreement Establishing the World Trade Organization, An Act to amend certain Acts as a result of the, S.C. 2002, c. 19, sections 1 to 18, in force	30 Sept., 2002	SI/2002-122 Vol. 136, p. 1989
Acts and instruments and to repeal the Fisheries Prices Support Act, An Act to amend certain, S.C. 2002, c. 17, in force	22 July, 2002	SI/2002-105 Vol. 136, p. 1829
Air Canada Public Participation Act, An Act to amend the, S.C. 2001, c. 35, in force	2 Feb., 2002	SI/2002-40 Vol. 136, p. 444
Anti-terrorism Act, S.C. 2001, c. 41,		
— Act, other than sections 52, 54 to 64, subsections 67(2) and (3) and section 74, in force	24 Dec., 2001	SI/2002-16 Vol. 136, p. 292
— section 52, subsections 67(2) and (3) and section 74, in force	12 June, 2002	SI/2002-86 Vol. 136, p. 1241
— sections 54 to 64, in force	6 Jan., 2003	SI/2002-164 Vol. 136, p. 2885
Budget Implementation Act, 2001, S.C. 2002, c. 9,		
— (a) the *Canadian Air Transport Security Authority Act*, as enacted by section 2, and (b) section 3, in force	1 April, 2002	SI/2002-63 Vol. 136, p. 854
— sections 1 and 2 of the *Canada Fund for Africa Act*, as enacted by section 45, in force	12 April, 2002	SI/2002-71 Vol. 136, p. 990
— sections 12 to 18, in force	17 April, 2002	SI/2002-76 Vol. 136, p. 1111
— sections 3 to 5 of the *Canada Fund for Africa Act*, as enacted by section 45, in force	27 June, 2002	SI/2002-101 Vol. 136, p. 1642
Canada–Costa Rica Free Trade Agreement Implementation Act, S.C. 2001, c. 28, in force	1 Nov., 2002	SI/2002-146 Vol. 136, p. 2591
Canada Foundation for Sustainable Development Technology Act, S.C. 2001, c. 23, in force	22 Mar., 2002	SI/2002-57 Vol. 136, p. 757
Canadian Commercial Corporation Act, An Act to amend the, S.C. 2002, c. 4, in force	19 April, 2002	SI/2002-77 Vol. 136, p. 1112
Cape Breton Development Corporation Divestiture Authorization and Dissolution Act, S.C. 2000, c. 23, subsections 7(2) and 8(2), in force	3 June, 2002	SI/2002-92 Vol. 136, p. 1500
Competition Act and the Competition Tribunal Act, An Act to amend the, S.C. 2002, c. 16, the Act, except for section 124.1 of the *Competition Act*, as enacted by section 15, in force	21 June, 2002	SI/2002-100 Vol. 136, p. 1641

Some print tables of proclamation are cumulative and some are not. As seen in the example, this table of proclamation covers only one period: January 2002 to December 2002. Therefore, in this example, each table must be searched in each of the successive annual volumes. In other words, you must look at the table in the volume of the year in which the statute was given royal assent, **as well as all subsequent volumes,** until you finally find the date of the proclamation.

You will note that you are referred to the volume and page number of the *Canada Gazette, Part II* or a volume and page number of a provincial or territorial gazette, rather than to a regulation number.

Finally, you must find the actual regulation. If you have the regulation number, you can go directly to the volume of regulations or statutory instruments and locate the regulation by date and regulation number.

For the most recent information on statutes coming into force, look in the softcover volumes of the federal or provincial gazettes, or contact the legislative library. Alternatively, use Thomson Carswell's *Legislation* (monthly) or the online CCH Canadian *Legislative Pulse*, both of which give very current coming into force dates.

A WORD ABOUT MUNICIPAL BYLAWS

The Constitution does not mention legislative powers of municipalities. Municipal law-making powers are delegated provincial powers. These powers are delegated through statute and give municipalities the powers to create bylaws (also called ordinances). Typically, each municipality has a governing (enabling) statute (often called a *Municipalities Act* or a *Cities and Towns Act*) which describes the areas in which municipalities have powers to make bylaws.

The process by which bylaws are adopted is different than that of statutes or regulations. Usually the method of adoption is outlined in the enabling statute or another bylaw.

Some bylaws require that certain procedures be followed prior to their introduction. These include such procedures as public hearings or public votes. Bylaws usually require three readings; however, all three readings are often conducted in one sitting of municipal council. The committee work is usually done prior to the bylaw being introduced and there is usually "reconsideration" of the bylaw at least one day after third reading.

Municipal bylaws may be found cited as primary authority in case law. However, because law students tend to focus primarily on case law, they are often unfamiliar with municipal law when they graduate.

At present, there is no commercial online service or public website that provides full text, or even a comprehensive listing, of the bylaws and ordinances of Canadian municipalities. As more references are made to them in judicial decisions, demand for such an online service will likely grow. Meantime, the only way to find and read municipal bylaws is either on the website of the municipality in question or at a local public or law library. Public libraries are often designated as an "official public depository" for municipal legislation.

SELF TEST

The answers to these questions are found at the end of the book in the "Answers to Self Tests" section.

1. What is a regulation?
2. Explain how regulations become law.
3. What is a consolidation of regulations?
4. How do you locate regulations?

SAMPLE EXERCISES — FINDING REGULATIONS

Objectives

At the end of this exercise you should be able to:

- Locate a federal regulation
- Locate a provincial regulation
- Use tables or indexes to update regulations
- Cite a regulation

Instructions

- Do background reading on how to locate and cite regulations.
- Keep a record of the time taken to complete the exercise.

Provincial Regulations

Answer questions 1–4 for the following regulation:

Christmas Tree Regulation (B.C.)

1. Record the proper citation for the statute that authorizes this regulation.

   Citation:

2. Record the basic citation of the regulation.

   Citation:

3. Record the citation for any amendments to the regulation.

   Amendments:

4. Find the regulation and record the date of deposit or date of filing.

Date of deposit or date of filing:

Federal Regulations

Answer questions 1–4 for the following regulation:

Honey Regulations (Canada)

1. Record the proper citation for the statute that authorizes this regulation.

Citation:

2. Record the basic citation of the regulation.

Citation:

3. Record the citation for the very first listed amendment to s. 2 of that regulation.

Citation:

4. Find the regulation and record the P.C. (Privy Council) number for that amendment.

P.C. number:

ANSWERS TO EXERCISES

Provincial Regulations

1. *Forest Act*, R.S.B.C. 1996, c. 157.
2. B.C. Reg. 166/2000.
3. None.
4. Date of deposit for Reg. 166/2000 is May 19, 2000.

Federal Regulations

1. *Canada Agricultural Products Act*, R.S.C. 1985 (4th Supp.), c. 20.
2. C.R.C. Vol. II, c. 287.
3. Section 2 was amended by SOR/91-524, s. 1.

4. P.C. number 1991-1631, Sept. 5, 1991.

(From Index volume Jan. 1, 1955 - Dec. 31, 2006)

Appendix 8A: Checklist: How to Find and Update Regulations

ELECTRONIC SEARCHES

Electronic versions of regulations can be found on most government websites and on most commercial online services. Therefore, if you know the name of the relevant statute under which your regulation was made, you will likely be able to find the regulation through one of these electronic sources.

However, you must still be familiar with the print sources to find the official version of the regulation and to confirm that the electronic version of the regulation is current and accurate. Unless you know the exact title of a regulation or the title of its enabling statute, it is best to first look at secondary sources to get the right title before searching electronic regulations databases. Here are some sources:

- **Internet:** The federal government website and most provincial government websites include full-text regulations. CanLII (<http://www.canlii.org>) and law libraries also either list regulations or provide links to the originating parliament or legislature. The federal list is called the *Consolidated Index of Statutory Instruments*, and you can go directly to it online (<http://canadagazette.gc.ca/ index-e.html>). On these sites, you can usually either browse a title list or search by keyword in a search template. A list of government sites is appended to Chapter 7 (How to Find and Update Statutes).

- **LN/QL and WL*e*C:** Both have databases containing federal, provincial, and territorial regulations. Within regulations databases, you can browse a title list or perform a keyword search of the full text.

When updating regulations using electronic sources, you will see that most of the online versions state whether the regulations database is consolidated (whether the amendments have been incorporated into the text). If it is consolidated, record the consolidation date then check the appropriate gazette (either online or in paper form) for any amendments to the regulations since the consolidation date.

LIBRARY SEARCHES

In the library you will find volumes of new regulations and consolidated sets of older regulations. Federal regulations are also known as statutory orders and regulations (SOR) or statutory instruments (SI). Each regulation is made pursuant to an "enabling" statute. In the library, you can locate a regulation by searching under the name of the enabling statute or by searching for the title of the regulation itself.

One handy tool is *Legislation* (a part of the *Canadian Abridgment*), which since 1989 has comes out monthly with lists of federal, provincial, and territorial regulations that have been issued, issuance date, SI or SOR number or regulation number, and enabling statute.

Step 1: Find the Name of the Regulation

Go to the most recent *consolidated* index of regulations or statutory instruments.

- For **federal regulations**, this index is entitled *Consolidated Index of Statutory Instruments*. It is published quarterly as part of *Canada Gazette, Part II*.

- For **provincial and territorial regulations**, the index has various titles. In British Columbia the *Index of Current B.C. Regulations* lists regulations under the titles of their enabling statutes.

- Some commercially published regulations consolidations are available, but only for more frequently used federal regulations and those of the larger provinces.

If You Know the Title of the Regulation but not its Enabling Statute

❑ If you know the title of the *regulation*, but not the enabling statute's name, you will need to use a specific table:

- For **federal** regulations, this table is included in the *Consolidated Index of Statutory Instruments* and is entitled Table I: *Table of Regulations, Statutory Instruments (other than Regulations) and Other Documents.* Simply look up the title of the regulation there, *e.g.*, *Foreign Ownership of Land Regulations, Letter Definition Regulations,* etc.

- For **provincial and territorial** regulations, the specific tables have various titles. In British Columbia it is called the

Regulation/Act Concordance and is located in volume 1 of the *Consolidated Regulations of British Columbia.*

❏ Record the number and year of your regulations and their citations. Note the index date, since you will need to update from that date forward.

If You Know the Title of the Statute but not the Name of the Specific Regulation

❏ If you know the title of the enabling *statute*, look for a different table that lists statutes and their corresponding regulations.

- For **federal** regulations this table is included in the *Consolidated Index of Statutory Instruments* and is entitled Table II: *Table of Regulations, Statutory Instruments (other than Regulations) and Other Documents Arranged by Statute.*

- For **provincial and territorial** regulations, this index or table has various titles. In British Columbia it is called the *Index of Current B.C. Regulations.* Regulations are listed under the name of their enabling statute.

❏ Record the number and year of all the relevant regulations and their citations. Note the index date so you can update from that date forward.

Step 2: Find the Regulation

Regulations are arranged chronologically by number. The citation of the regulation tells you both the year and the number to look for in each of the annual volumes of the Gazettes (*e.g., Canada Gazette, Part II*). When looking for federal regulations, C.R.C. refers to the *Consolidated Regulations of Canada, 1978* — the last official print consolidation of federal regulations.

Issues of the *Canada Gazette, Part II,* include both SOR and SI, mixed together. SORs precede SIs within each issue of the Gazette, so look for the SOR or SI prefix when looking for your regulations. As explained above, the *Consolidated Index* for The *Canada Gazette, Part II* lists the regulations under their enabling Act, and provides the regulation number, Gazette date, and page (*e.g.,* SOR/79-416, date 13/06/79, and page 2113). Note that SOR and SI numbers are composed of the year and regulation number, *e.g.,* SOR/2002-345 or SI/79-23. Most provincial regulations numbering is composed of regulation number then year, *e.g., Bee Regulation,* B.C. Reg. 373/88.

Step 3: Update the Regulation

❑ To locate the most recent amendments to regulations, look in the index or table of contents of *each* of the softcover issues of the jurisdictional Gazette published after the most recent consolidated index or table (as described above). For federal regulations, these are the biweekly issues of the *Canada Gazette, Part II*. For provincial or territorial regulations, read the printed jurisdictional gazette. Or, for all jurisdictions, use Carswell's *Legislation* monthly issues.

❑ To further update, look at electronic gazettes online from the various provincial governments.

❑ To be absolutely up to date, you should contact the office of the minister named in the enabling statute and ask if there have been any very recent updates that have not been published.

How to Find and Update Cases 9

Case law research involves locating relevant cases, seeing whether these cases have been appealed (updating), and locating later cases that have considered those cases (noting up). Thousands of cases are decided each year provincially, federally, and internationally. In order to locate these judicial decisions, researchers must become familiar with how cases are published, how they are arranged in law libraries and databases, and the tools available to assist in locating them.

This chapter describes what cases are, how to read cases, and how cases are published in reports and displayed online. It then describes step-by-step how to locate cases, and explains how to cite cases.

LEARNING OBJECTIVES

At the end of this chapter you will be able to:

- Read a case and define its parts
- Describe how cases are published or displayed online
- Name a few specific case reports
- Locate a case by case name or citation
- Locate a case by subject
- Update and note up a case
- Use proper case citation

WHAT IS A CASE?

A case is a decision of a judge or a tribunal. It is the written outcome of a dispute that has been tried in a court or an administrative tribunal. Since Canadian judges are required to follow previously decided similar cases, these cases must be made available to the judges and the public. Cases form a very significant part of the common law in Canada.

HOW TO READ A CASE

The ability to read a case is critical to legal analysis but also equally important to the task of locating *relevant* cases. If you can read cases quickly and accurately you can efficiently detect those cases that are relevant and exclude those that are not.

Reading cases involves some skill. Most cases follow a particular format and, after reading several cases, the researcher should be able to quickly find relevant information without getting bogged down in irrelevant information.

At the most basic level, researchers should be familiar with the format of published cases. A description of this format is provided in Appendix 9A. This format is also important for computer research since you can narrow down your search by asking the computer to search only certain locations in the text of reported cases (*e.g.*, the parties or the date).

HOW CASES ARE PUBLISHED

The system of common law and the doctrine of precedent require that judges follow past judgments to the extent that they are similar and binding. Therefore, in a common law system, it is very important that judgments be written and published. This process is called case reporting.

Although many cases are in electronic form, computers are not always the most effective or efficient method of finding cases. As well, not all electronic cases are recognized by the courts and not all cases are in electronic form.

The location of cases in computer databases is similar to their location in paper compilations in the library. For example, the same cases from the *Dominion Law Reports* are found both on QL/LN (electronic format) and in the printed reporter by that same name.

What Are Case Reports?

Case reports are sets of books containing decided cases. Case reports are also called case reporters, law reports, or case reporting series.

Various commercial publishers and government bodies collect the decisions of courts and administrative bodies and assemble and publish them for resale. There are over 100 distinct case reports in Canada. It is important to know that *not all cases are reported in print*. Usually only those that change or clarify the law are reported.

Each case report consists of many volumes of bound books, which are arranged in chronological order on the library shelves. Each hardbound volume contains many cases. As you can imagine, there are thousands of volumes of case reports, containing millions of cases, on the shelves of law libraries. Each case has a set of keywords and a headnote or summary of the issues at the top. These are written by editors and occasionally include case comments and references to other cases. These headnotes are rarely found in electronic versions of cases unless the cases were originally published in hard copy or the editors can charge for the value added by this service.

When locating cases, particular attention should be paid to the publishers of legal materials. Although it may seem strange to the new researcher, the way in which cases are published directs much of legal research. This is because each publisher decides which cases are published, how they are categorized, and how they are indexed. In order to locate cases, therefore, researchers should be aware of the different publishers' indexing systems.

Which Cases Are in Case Reports?

Cases are organized and published in a number of ways. There is no single complete set of all decided cases in Canada. Cases from different jurisdictions and on different subjects are published in different case reports. This is one of the main reasons why legal researchers need research aids to assist them in locating cases.

Although computer research can eliminate some of this problem, at present there is no single computer system that contains all decided cases. The same case can often be found in several case reports. Most case reports include a list of what cases they publish and it is always a good idea for new researchers to check and ensure that the cases they are looking for are in that particular report. The following are some examples.

Federal Case Reports

There are three case reports that publish cases from the two Canadian federal courts: the *Supreme Court Reports* (S.C.R.), the *National Reporter* (N.R.), and the *Federal Courts Reports* (F.C.R. (formerly F.C.)). The *Supreme Court Reports* contains only Supreme Court of Canada decisions. The *National Reporter* publishes all of the judgments of the Supreme Court of Canada, the Federal Court of Appeal, and some decisions from the Federal Court (the trial court of the federal court system). The *Federal Courts Reports* is the official report of the Federal Courts of Canada and contains all of the decisions of the Federal Courts (which typically involve matters of taxation, immigration, and other areas of federal jurisdiction).

General Case Reports

The only case report that publishes cases from all the provinces as well as the two federal courts is the *Dominion Law Reports* (D.L.R.). It is the best-known case report in Canada.

Provincial Case Reports

Most provinces have their own set of case reports that include court decisions from that particular province and cases that are important to the law of that province. Examples include the *British Columbia Law Reports* (B.C.L.R.) and the *Ontario Reports* (O.R.). These case reports are published by private publishers and are generally recognized by courts, practitioners, and the law society of the province as "semi-official" reports for that jurisdiction in the absence of any sets published by the government itself.

Regional Case Reports

Regional case reports include cases from regions of Canada. For example, the *Western Weekly Reports* (W.W.R.) includes cases only from the western provinces and the *Atlantic Reports* (A.R.) includes cases only from the four Atlantic provinces.

Subject Case Reports

Over the past 30 years or so, there has been an increase in case reports that only include cases on particular subjects. This is because lawyers tend to specialize and will often only purchase case reports containing cases that are relevant to their particular specialty. *Canadian Criminal Cases* (C.C.C.) and *Canadian Cases on Employment Law* (C.C.E.L.) are examples of such subject specific reports.

Administrative Tribunal Case Reports

The decisions of administrative tribunals are published in separate reports from those of cases decided by judges. Reports that include court cases do not, as a rule, include decisions of administrative bodies because they are not *per se* part of the common law (*i.e.*, law of general applicability made by judges). An example of an administrative tribunal case report is the *Canadian Labour Relations Board Reports* (C.L.R.B.R.). It includes labour tribunal decisions from across Canada. Tribunal decisions traditionally have been published "in house" by the board, commission or tribunal rendering the decision. Obtaining copies of such decisions has been difficult until recently because they were not widely disseminated. One exception is the *Canadian Human Rights Reporter* (C.H.R.R.) which is privately published (see Chapter 5) and widely purchased in print and online.

Digests of Cases

There are some so-called case reports that include only digests or summaries of cases. Researchers typically use these reports to keep current on cases as they come out or to locate recent cases.

Digests are useful not only because they are very current but also because they enable you to quickly decide whether the case is worth reading in full. Most practising lawyers subscribe to digest services in order to stay current on the law. The digests are organized by subject area, so a busy lawyer only needs to read those summaries that are relevant to his or her practice area.

For example, *All Canada Weekly Summaries* (A.C.W.S.) consists of digests of cases that will ultimately be published in full in *Dominion Law Reports* (D.L.R.).

The most comprehensive set of Canadian digested cases is the *Canadian Abridgment, Case Digests,* which is published by Carswell. The digests are collected in a multiple-volume set and sorted by a subject classification scheme. In order to locate digests you need to figure out the classification for your particular topic.

As this book went to press, Carswell was issuing the Third Edition of the *Canadian Abridgment.* This is the first reorganization of this set of helping tools since 1986 and Carswell has combined many similar legal topics into a more modern classification in order to reflect the profound changes in Canadian law in the intervening 25 years. Because the changeover to the Third Edition is happening now, some of the examples in this chapter refer to "Second and Third Editions". Once the new edition is complete, all references will be to that set.

LN/QL and WL*e*C have digest databases and the digests are hyperlinked to the full-text version of the case (where available online), which simplifies the research process.

Format of Case Reports

Most cases are published in case reports as soon as they are issued by the courts. However, this process of publication may take some time. Case reports may not be received in hard copy by law libraries until about four to six months after the decisions are written. Therefore, it is always important to check for most recent cases online or directly through the courts.

Usually, case reports have tables of cases and subject indexes in each volume to assist in locating cases quickly. Some also have other aids for research, such as annotations of cases and statute indexes. When looking at a new case report, a researcher should try to become acquainted with the available research aids and the format of the particular case report.

Many case reports have been divided into several series (*e.g.,* 1st, 2d, and 3d series). For example, *Dominion Law Reports* has several series. This means that the numbering of the volumes begins over again every so often. In each series, the volumes are numbered consecutively for many years. At some point, the publishers decide to begin the numbering again and call it a new series. For example, a 2d series will begin once the numbering in the first series becomes unmanageable. A 2d series is not a second edition or reprinting of the cases in the first series, but rather a continuation of the set with new volume numbers that start over again at Volume 1. The series number is important for locating cases.

What is NOT a Case Report?

Beginning legal researchers often are confused about this question. During the course of a trial, many types of documents are prepared and collected in the court's file for that case. These may include briefs, pleadings and evidentiary materials prepared by or collected by both sides and presented to the court. They do not form part of any judicial decision. To obtain copies of these types of documents, you must obtain them from the clerk at the courthouse where the case was heard. They are not collected by law libraries anywhere and are not generally available online in Canada, although this may change in the near future.

One particularly interesting type of "docket" material is a transcript, which is a word-for-word account of everything that was said by all parties during a trial. The rules for retention of transcripts vary by jurisdiction and, again, must be obtained from the court clerk. Often, if a lawyer decides to appeal a case he or she will want to look at transcripts or other docket materials associated with the case at any lower levels. Journalists and historians may also have an interest in these types of materials.

A Word about "Unreported" Cases

Since the mid 1980s, many decisions that have not been chosen for printing in reporters have been digitized and put into online databases managed by LN/QL, WL*e*C, Maritime Law Book Online, and other providers such as CanLII (see Chapter 5 for names of other providers). Courts have been increasingly willing to share electronic versions of their decisions with online providers so that more law is more easily accessible to everyone. It is imperative for the legal researcher to understand that these "unreported" cases are valid Canadian decisions and may certainly be cited as authority. The only distinction between then and "reported" decisions is that the latter show up in print and the former are simply online.

Some decisions may stay in the grey area of "not yet reported" for some period of time. Usually, if a decision is not included in a printed reporter for approximately two years, it will remain "unreported" forever and therefore only available online, if at all.

Jury Trials

When a trial is conducted by a jury, the judge does not render a decision but rather requires the jury to do so. Hence, there is no written decision in a jury trial because the jury does not have to justify its reasons for deciding a case a certain way. There will be a docket file in the courthouse where the trial occurred, stating the outcome of the trial and the sentence rendered, but no written judicial decision will exist. Should the case be heard by an appellate court, that panel of judges will produce a written decision which would appear in print or online, or in both formats.

HOW TO FIND CASES

There is no simple way to find relevant cases. It is an art as well as a skill. The main rule to keep in mind is to be systematic. If you proceed in a systematic way and record your steps as you go, it is unlikely that you will get off track or duplicate steps. Ideally, you should have a strategy or plan of attack before you enter the library. Developing a research plan is discussed in Chapter 12.

Before beginning your search, you should ask yourself the following questions. The answers will help you narrow down the sources you will look at.

- Do you want the full text of a case?
- Do you just want the citation of the case?
- Do you want a summary or digest of the case?
- Do you want a reported or a not-yet-reported case?
- Do you want a list of all the cases related to your case?
- Do you want the history of your case (*e.g.*, appeals)?

There are essentially two ways to find cases: by case name (or citation) or by subject. If you know the name of a particular case, it can be searched for by its title in various tables, case reports, and databases. If you know only the subject, other tools must be used. No matter what method you employ, once you find a case you must update it (find any subsequent history of any appeals) and note it up (find later cases that have referred to your original case).

How to Find a Case by Name or Citation

In some situations you may have enough information to locate a case by searching an electronic database or going to the print volume on the library shelves. Often, however, you have only a case name, maybe with a date.

Finding a case by its name is reasonably straightforward, whether in the library or on your computer.

To locate a case by name or citation you can use any of the following sources:

- the *Consolidated Table of Cases* (*Canadian Abridgment*) in print or through WL*e*C;
- online case databases through LN/QL, WL*e*C, or other commercial online providers; or
- public access websites such as CanLII and some law library websites.

Although your first impulse may be to conduct an electronic search, sometimes a quick library search can be faster and less expensive, particularly if you need an original copy of the published version of the case as required by some courts.

Source 1: The Consolidated Table of Cases

The *Consolidated Table of Cases* (one part of the larger set known as *The Canadian Abridgment*), published by Carswell, is a comprehensive list of thousands of reported Canadian cases. It includes the titles of almost all published cases in Canada and of many British cases. It contains case histories (*e.g.*, appeals) and citations for each case. Carswell publishes new cumulative revisions of the *Consolidated Table of Cases* from time to time. It is also available online through WL*e*C.

Illustration 9.1
Consolidated Table of Cases (Canadian Abridgment)

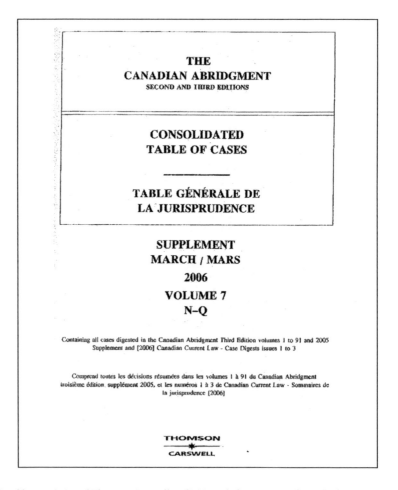

Reprinted by permission of Thomson Carswell, a division of Thomson Canada Limited.

Illustration 9.2
Consolidated Table of Cases Entry

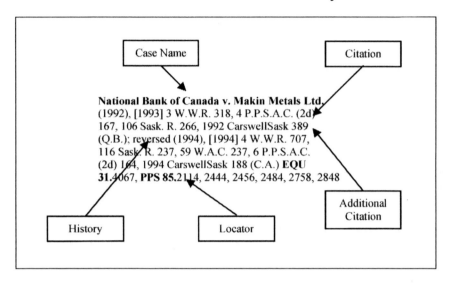

The Canadian Abridgment Third Edition "Consolidated Table of Cases — Supplement March/Mars 2006" Volume 7 N-Q. Reprinted by permission of Thomson Carswell, a division of Thomson Canada Limited.

The *Canadian Abridgment* set is a major research tool for Canadian law. The *Consolidated Table of Cases* is just one of a host of aids within the *Abridgment*. Use of the *Abridgment* is described in more detail below, but the main rule when searching any of the parts of the *Abridgment* is to search in the hardbound volumes first, then the softbound volumes, then the loose-leaf volumes (*i.e.*, search from oldest to most recent). Once you have located a case citation in the *Abridgment,* it is always advisable to go to the actual case report and make sure the citation is correct.

Source 2: Online through LN/QL and WLeC

LN/QL and WLeC have hundreds of databases of cases: reported, unreported, and in digest form. Many of the databases are combined into global databases to make the searching of multiple case collections easier. Researchers have the ability in LN/QL to make up their own customized combinations of databases and save these combinations for repeated use.

If you know what database your case is likely to be in, you can do a word search in those databases for the name of one of the parties or search by citation.

Both LN/QL and WLeC have a quick way to search for a case by case name or citation. You can simply search by citation and your case will be located. This is because lawyers often conduct these particular types of searches. In practical terms this means that you can do a very quick search without having to search through several different databases. The search engine will use the citation to search only relevant databases.

Source 3: Websites

There are several websites that include free access to collections of cases. For example, CanLII, some law library websites, and some sites sponsored by non-governmental organizations provide access to some electronic cases, but these only go back in time to the year when the courts first begin providing them, in most instances only back to the mid-1990s.

The main difference between free access case collections and those provided online through commercial providers is that the free websites are not truly "value added" creatures. This means that the cases have not been edited, may have no headnotes, indexes, summaries, or key numbers, and do not have formal citation capabilities such as histories or judicial considerations of the cases. For example, CanLII is not a "value-added site" in the sense that it only provides links to the law from the originating sources. However, there are key terms, automatically generated, that are associated with every decision retrieved.

CanLII provides helpful hypertext linking between its case law and legislation content and also the capability to note up case law to some extent.

How to Find a Case by Subject

A case is more difficult to locate by subject than by title. As mentioned above, cases are published in a variety of ways in a variety of case reports and in a variety of databases.

Publishers have recognized this problem and have developed aids to assist researchers in finding cases by subject. One publisher, Carswell (in the *Canadian Abridgment* set of books), has developed a subject classification scheme and has organized its published summaries of cases into these classifications. Therefore, researchers need only find the way in which the subject they are researching is categorized in order to find summaries (digests) of cases in that category. From the summary, the researcher quickly can decide if the decision is worth reading for the issue being researched.

This may sound easy, but in order to locate a case by subject you must first know the particular subject area and how it is categorized. As you can imagine, this is not an easy task for a person unfamiliar with a particular area of law. Many legal subjects fall into a host of areas of the law; different publishers often categorize the subjects differently and those categorizations may not be consistent with your thinking. To avoid searching under the wrong subject, most researchers read about the law generally to achieve a clearer sense of the way the law is categorized before delving into subject classification schemes and case reports.

The sources used to locate cases by subject are:

- the *Canadian Encyclopedic Digest* (CED), or *Halsbury's Laws of Canada*, or textbooks in the library;
- the *Case Digests (Canadian Abridgment)* in the library;
- online case databases through LN/QL and WL*e*C;
- public access websites including CanLII or law library websites.

Source 1: Legal Encyclopedias and Textbooks

Halsbury's Laws of Canada, the *Canadian Encyclopedic Digest* (CED) and textbooks are summaries or overviews of the law. Typically, researchers use these secondary materials to gain a general understanding of the law and, at the same time, to gather citations of cases and statutes. These cases often provide a springboard for further case research. Use of these and other secondary materials is discussed in more detail in Chapter 6 (How to Find Secondary Materials).

The CED is available on WL*e*C, and can be searched fairly easily. The only problem is that you might uncover too much information. Therefore it is best to start by reviewing the list of topics (Index) before delving into the text of the CED.

In order to locate a case by subject in the print version of the CED, you must find your subject in the classification scheme, which is contained in the first few volumes. These volumes are thick loose-leaf volumes that contain a *Contents Key* and *Index*. Both list legal topics and either is a good starting point for research.

Each volume of *Halsbury's Laws of Canada* is divided into logical divisions and detailed subheadings about each particular topic. At the end of each volume is a detailed subject index, a recommended list of additional secondary sources for further research, and a glossary of relevant terms. Once the entire set of 57 volumes is complete, there will most likely be a master index and consolidated outline of the topics and subdivisions to aid the researcher.

Very few textbooks are available electronically but more and more journals are becoming available through aggregated collections sold by commercial online providers such as HeinOnline and Oxford Journals (from Oxford University Press). Please refer to Chapter 6 to learn more about these sources and how to use them.

Source 2: Case Law Digests

The part of the *Canadian Abridgment* known as *Case Digests* is another tool which can be used to locate cases by subject. These *Case Digests*, which were discussed above, are summaries of cases. The entire set of digests includes almost every reported Canadian case and many more recent unreported cases, and consists of about 150 volumes. These digested cases are arranged by subject pursuant to a classification system very similar to that used in the CED. This is because Carswell is the publisher of both tools.

In order to locate a case by subject in the *Canadian Abridgment*, it is best to find your subject in the classification scheme, which is contained in the first volume, called the *Key & Research Guide*. The *Key* is a thick, single loose-leaf volume that contains the *Key Classification System* and a *Subject Titles Table*. Both list legal topics and either is a good starting point for research.

Illustration 9.3
Canadian Abridgment, Key & Research Guide: Subject Titles Table

SUBJECT TITLES TABLE

> **EDITOR'S NOTE:** The list of subject titles below is supplemented in the Key by an extensive system of cross-references. The cross-references appear in bold-face and may be of assistance in locating specific topics or related issues. In addition, each subject title includes a Scope Note describing its contents and the location of related issues in other subject titles.

Subject Title	Page
Aboriginal law	2-3
Administrative law	2-11
Alternative dispute resolution	2-19
Bankruptcy and insolvency	2-25
Bills of exchange and negotiable instruments	2-39
Business associations	2-51
Civil practice and procedure	2-69
Commercial law	2-109
Communications law	2-125
Conflict of laws	2-129
Constitutional law	2-137
Construction law	2-149
Contracts	2-157
Criminal law	2-169
Debtors and creditors	2-243
Education law	2-261
Environmental law	2-267
Equity	2-273
Estates and trusts	2-277
Estoppel	2-299
Evidence	2-303
Family law	2-325
Financial institutions	2-351
Guarantee and indemnity	2-359
Health law	2-365
Human rights	2-373
Immigration and citizenship	2-379
Information technology	2-389
Insurance	2-393

i   Key & Research Guide 2006–2

The Canadian Abridgment Key and Research Guide, Third Edition. Reprinted by permission of Thomson Carswell, a division of Thomson Canada Limited.

Illustration 9.4
Canadian Abridgment, Key Classification System

CANADIAN ABRIDGMENT
KEY CLASSIFICATION SYSTEM

EDITOR'S NOTE: *All case digests in the Abridgment are classified and organized according to the subject titles which form part of the Abridgment's classification system. To facilitate research, each of the subject titles has a Scope Note describing its contents and parameters. In addition, an extensive system of cross-references enables the researcher to locate specific topics and related issues*

AB INITIO — *see Torts XX.1.d*

ABANDONMENT — *see Natural resources II.3.c v; Public law II.12 a.v.A; Real property V.10.b.iv.D*

ABATEMENT — *see Estates and trusts I 6.i; Public law II 12 a v C*

ABDUCTION — *see Criminal law VI 2–VI.6, VI.52, VI.72, VI 93*

ABETTING — *see Criminal law I 7 c*

The Canadian Abridgment Key and Research Guide, Third Edition. Reprinted by permission of Thomson Carswell, a division of Thomson Canada Limited.

In addition, the first volume consists of *General Index*, which is an alphabetical subject index of legal concepts arising out of the case law digests.

Illustration 9.5
Excerpt from the Main Set of the Canadian Abridgment, Case Law Digests, Volume R29

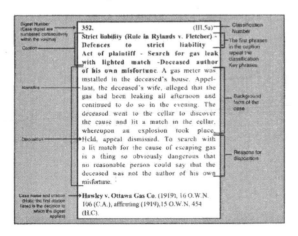

From A Short Guide to the Canadian Abridgment and Related Products, *October 2001. Reprinted by permission of Thomson Carswell, a division of Thomson Canada Limited.*

As you can see from the excerpt in **Illustration 9.5** these digests are in order by "classification number" (see top right hand of digest: III.5.a) and that the case of *Hawley v. Ottawa Gas Co.* was classified under III.5.a. If you look in the classification scheme below in **Illustration 9.6**, you will see that III.5.a represents the following subjects:

Negligence
III: Strict Liability (Rule in *Rylands v. Fletcher*)
5: Defences to strict liability
a: Act of plaintiff

Illustration 9.6
Excerpt from the Canadian Abridgment, Key Classification System

NEGLIGENCE
III. **STRICT LIABILITY (RULE IN RYLANDS v. FLETCHER)** — *liability for environmental damage, see ENVIRONMENTAL LAW I.2; strict liability in nuisance, see TORTS IX.3.a vicarious liability, see IV*
1. **General principles**   a. Non-natural user of land   b. Escape
2. **Particular dangers**   *— liability of owners of animal, see ANIMALS III, tortious liability of public utilities generally, see PUBLIC UTILITIES III.2*
5. **Defences to strict liability**   a. Act of plaintiff   b. Act of stranger   c. Act of God   d. Mutual benefit   e. Statutory authority   f. Due diligence   g. Miscellaneous issues

From A Short Guide to the Canadian Abridgment and Related Products, *October 2001. Adapted by permission of Thomson Carswell, a division of Thomson Canada Limited.*

Remember that when using the library set of the *Abridgment* you must look in *all* of the following parts:

❑ *Key & Research Guide*: Look in the *Subject Titles Table* and *Key Classification Scheme*.

❑ *Main Set*: Look under your title (*i.e.*, subject), note the classification number, and refer to the pages and specific digest numbers.

❑ *Supplements* (softcover): Refer to your classification number.

❑ *Canadian Current Law – Case Digests* and *Canadian Case Citations*:[1] Look at these for further updates.

Many Canadian researchers have become frustrated with the *Canadian Abridgment*, arguing that it is too difficult to use because of the number of supplements. This requires explanation. Because the *Canadian Abridgment* is a vital aid to case law research, it is important that researchers understand the underpinnings of the system.

All of the books in the *Canadian Abridgment* are out of date as soon as they are published. Therefore, the publisher must continually update these hardbound volumes with supplements. As soon as the supplements accumulate to a certain point, these supplements are bound. This process is continuous so that each source typically has one original volume or volumes (called the *Main Set*), as well as both hard- and softbound supplements. Periodically, the entire set is consolidated. When the edition gets out of date, a new, entirely reorganized edition is published. As noted above, this is now occurring with the Third Edition.

As a result of this ongoing process, the researcher is required to look in a number of volumes to find the information needed. As a rule of thumb, the three general steps in using the *Canadian Abridgment* are as follows:

1. Hardbound
2. Softbound
3. Loose-leaf

If you search in each of these volumes, you can ensure that your information is correct and up to date. If you are confused, ask a law librarian for assistance. Once you know the basic steps, the *Abridgment* becomes an invaluable aid.

Source 3: Online through LN/QL and WLeC

These two commercial online providers have hundreds of databases of cases: reported, unreported, and in digest form. When searching by subject you must use the templates and research tools that they provide. Before you construct a search, however, you usually must know what database your case is likely to be in. More information on each of these providers and a sample search for each is in Chapter 5 (Law Libraries and Electronic Collections of Law).

---

[1] These are other parts of the *Canadian Abridgment*.

Source 4: Free Websites

There are several websites, including CanLII, that include collections of recent cases. Because these cases are not edited or compiled by publishers, they may not be as easy to search as those on commercial services. Nor do they often contain headnotes, so your subject search may be very cumbersome. It is always best to refine your search as much as you can before going online or you may be overwhelmed by all the information available. However, if you are fairly sure about the court that decided your case, you can search CanLII using that court database.

How to Update and Note Up Cases

After you have located the cases that are relevant to your situation, you will need to update them and note them up. This means ensuring that the cases are still "good law" and requires:

- Updating: Find the history of the cases. Have they been appealed or overturned?
- Noting-up: Find the judicial treatment of the cases. Have they been considered in other cases, and have these cases overruled them or followed them, *etc.*?

There are two print research aids specifically designed to answer these two queries: tables of cases, which list all decided cases and their history, and case citators, which list all cases, their history, and their treatment (how they were considered in other, later cases). The two main Canadian sources are published by Carswell and are also available on WLeC:

- To update, use the *Consolidated Table of Cases (Canadian Abridgment)*.
- To note up, use the *Canadian Case Citations (Canadian Abridgment)*.

Tables of Cases

The *Consolidated Table of Cases (Canadian Abridgment)* lists alphabetically almost every Canadian case, the history of the case, and citations. It is typically used to locate the citation of a case or to find out if a case has been appealed. It is available in print and on WLeC. (See above for a detailed discussion of the *Consolidated Table of Cases*.)

Some individual case reports, both topical and jurisdictional, also have indexes that provide information about the history and judicial treatment of cases. A researcher could consult case tables in those case reports where a case would likely be reported to locate this information. For example, if looking for a British Columbia tort case, a researcher might look in *British Columbia Law Reports* (B.C.L.R.) or *Canadian Cases on the Law of Torts* (C.C.L.T.).

Citators

The main tools used to update or note up cases are called case citators. These citators are lists of cases that are compiled by editors. Under each case there is information about whether the case has been appealed (history) and how the case has been considered in other cases (treatment). These tools greatly assist the ability of our courts to apply the rule of precedent.

The only cross-Canada print citator is called *Canadian Case Citations* (*Canadian Abridgment*). It consists of a set of 10 hardbound volumes and supplements. It contains two types of information: prior and subsequent history (*e.g.*, the prior or subsequent treatment of that case in a lower or higher court), and treatment of the case by other cases.

LN/QL and WL*e*C both have their own powerful citators. Electronic citators can be used in two ways:

1. If you are in the case you need, you can select the citator function and you will be hyperlinked to all the history and judicial treatment of this case.

2. You can go directly into the particular citator database and you can do a word search for your case. Just as in the paper version, it will list all those cases that mentioned your case.

Illustration 9.7
Canadian Abridgment: Canadian Case Citations

Cuddy Chicks Ltd. v. Ontario (Labour Relations Board) ——— The decision of the Ontario Labour Relations Board can be found in all of these reports
(May 6, 1988), Doc. 0310-87-R
[1988] O.L.R.B. Rep. 468, 88 C.L.L.C.
16,049 19 C.L.R.B.R. (N.S.) 286 (Ont.
L.R.B.)

affirmed/confirmé (November 2, 1988), ——— The decision of the Ontario Labour Relations Board was affirmed by the Ontario Divisional Court
Doc. 469/88 (1988), 66 O.R. (2d) 284,
32 O.A.C. 7, 88 C.L.L.C. 14,053,
33 Admin. L.R. 304 (Ont. Div. Ct.)

The decision of the Ontario Divisional Court was affirmed by the Court of Appeal for Ontario ——— **which was affirmed/qui a été confirmé** (September 8, 1989) Doc. CA 67/89 (1989), 39 Admin L.R. 48, 62 D.L.R. (4th) 125, 35 O.A.C. 94, 89 C.L.L.C. 14,031 44 C.R.R. 75, 70 O.R. (2d) 179, [1989] O.L.R.B. Rep. 989 (Ont. C.A.)

which was affirmed/qui a été confirmé ——— The decision of the Court of Appeal for Ontario was affirmed on appeal to the Supreme Court of Canada
(June 6, 1991), Doc 21675 (1991), 91
C L.L.C. 14,024, 3 O.R. (3d) 128 (note). 50
Admin. L.R. 44, 122 N.R. 361, 81 D.L.R.
(4th) 121, [1991] O.L.R.B. Rep. 790, 47
O.A.C. 271, 4 C.R.R. (2d) 1, [1991] 2 S.C.R.
5 (S.C.C.)

The Ontario Divisional Court ——— **Cases citing Ont. Div Ct.**
decision was followed in this case
Ⓕ B.G. (L.G.A.), Re (1989), 101 A.R. 92
(Alta. Prov. Ct.)

The Ontario Court of Appeal ——— **Cases citing Ont. C.A.**
decision was considered in
these cases
Ⓒ R v. Lepage (1994), 23 C.R.R. (2d) 81
(Ont. Gen. Div.)

Ⓒ Health Sciences Assn. of Alberta v.
Calgary General Hospital (1991), 91
C.L.L.C. 16,044 (Alta. L.R.B.)

Cases citing S.C.C.

Ⓕ K. Mart Canada Ltd. v. U.F.C.W., Local ——— The decision of the Supreme Court of Canada was followed in these cases
1518 (1994), 24 C.L.R.B.R. (2d) 1
(B.C.L.R.B.)

Ⓕ Canada (Minister of Employment &
Immigration) v. Agbasi (1993), 10 Admin.
L.R. (2d) 94 (Fed. T.D.)

Ⓕ Tétreault-Gadoury v. Canada
(Employment & Immigration
Commission) (1991), 91 C.L.L.C. 14,023
(S.C.C.)

Ⓓ P&S Investments Ltd. v. Newfoundland ——— The decision of the Supreme Court of Canada was distinguished in this case
(Human Rights Commission) (1994), 2
C.C.E.L. (2d) 287 (Nfld. T.D.)

The decision of the Supreme ——— Ⓒ G.(M.)c. Gazette (The) (November 28,
Court of Canada was considered 1996), no C.A. Montreal 500-09-002434-
in these cases 967, 500-09-002305-969 (Que. C.A.)

Ⓒ Falkner v. Ontario (Ministry of
Community & Social Services) (1996),
140 D.L.R. (4th) 115 (Ont. Div. Ct.)

From A Short Guide to the Canadian Abridgment and Related Products, *October 2001. Adapted by permission of Thomson Carswell, a division of Thomson Canada Limited.*

Illustration 9.8
Terms and Symbols Used in Canadian Case Citations
(Canadian Abridgment)

Affirmed *Decision affirmed on appeal or on reconsideration, or application for judicial review refused.*

Amended *Correction of wording of decision by decision maker to conform to intended meaning*

Additional reasons *Additional reasons for decision*

Allowed leave to appeal *Leave to appeal to an appellate court allowed*

Refused leave to appeal *Leave to appeal to an appellate court refused*

Referred for further consideration or clarification *Decision referred back by an appellate court to lower level for further consideration or clarification*

Reconsideration or rehearing granted *Application for reconsideration or rehearing of decision by same court granted*

Reconsideration or rehearing refused *Application for reconsideration or rehearing of decision by same court refused*

Reversed *Decision reversed on appeal or on reconsideration*

Set aside or quashed *Decision set aside or quashed*

Varied *Decision varied or modified by either the decision maker or an appellate court without reversing the result*

○ **Not followed/overruled** *Cited case wrongly decided*

⊕ **Followed** *Principle of law in cited case adopted or decider's reasoning applied*

◐ **Distinguished** *Cited case inapplicable because of difference in facts or law*

○ **Considered** *Some consideration given to cited case*

From A Short Guide to the Canadian Abridgment and Related Products, *October 2001. Adapted by permission of Thomson Carswell, a division of Thomson Canada Limited.*

HOW TO WRITE A CASE CITATION

The citation of cases is fairly rigid. This is primarily because each component of the citation is necessary to enable a person to locate a case.

An example of a case citation is as follows:

Style of Cause	Date	Volume	Case Report	Series	Page	Court
⬇	⬇	⬇	⬇	⬇	⬇	⬇
Jones v. Gas Co.	(1980),	2	D.L.R.	(2d)	555	(B.C.C.A.)

The following are some basic rules of case citation. For detailed rules of citation it is best to refer to a specific book on the topic.

Style of Cause

The style of cause is the title of the case or the names of the parties involved in the action. Some of the rules of citation of the style of cause are as follows:

- Always underline or italicize style of cause, including the *v.* which stands for *versus*.
- Do not use full names of parties.
- Refer to the Crown as *R.*
- *Re* means "References" or "in the matter of a party named". These cases are usually applications to a court for an opinion or interpretation of someone's rights.
- Omit "the" before most styles of cause.
- *Ex Parte* means "on application of a party who is not present".
- In some family or sexual assault matters only initials are given (*e.g.*, *M. v. L.*).

Date/Year

The year in the citation means either the date the case was published or the date of judgment.

If there are round brackets around the year, it means the date of judgment. If only round brackets are in the citation, you also need the volume number to locate the case. Square brackets are used to enclose the year of publication. In some cases it may be necessary to include both square and round brackets.

Volume

The volume is the number of the volume in which the case is published. Some reports resume numbering at volume 1 at the beginning of each year. Citations to these reports will have a year in square brackets followed by a volume number.

Case Report

The title of the case report is abbreviated. There are specific books in the library that provide the abbreviation of case reports.[2] Do not try to guess what the abbreviation is.

---

[2]   *E.g.*, Iosipescu & Whitehead, *Legal Writing and Research Manual*, 6th ed. (Markham, Ont.: LexisNexis Butterworths, 2004); *Canadian Guide to Uniform Legal Citation*, 6th

One handy free website for interpreting abbreviations is the *Cardiff Index*, at <http://www.legalabbrevs.cardiff.ac.uk/about.jsp>.

Series

The series number is an essential piece of information. Many case reports have several series spanning many years (*e.g.*, 1st, 2d, and 3d series). When citing a case report, you must cite the series in brackets after the title (*e.g.*, D.L.R. (2d)).

Page or paragraph number

The citation includes the page at which the report begins. If you are referring to a specific page within a case, include that page number at the end of the citation, preceded by "at" (*e.g.*, 434 at 437).

Most modern judicial decisions now have numbered paragraphs. Numbering begins with the first paragraph of the judge's actual words and ensures very accurate reference to the exact text you wish to point out. Everything above that is editorial matter and is not numbered. If you wish to refer to a specific paragraph within a case, include that paragraph number at the end of the citation, preceded by "at para." (*e.g.*, 345 at para. 21). Alternatively, this information can be indicated by use of the paragraph symbol (*e.g.*, 345 ¶ 21); do not put "at" before the symbol.

Court

The court is also part of the citation, and each court has its own particular citation (*e.g.*, B.C.C.A. stands for the British Columbia Court of Appeal). If the court is obvious from the title of the report, then the court does not need to be included in the citation (*e.g.*, S.C.R. includes only decisions of the Supreme Court of Canada).

Parallel or Alternate Citations

A parallel or alternate cite is another citation of the same case in a different case report or online. This is to assist those who may only have access to certain case reports or online services.

---

ed. (the "McGill Guide") (Scarborough, Ont.: Carswell, 2006); and Carswell's *Canadian Abridgment, Consolidated Table of Cases*, at the beginning of Volume 1.

The date does not need to be repeated in an alternate cite, but square bracketed years must be included when they are necessary to locate the case by volume. Alternate citations are separated by a comma.

See below for discussion of the recent "neutral citation" innovation for identifying cases.

Punctuation

General Rules about Punctuation in Citation	
Comma	Precedes date in square brackets Follows date in round brackets Between parallel citations
Period	After all abbreviations At end of citation
Brackets	Around date (round if date of judgment; square if date of volume) Around court Around series
Underline or italicize	Style of cause only, including the "v."
Semicolon	Between citations of different cases

History of a Case

The history of a case is the course of a case through all levels of appeal. Prior history means all that happened before. Subsequent history means all that happened after.

Use of *sub nom.*

The term *sub nom.* is the abbreviation for the Latin *sub nomen*, meaning "under the name of". It implies that the case also has an alternate title. In the citation, this other name appears in round brackets before the name of the case report in which it appears.

For example, *W. v. R.* (1984), [1985] 1 W.W.R. 122, (*sub nom. Re Walton and A.G. of Canada*) 13 D.L.R. (4th) 379 (Ont. C.A.).

ELECTRONIC CITATIONS

If a case is taken from an electronic source it is necessary to add that information to the citation. After the citation (above) add a comma and then the word "online" followed by a colon. If a commercial online system was used, add the abbreviation for the provider (*e.g.*, LN/QL). If a free public website was used, add the name of the website followed by the name of the specific part of the site, then the URL (Uniform Resource Locator) in angled brackets.

NEUTRAL CITATION

Starting around 2000, Canadian courts began assigning a "neutral" citation to each decision they released. This number provides the year, court and unique decision number of each case, so that such a decision can be identified regardless of which printed reporter and/or online database published it.

Here is a fictitious example of a typical "neutral" citation:

Smythe v. Myers Upholstery Ltd., 2003 ABQB 312 at para. 16.

This fictitious case is the 312th decision released in 2003 by the Alberta Court of Queen's Bench. The information following the names of the parties is assigned by the court and cannot be changed. Note that the jurisdiction (AB) and level of court (QB) are shown in the neutral citation and do not have to be repeated elsewhere in the citation, nor does the year (2003). There are no periods in the identifiers for the court and jurisdiction. In the example, the reader's attention is drawn to paragraph 16 of the case by adding "at para 16." at the end. (Alternatively, this can be signified by "¶ 16".)

Current guidance suggests that a reference to a printed reporter should follow as a parallel citation to the neutral citation. In this fictitious example, this decision was reported in the *Alberta Law Reports* (abbreviated A.R.), second series, on page 109 of volume 97. Thus, the recommended form would be:

Smythe v. Myers Upholstery Ltd., 2003 ABQB 312, 97 A.R. (2d) 109 at para. 16. (Alternatively, this can be signified by "¶ 16".)

At the present time, there is no universal agreement about how to use the "neutral citation" in conjunction with "unreported" decisions that appear ***only*** in databases of commercial online providers. If a researcher locates an "unreported" (or perhaps a "not yet reported") decision on one or more of the commercial online services, common sense dictates that a parallel citation to that service be provided, as a help to his or her readers. Thus, in the fictitious example above, if the case had never appeared anywhere in a printed reporter BUT had been captured online by, for example, LN/QL, one might use the following form:

Smythe v. Myers Upholstery Ltd., 2003 ABQB 312, [2003] A.J. 808 at para. 16. (Alternatively, this can be signified by "¶ 16".)

Upon seeing the above parallel citation, a reader would quickly discern that he or she could find the case in LN/QL because of the designation [2003] A.J. 808.

Similarly, if the decision has been captured by WL*e*C, one might use the following form:

Smythe v. Myers Upholstery Ltd., 2003 ABQB 312, 2003 CarswellAB 3560 at para. 16. (Alternatively, this can be signified by "¶ 16".)

Upon seeing the above parallel citation, a reader would quickly discern that the case appears in WL*e*C because of the designation 2003 CarswellAB 3560.

Neutral citation is a dynamic subject at present. The best guidance for new legal researchers is to inquire about neutral citation from a law librarian, work supervisor, or legal editor, or follow the lead of local practitioners.

For a more detailed discussion of neutral citation, see: <http://www.lexum.umontreal.ca/ccc-ccr/index_en.html>.

SELF TEST

The following is a self test based on the information provided in this chapter. The answers to these questions are found at the back of the book in the "Answers to Self Tests" section.

1. Describe what a case report is.
2. Name a few case reports.
3. Name a research aid that assists in locating a case by name.
4. Name a research aid that assists in locating a case by subject.
5. What does "updating" a case mean?
6. Name a research aid that assists in updating a case.

SAMPLE EXERCISES —
FINDING AND UPDATING CASES

Objectives

At the end of this exercise you should be able to:

- Locate cases by title
- Locate cases by subject using the *Canadian Abridgment, Case Digests*
- Locate case reports

- Update and note up cases
- Cite cases properly

Instructions

- Do background reading on how to locate, update, and cite cases.
- Keep a record of all the steps and the time taken to complete the exercise.

1. *Find Cases by Title*

Go to the *Canadian Abridgment, Consolidated Table of Cases* and give the proper citation for the following case. Provide an alternate citation as well.

Berwick v. Canada Trust Co. (S.C.C.)

Citation:

Alternate citation:

2. *Find Cases by Subject Using the Case Digests (Canadian Abridgment)*

Read the following research situation and answer the following questions.

Research Situation

Ms. Keener

Your client, Ms. Keener, a recent graduate from law school, has been going through the articling interview process over the last few weeks. She has received no offers and, although she admits that there is a recession, she has recently become suspicious of the interviewing process. In particular, at her last two interviews, she was asked whether she had ever been to a psychiatrist or suffered from any mental disorder. Being an honest person, Ms. Keener told both interviewers that she had indeed been to a shrink and has a family history of mental disorders. She has asked you to find her some case law that defines discrimination in order to determine whether her human rights have been violated.

Questions

a. Before entering the library, brainstorm for possible legal subject areas. List five or more words relating to the above research situation that you might search for in the library.

Words:

b.   Go to the *Canadian Abridgment, 3d ed., Key & Research Guide* and look at the section entitled *Key Classification System*. Find subjects relevant to the research situation. List one or two relevant subject titles, and also their subtitles and reference numbers (*e.g.*, Torts; XVI Negligence; 2. Duty and Standard of Care; e. After accidents.

Titles; Subtitles; Reference Numbers:

c.   Using these Key Classification numbers, go to the multi-volume set of *Canadian Abridgment, 3d ed., Case Digests* and find the volume that contains your subject. Within that volume, find a case that appears to discuss your research situation. Give the citation for that case. Recall that you must look in the hardbound and softbound volumes.

Citation:

3.   Find Case Reports Using the Canadian Abridgment, Canadian Case Citations

Go to relevant case report and then the *Canadian Abridgment, Canadian Case Citations* and give citations for the following cases.

a.   [1973] 4 W.W.R. 417.

Citation:

b.   (1976), 12 O.R. (2d) 253.

Citation:

Alternate Citation:

c.   (1982), 139 D.L.R. (3d) 407.

Citation:

Alternate Citation:

4.   Find the History of a Case

Go to the *Canadian Abridgment, Canadian Case Citations* and list the courts that heard the following case. Provide one citation for each level of court that heard the case, starting with the highest level of court.

Industrial Acceptance Corp v. Canada Permanent Trust Co.
(Supreme Court of Canada)

Courts:

Citation one (S.C.C.):
Citation two (S.C.C.):
Citation three (S.C.C.):
Citation four (N.B.C.A.):
Citation five (N.B.K.B.):

5. *Find Cases Judicially Considered*

Go to the *Canadian Abridgment, Canadian Case Citations* and give the citation for the case by the Alberta Court of Queen's Bench that followed *Slavutych v. Baker*, [1976] 1 S.C.R. 254.

Citation:

ANSWERS TO EXERCISES

1. Find Cases by Title

Berwick v. Canada Trust Co., [1948] S.C.R. 151.

Alternate citation: [1948] 3 D.L.R. 81 (S.C.C.).

2. Find Cases by Subject Using the *Case Digests (Canadian Abridgment)*

a. Human Rights; Discrimination; Employment; Labour; Articling.
b. Human Rights; III. What Constitutes Discrimination; 7. Handicap;
    b. Mental Handicap; ii. What constitutes: III.7.b.ii.
c. In volume 50 [HUM], Human Rights, under section III.7.b.ii there
    are many cases. One is *Walmer Developments v. Wolch* (2003), 67 O.R.
    (3d) 246, 230 D.LR. (4th) 372 (Ont. Div. Ct.).

3. Find Case Reports Using the *Canadian Abridgment, Canadian Case Citations*

a. *Bank of Montreal v. Sperling Hotel Co.*, [1973] 4 W.W.R. 417 (Man.
    Q.B.).

    Alternate Citation: (1973), 36 D.L.R. (3d) 130 (Man. Q.B.).

b. *Mahood v. Hamilton-Wentworth (Region) Commissioners of Police* (1976),
    12 O.R. (2d) 253 (Ont. H.C.).

    Alternate Citation: (1976), 68 D.L.R. (3d) 437 (Ont. H.C.).

c. *Sherwood v. Sherwood* (1982), 139 D.L.R. (3d) 407 (N.S.T.D.).

    Alternate Citation: (1982), 29 R.F.L. (2d) 374; *or* (1982), 52 N.S.R.
    (2d) 631; *or* (1982), 106 A.P.R. 631.

4. Find the History of a Case

Courts: Supreme Court of Canada (3 times), New Brunswick Court of
         Appeal, and New Brunswick King's Bench.

Citation one:	[1932] S.C.R. 661 (reversed)
Citation two:	[1931] S.C.R. 652 (set aside)
Citation three:	[1931] S.C.R. 503 (refused leave)
Citation four:	[1931] 4 D.L.R. 348 (N.B.C.A.) (affirmed)
Citation five:	[1931] 2 D.L.R. 663 (N.B.K.B.)

This is a good exercise because it is such a complicated example. These are five decisions by five courts about the same situation. The case was first heard in the N.B.K.B. and then the N.B.C.A. It was considered by three different sittings because leave was sought, refused, then overturned, and eventually heard.

5. Find Cases Judicially Considered

Dudley v. Jane Doe (1997), 53 Alta. L.R. (3d) 272 (Q.B.) (followed)

Appendix 9A: Format of a Printed Decision

1. The *style of cause* names the parties in the case. The name of the plaintiff (or on an appeal the name of the appellant) appears first.

2. The *name of the court* that decided the case.

3. The *name of the judge or judges*.

4. The *date of the judgment* is the date that the judgment was handed down, not the date it was heard or published.

5. The *keywords* classify the issues in the case. They are selected by publishers to fit a subject classification scheme.

6. The *headnote* is a brief summary of the case. It is written by the editors of the case report.

7. The list of *authorities* is those sources referred to by the court (e.g., cases, statutes, and literature).

8. The *history of the case* advises where the case originated.

9. The *names of counsel are the lawyers* representing the parties in the case.

10. The *name of the judge* who delivered or wrote the decision.

1

BUDAI v. ONTARIO LOTTERY CORP.

2

Ontario High Court of Justice, Divisional Court O'Leary J. January 20, 1983.

4

3

Torts — Negligent misstatement — Plaintiff wrongly informed that he had won lottery prize — Plaintiff spending money to celebrate — Whether defendant liable for prize or for money spent.

5

The plaintiff was, because of a computer error, wrongly informed by the defendant that he had won $835.40 in a lottery. He spent $480 U.S. in an evening's celebration, but was informed the next day of the error. An action for the $835.40 succeeded at trial. On appeal to the Divisional Court, held, allowing the appeal in part, the plaintiff had not, by the rules of the lottery, won the prize. However, the defendant was liable for negligently misinforming him, the extent of the liability being the money lost by the plaintiff in reliance on the misstatement, in this case $480 U.S.

6

Statutes referred to

Ontario Lottery Corporation Act, R.S.O. 1980, c. 344

Rules and regulations referred to

7

O. Reg. 251/75, s. 9 (now R.R.O. 1980, Reg. 719, s. 8)

8

APPEAL from a judgment in favour of the plaintiff in an action for a lottery prize.

9

K. C. Cancellera, for appellant, defendant, Ontario Lottery Corporation
Robert Roth, for *amicus curiae*.
No one appearing for respondent, plaintiff, Jim Budai.

O'Leary J.:—This appeal involves the question of the right of the purchaser of a lottery ticket, who has been incorrectly and negligently told by the lottery operator that he is a winner, to collect from that operator some or all of the amount he was incorrectly told he had won where, prior to learning of the error he has squandered part of his expected winnings.

10

The appeal is brought by the defendant, Ontario Lottery Corporation, from the judgment dated February 29, 1980, of His Honour Deputy Judge D. Ceri Hugill, wherein he awarded the plaintiff the sum of $835.40. The plaintiff, at a cost to him of $7, in effect purchased seven tickets on a lottery operated by the defendant.

Appendix 9B: Checklist: How to Find and Update a Case

HOW TO FIND A CASE BY NAME OR CITATION

You can find a case by name or citation by using any of the following sources:

- *In the library*: Use the *Canadian Abridgment's Consolidated Table of Cases*. This multi-volume set lists all cases alphabetically. Each volume has a supplement containing more recent cases. Locate your case in the Table and note its citation. This is where it is located in the *Canadian Abridgment's* print and electronic case digests.

- LN/QL and WL*e*C allow "find by citation" searching at their main screens. Alternatively, you may select a specific jurisdiction, then do a keyword search using the template.

- *Internet*: Search free public websites such as CanLII <http://www.canlii.org>. These free access sites provide many current full-text cases, but relatively few older historical cases. Search by case name in the search templates provided.

Your accuracy in electronic searching will improve if you know how to conduct Boolean searches, recognize the limitations of electronic searching, and understand the workings of the search engines. Spend time reading the online information on how to search and use advanced search templates where available.

HOW TO FIND A CASE BY SUBJECT

When you know your topic but do not have any case names, the most direct way to identify relevant cases is by reading secondary materials and noting the cases mentioned. See Chapter 6 (How to Find Secondary Materials). Unless you are an expert, conducting an electronic keyword search will either pull up too many cases or, worse, not locate the relevant cases. The following useful secondary materials are the best way to begin research:

- ❏ Read about your topic in texts, the *Canadian Encyclopedic Digest* (CED), *Halsbury's Laws of Canada*, and periodical articles.

❑ Use the *Canadian Abridgment's Key & Research Guide* volume to discover how your subject is categorized in its *Key Classification Scheme*. Write down the key classification number (*e.g.*, *Torts, X.3.a.*)

❑ Using this key classification, find the relevant *Canadian Abridgment, Case Digests* main and supplement volumes containing your topic and key classification number. Read the digests and record the citations of all relevant cases. Locate these cases in print or electronic sources. Read each case and do not depend on summaries.

❑ Once you have a better sense of your subject, do a keyword or phrase search in commercially provided databases, such as LN/QL or WL*e*C. First, to save time, search case digest databases to find and read summaries, then search full-text databases to read only the most relevant cases. Alternatively, use a free public website (*e.g.*, CanLII), remembering that these usually do not have "summary" or "digest" databases.

How to Update and Note Up a Case

Ensuring that cases are still "good law" requires both **updating** cases and **noting up** cases. *Updating* means finding the history of the cases and ensuring your cases have not been appealed or overturned by a higher court. *Noting up* cases means finding judicial treatment to ensure the cases have not subsequently received adverse judicial consideration in later decisions.

In the Library: Two parts of the print *Canadian Abridgment* are specifically designed for *updating* and *noting up* cases:

• To **update** cases, use the *Consolidated Table of Cases (Canadian Abridgment)*. It lists all decided cases alphabetically and their history.

• To **note up** a case, use the *Canadian Case Citations (Canadian Abridgment)*. It lists all cases alphabetically, their history and their judicial treatment (*i.e.*, later cases considering them).

Electronic: The most comprehensive electronic case citators are LN/QL's *Quickcite* and WL*e*C's *KeyCiteCanada* (the latter is simply the online version of the printed *Canadian Case Citations*).

❑ You can check these citators in two ways: (1) search the citator database directly for your case; or (2) link to the citator from a case that you are viewing on screen. To ensure comprehensive research, it is a good idea to compare both of these case citators because the subsequent cases listed and the treatment codes used often vary from one case citator to another.

Appendix 9C: Courthouse Electronic Cases

CANLII attempts to bring together on one free, easily searchable website, many newer cases from most Canadian jurisdictions. However, a number of the free public websites listed below contain some cases that are older than those now available through CanLII.

Jurisdiction	URL
Supreme Court of Canada	<http://www.scc-csc.gc.ca> (official site for history, *etc.*) OR <www.lexum.umontreal.ca/csc-scc/en/index.html> (for judicial decisions)
Federal Court of Appeal	<http://decisions.fca-caf.gc.ca/en/index.html>
Federal Court	<http://www.fct-cf.gc.ca/>
Tax Court of Canada	<http://decision.tcc-cci.gc.ca/en/index.html>
British Columbia	<http://www.courts.gov.bc.ca>
Alberta	<http://www.albertacourts.ab.ca>
Saskatchewan	<http://www.sasklawcourts.ca>
Manitoba	<http://www.manitobacourts.mb.ca>
Ontario	<http://www.ontariocourts.on.ca/english.htm>
Quebec	<http://www.jugements.qc.ca>
Newfoundland and Labrador	<http://www.justice.gov.nl.ca/just/LAWCOURT/appeal.htm>
Prince Edward Island	<http://www.gov.pe.ca/courts/>
Nova Scotia	<http://www.courts.ns.ca/>
New Brunswick	<http://www.gnb.ca/cour/index-e.asp>
Yukon	<http://www.justice.gov.yk.ca/prog/cs/courts.html>
Northwest Territories	<http://www.justice.gov.nt.ca/dbtw-wpd/nwtjqbe.htm>
Nunavut	<http://www.nucj.ca/decisions.htm>

Introduction to Legal Analysis 10

The skill of legal analysis is one that evolves over years of practice. It is sometimes called "thinking like a lawyer" and involves determining what law is relevant, understanding it and applying it to the situation at hand. In simple terms, you must take all the law that you have found, read it, interpret it, and apply it to your facts.

Each of the skills of reading, interpreting, and applying the law are continually learned throughout law school, professional legal training, and in practice. However, to complete the full five steps in the FILAC model of legal problem solving you need to know how to do legal analysis. This chapter, therefore, serves as a basic introduction to the skill of legal analysis.

Legal analysis requires researchers to construct a picture of the law and apply this picture to a set of facts. This chapter explains how to analyze cases and statutes and how cases build upon each other and combine with statutes to form the law. It teaches legal analysis in a direct and simple manner and is not intended to replace the long-term development of legal analysis skills.

LEARNING OBJECTIVES

At the end of this chapter you will be able to:

- Describe the doctrines of precedent and *stare decisis*
- Name the three basic levels of court in Canada
- Name the three steps in case analysis
- Define what is meant by synthesizing the law
- Explain what "distinguishing between cases" is
- Name a rule of statutory interpretation

CASE ANALYSIS

The ultimate goal of research is to find cases and statutes that are relevant to a particular situation, analyze them, and apply them to that situation.

Analysis of cases involves determining the relevance of cases, reading these cases, and synthesizing them into a statement of law. It involves asking the following questions about the cases you find:

- Does the case apply to the situation? (determining relevance of cases)
- What does the case say? (reading cases)
- What does the case mean? (synthesizing cases)

Only after completing these three steps and doing a similar type of analysis for relevant statutes can you synthesize the law and then apply it to your legal problem. Each step is discussed here.

Determining Relevance of Cases

The first step in case analysis is determining whether the cases you have found apply to your situation or will be considered relevant by a court.

Relevant cases are those that have similar facts and issues and are persuasive or binding on the court that is likely to hear the case if it goes to trial.

Therefore, determining the relevance of cases involves determining which cases are similar, binding, or persuasive. An understanding of the system of common law and the Canadian court system is necessary to be able to determine relevance.

The Common Law

The system of common law developed through the use of precedents or decided cases. Precedents were, and continue to be, used as examples or authorities to assist judges in deciding cases.

From the system of precedent evolved the doctrine of *stare decisis*, which literally means "to stand by the decision". *Stare decisis* requires courts to follow prior decisions of courts from the same jurisdiction to the extent that those cases have similar facts and issues.

The doctrines of precedent and *stare decisis* promote consistency in law, ensure certainty, and provide tools to predict the likely outcome of a case. A coherent body of law results if these doctrines are applied consistently.

The Court System

The court system in Canada is structured in tiers of increasing authority. The courts form a hierarchy, whereby appeals from lower courts are heard by the higher courts and lower courts are bound by the decisions of higher courts. In Canada, there are three levels of courts: trial level, appellate level, and court of last resort. Each province has a trial and an appeal court. The court of last resort is the Supreme Court of Canada.

Trial courts are courts of original jurisdiction. This means they are the first courts to hear cases and make determinations about both fact and law. Often trial courts are divided by type of claim, amount of claim, or territorial jurisdiction. For example, the provincial court in British Columbia consists of the following divisions: Family Court, Criminal Court, and Small Claims Court.

Appellate courts hear appeals from trial courts. They do not, as a rule, review factual determinations of trial courts, but review errors of law. There is no trial *per se* in the appellate court since no evidence is heard. The court instead reviews written briefs on the law (*i.e.*, factums) and hears arguments only.

The court of last resort in Canada is the Supreme Court of Canada. Prior to 1949 the court of last resort was the British Privy Council. Today, the Supreme Court of Canada hears cases that are appealed from the various appeal courts. It also hears cases that are specifically referred to it for a determination about the meaning or application of a law. These are called "references".

There is also a federal court system that deals exclusively with federal matters, such as immigration and tax law. The system includes a trial and an appeal level: the Federal Court and the Federal Court of Appeal. Appeals from this court go to the Supreme Court of Canada. There are also a federal Tax Court of Canada and a Court Martial Appeal Court of Canada, which hear cases limited to tax issues and appeals from military court martials, respectively.

Illustration 10.1
Canadian Court Structure

Supreme Court of Canada
↗   ↖
Provincial Courts of Appeal   Federal Court of Appeal
↑   ↑
Provincial Trial Level Courts   Federal Court

In Canada, all courts are bound by decisions of the Supreme Court of Canada and all courts are bound by higher courts in their own jurisdiction. For example, trial courts are bound by appeal court decisions. Appeal courts from one jurisdiction are not bound by appeal courts from another jurisdiction. For example, the British Columbia Court of Appeal does not bind the Alberta Court of Appeal.

Similar, Binding, or Persuasive

Those cases most similar to your legal problem are the best indicators of the likely outcome of your case. In other words, a case's predictive value is greatest when its facts and issues are most similar to yours. The converse is also true.

If a court is compelled to follow a case, that case is considered to be *binding*. There are a number of factors that will determine whether a case is binding on a court: the level of court, the jurisdiction of the court, the history of the case, the judicial consideration of the case, and how current the case is. In other words, when determining whether a case is binding, the following questions should be asked about each case:

Court Level: What is the court level? Is the decision from a higher level court?

Jurisdiction: What is the jurisdiction? Is the decision from the same jurisdiction?

History: What is the history of the decision? Has the decision been appealed or overturned by another court?

Judicial Consideration: Has the decision been considered by another court? (*e.g.*, distinguished, applied, or followed)

Currency: Has the decision been superseded by legislation?

The answers to these questions will not only determine whether a case is binding but will also contribute to the amount of weight the decision will be given by a court. Precedents that are binding are referred to as "mandatory", whereas those that are not binding are referred to as "persuasive". Although not binding, persuasive cases often assist judges in deciding cases. For example, a case from the United States will not be binding on a Canadian court but may be persuasive if the facts and issues are similar.

After selecting relevant cases, the researcher must read them and synthesize them into a coherent whole.

Reading Cases

Reading cases involves some skill. Most cases follow a particular format and, after reading several cases, the researcher should be able to quickly find relevant information without getting bogged down in irrelevant facts.

At the most basic level, researchers should be familiar with the format of published cases. A description of this format is provided in Appendix 9A. This format is also important for computer research, since computer searches are often conducted by selecting a specific location in the text of reported cases (*e.g.*, by title or date).

Each case is the result of a judge's attempt to move through the legal problem solving process. Therefore, as you read cases you will learn how to elicit from each case the products of the legal research process: FILAC — facts, issues, law, analysis, and conclusion. By reading and dissecting cases, researchers enhance their problem solving skills.

Synthesizing Cases

After all the relevant cases have been gathered and read they must be synthesized into a coherent description of the law. Synthesis requires comparing cases, recognizing their similarities and differences, and attempting to weave them together into a single picture of the law. It involves the exploration of the relationships between cases.

Judges do exactly this in their decisions as they apply the rule of precedent. Since similar cases must be decided in a similar manner, a crucial step for judges is to recognize the differences and similarities between the facts and issues of decided cases and the facts and issues of the case before the court.

Synthesis involves briefing cases, comparing them, and then constructing a description of the law.

Briefing Cases

A skill that can greatly assist researchers in synthesizing cases is briefing cases. Most law students become fairly proficient at the skill of summarizing cases into briefs, since much of law school learning is through cases.

Briefing cases involves summarizing cases into short, organized, and easily understandable formats. The basic format of a case brief is as follows:

1. **Style of Cause:**   Name and citation of the case
2. **Procedural History:**   Previous judicial treatment of case
3. **Facts:**   Summary of relevant facts in the case
4. **Issues:**   Specific legal questions that the court must answer
5. **Decision:**   Disposition by the court of the case
6. **Reasons:**   Reasons provided by the court for the answers to the legal issues
7. ***Ratio Decidendi*:**   Rule of law for which the case stands
8. **Commentary:**   Dissenting opinions, personal views on the case, and connections to other cases

Attached as Appendix 10A to this chapter is a sample case brief.

The obvious benefit of a briefed case is that it is in a form that can be quickly reviewed. Case briefs provide snapshots of the law as applied to a particular situation. These snapshots can then be pulled together to form a complete picture of the law.

Comparing Cases

The goal of legal research is to find cases that are so similar that they will predict the results of the current situation.

In order to find similar cases, the facts and issues of each case must be compared and reconciled with other cases and your situation. This is called analogizing and distinguishing. Analogizing is extracting the similarities between the cases. Distinguishing is noting the differences. Analogizing and distinguishing are very important intellectual skills in case analysis.

Whether a case is viewed as similar or different often depends on the level of generality and creativity applied. For example, a case that held that a landlord must supply a tenant with a heater could be considered similar to a situation in which a tenant complained that she had no running water. On the other hand, the case could be seen as fundamentally different because heating is a necessity of life but running water is not.

Often it is useful to gather together all of the case briefs into a one-page schedule like the following.

Illustration 10.2
Case Comparison Schedule

	Case 1	Case 2	Your Facts
Binding or Persuasive			
Facts			
Issues			
Decision			
Reasons and *Ratio*			
Commentary			

When comparing cases, sometimes it is best to compare the decision of the court first and work back through the reasoning of the judge. For example, if the facts and the issues are very similar but the decisions are not, working back through the analysis might enable you to locate the distinguishing features or perhaps the different approaches taken by different judges. Do not assume, however, that because the decisions are the same, the same analysis was applied.

Constructing a Description of the Law

After a comparison of the relevant cases, the law should be synthesized into one general statement.

Synthesis involves pulling all the individual relevant cases together to form a complete picture of the law. Synthesis involves finding a collective meaning from the relevant cases. Synthesis does not simply involve describing case after case, but, rather, describing the law as a unified whole. Synthesis weaves the law together like a spider web. The result of synthesis is the development of a new "rule" from all of the cases that have been decided as they apply to your particular fact situation. Synthesis takes practice and is a skill that develops over time.

The difficulty of synthesis is finding common ground among the cases when there are wide-ranging similarities and differences. The following is a simple example of a synthesis.

Example of Synthesis

Slip and Fall

Facts: A woman slipped and fell on a banana peel on the sidewalk in front of her neighbour's house. The banana had been on the sidewalk for days and had rotted in the sun, making it particularly slippery. She has sued the neighbour for negligence.

Case 1: A man fell on an icy sidewalk of a big department store. The sidewalk had been cleared of ice daily but there had recently been a massive snowfall. The department store was not liable because, although it was foreseeable that such an accident could occur, the store did all it could do to prevent the accident.

Case 2: A boy slipped and fell on an icy sidewalk. The ice was caused by faulty eavestroughs, which dripped water onto the sidewalk. The owner was liable because he could have foreseen the accident and did nothing to prevent it from occurring.

Case 3: An owner posted a sign on her property stating "enter at own risk" because she had flooded her property for irrigation purposes. A man slipped in the mud. The owner was not held liable because she had posted a warning.

Possible Synthesis: An owner or occupier of property will be held liable for injuries that occur on his or her property if the injury was reasonably foreseeable and the owner did nothing to prevent the injury from occurring.

> **Application to the Facts:** The neighbour will likely be liable to the woman who slipped on the banana peel. Because the banana peel had been there for days, it was likely reasonably foreseeable that such an accident might occur. In addition, the owner did nothing to prevent the accident from occurring.

STATUTE ANALYSIS

The system of common law has been altered significantly by the introduction of statutes. Indeed, some academics have argued that the law in Canada is no longer a true system of common law because of the weighty effect of statutes on almost every area of the law.

Statutes are codifications of the law. They are legal rules set out in legislative form to alter or clarify case law or create new areas of law. They cannot be separated from case law.

The law develops through both the creation of statutes and the interpretation of statutes by the courts in deciding cases. The rule of precedent suggests that the courts must apply statutes similarly to each set of facts.

Similar to case analysis, statute analysis involves finding relevant statutes, reading these statutes, and interpreting them. It involves asking the following questions about the statutes you find:

- Does the statute apply to the situation? (relevance)
- What does the statute say? (reading statutes)
- What does the statute mean? (interpreting statutes)

Relevance

The first step in statute analysis is to determine whether the statute applies to a particular situation. This entails reading a statute and determining if the legislation was designed to cover the current situation.

Like case analysis, statute analysis involves distinguishing and analogizing the facts. The "facts" in a statute, however, are the words used in the statute. These words describe whether and how the statute applies. These "facts" must exist in order for a statute to apply to a situation. For example, all criminal law offences require that there be an act (*actus reus*) and intent (*mens rea*). Thus, a legal problem must involve both an act and intent to be considered a criminal offence.

Statutes are rules that apply to specific people or activities. If the current situation involves those specific people or activities referred to in the statute, then the statute probably applies. Often statutes have definitions at the beginning of the statute that describe the persons and activities covered in the statute. For example, s. 2 of the British Columbia *Insurance Act*[1] states as follows:

> This Act, except as provided, applies to every insurer that carries on any business of insurance in British Columbia and to every contract of insurance made or deemed made in British Columbia.

If it is not readily apparent whether the statute applies, you may need to resort to the rules of statutory interpretation described below.

Reading Statutes

If a statute is applicable, you must read those parts of the statute that are relevant.

Most statutes follow a particular format. Recognizing this format will help you better read and interpret statutes. The six components of a statute are essentially as follows:

1. Long title
2. Chapter number
3. Date of Royal Assent
4. Short title
5. Definitions
6. Parts, sections and subsections

Statutes are discussed in detail in Chapter 7 (How to Find and Update Statutes).

Interpreting Statutes

Statutory interpretation involves some skill. There are three different, and often competing, approaches taken by the courts in interpreting statutes. They are as follows:

Literal or Grammatical Method

The literal or grammatical method of statute interpretation stresses the literal or plain meaning of a statute. This method assumes that complete understanding of the statute can be found within the ordinary meaning of the words of the statute. Therefore, interpretation is restricted to the actual text of the statute.

Aids used to interpret the statute, outside of the text, such as the intent of the legislators and previous versions of the statute, are not considered relevant. Taken to the extreme, this method requires

---

[1]   R.S.B.C. 1996, c. 226, s. 2.

interpretation of the ordinary meaning of the words within the statute even if it leads to an absurdity or inconsistency within the statute. Although the literal method is not appropriate where the wording of a statute is ambiguous, it is still the primary and preferred approach to interpreting statutes.

Contextual Method

The contextual method of statutory interpretation employs the "Golden Rule". This rule allows the court to depart from the literal meaning of a statute if it would lead to absurdity. Contextual interpretation is based on the assumption that statute law is meant to be rational and coherent. All legislation should be internally coherent and each must be coherent with any higher enactments; *e.g.*, a regulation must be coherent with its authorizing statute. Thus, the plain wording of a statute should be interpreted in a manner that will avoid any absurdity or inconsistency.

Purposive Method

Purposive interpretation of a statute gives primary importance to the intent of the legislators, rather than the words used, in enacting the legislation. This approach is called the "Mischief Rule". The original aim of this rule was to determine what mischief the legislators sought to overcome in enacting the legislation and to see that their goal was met. Today purposive interpretation of a statute is not limited to remedying mischief but rather to determining the purpose behind the legislation. With this method, in contrast to a literal interpretation, external aids such as legislative committee reports may be crucial to determining the purpose of the legislation.

Synthesis of the Three Approaches

According to E.A. Driedger in the *Construction of Statutes*, there is only one approach to statutory interpretation:

> the words of an Act are to be read in their entire context, in their grammatical and ordinary sense harmoniously with the scheme of the Act, the object of the Act, and the intention of Parliament.[2]

Just as important to statutory interpretation are court decisions that have construed statutes. These cases provide the opinions of both lawyers and judges on how the statute applies and what the statute means. The cases can be from other jurisdictions if those jurisdictions have similar statutes.

Thus, when looking at a statute, you should look at the specific words, the entire statute (*i.e.*, context), the history or creation process, the rules of construction of statutes, and cases that have considered the statute.

Because there will always be several interpretations of a statute, the skill required in statutory analysis, like case analysis, is to use analogy to

---

[2]   E.A. Driedger, *The Construction of Statutes* (Toronto: Butterworths, 1974), at p. 67.

extend or limit the application of the statute. For example, a statute that restricts vehicles from parks may or may not extend to skateboards or roller skates, depending on the interpretation.

This discussion is by no means exhaustive and other tools of interpretation can be found in treatises dealing specifically with statutory interpretation.

Recall the situation of Paul and Melody first mentioned in Chapter 2 (Factual Analysis). They were separating and Melody wanted to keep the $20,000 gift that her grandmother had given to her. We saw that the *Family Property Act* (fictitious) applied to all residents of British Columbia and all marriages entered into in British Columbia. We also saw that ss. 8 and 9 of that statute related to the division of family property upon marriage breakdown. One case had considered this statute. A synthesis of the statute and case law might look like this:

Example of Synthesis of Law

Paul and Melody

Statutory law in British Columbia provides that upon marriage breakdown, "family assets" must be shared equally between the marriage partners. Family assets include gifts and inheritances obtained while in the marriage. However, a court may alter this division if the division would be unfair, having regard to a number of factors including "the extent to which property was acquired by one spouse through inheritance or gift". Cases that have interpreted this statute primarily look at whether the gift was intended to become part of the family assets. For example, in those circumstances where a gift of money was kept in a separate bank account and was received fairly close to the time of the marriage breakdown, the gift was not considered to be part of the family assets.

APPLYING THE LAW TO THE FACTS

Once the cases and statutes have been read, analyzed, and synthesized, and the researcher has a good understanding of the law, the law may be applied to the current facts. This involves looking at the current facts and attempting to predict what would happen if the situation were brought to trial.

At this point, researchers should place themselves in the position of a judge. This entails looking at the law and stating how and why the law applies to the current facts. However, since researchers are not judges, they should not reach a final decision, but should only provide a best assessment of the outcome. In describing the outcome, words such as "probably" or "likely" should be used to show that the conclusion is only a prediction and not an absolute.

An example of application of the law, to the Paul and Melody situation, might look something like this.

Example of Application of Law

Paul and Melody

It is likely that Melody will be able to keep the $20,000 gift from her grandmother and not share it with Paul when they separate.

Although the gift would likely initially be included in the "family assets" which must be shared equally between the marriage partners on marriage breakdown, it is likely that a court would alter this division on the basis that the division of the $20,000 would be unfair. Case law indicates that it would be considered unfair because the money was not intended to become part of the family assets. This is evidenced by the fact that the money was kept in a separate bank account and was received fairly close to the time of the marriage breakdown.[3]

A WORD ON POLICY

When analyzing the law, policy should also be considered. Policy refers to the purpose or intent of the law or the reason behind the law. Policy usually relates to the underlying rights, interests, and obligations the law attempts to protect. Examples of policy are often found in the reports and other publications of law reform commissions at the federal, provincial and territorial levels. Occasionally these secondary sources are presented to courts as persuasive authority to be considered in judicial decisions, but they are not binding because they are only an interpretation of where the law stands or what it might become.

Policy can be used in two ways. It can be used to support the *status quo* or to introduce a change in the law. Often, if a case appears to be unfair, there is an underlying policy reason for the decision. This policy reason may be referred to when comparing cases and reconciling the differences.

As mentioned, courts are concerned with consistency in law and, therefore, will refer to policy in ensuring that the results reflect the intention of the law. But policy is not the law and should be used sparingly in legal analysis.

SELF TEST

The answers to these questions are found at the end of the book in the "Answers to Self Tests" section.

---

[3]   This is an example only and should not be taken as an accurate description of the law.

1. What is the doctrine of precedent?
2. What is meant by *stare decisis*?
3. What are the three basic levels of court in Canada?
4. What are the three steps in case analysis?
5. Define what is meant by "synthesizing the law".
6. What is the "Golden Rule" of statutory interpretation?

SAMPLE EXERCISE AND ANSWERS

The following exercise and answers demonstrates how the steps of legal analysis come together.

Try to do a legal analysis for the following fictional problem by reading the law (statutes and cases), determining its relevance, synthesizing it, and applying it to the following facts.

Problem

Janet Smith

Janet Smith is a single woman who lives alone in Edmonton in a second-floor apartment with a balcony. She was recently the victim of an attempted sexual assault. A series of similar sexual assaults on single women living alone in second- and third-floor apartments with balconies had occurred recently, all within a few blocks of Smith's home. Although the police were aware of the assaults, the investigating constables chose not to warn women at risk, partly for fear of causing hysteria.

It was discovered that the chief of police had reassigned several officers from Ms. Smith's neighbourhood to the downtown area to protect personal property in response to rumours of rioting. As well, the board of police commissioners had decided to allocate funds to public relations rather than to a seminar for police officers entitled "The Female Victim and the Myth of Hysteria".

Question

You have been asked to answer the following question: Did the police constables breach a private law duty of care by failing to take steps to warn Smith about her particular risk from this attacker?

The Law

The following is a brief fictional description of the law relating to the duty of care of police officers. It consists of the *Police Act* (fictitious) and the following four cases.

The *Police Act* applies to all police officers in Alberta. It sets out the duties of a municipal police force and liability for police action. The relevant section of the Act is as follows:

> 21(1) No action for damages lies against a police officer ... for anything said or done or omitted to be said or done in the performance or intended performance of duty or in the exercise of power or for any alleged neglect or default in the performance or intended performance of duty or exercise of power. (fictional)

Four cases that discuss the duty of care of public officials are as follows:

Anders v. Calgary Council (Alta. C.A., 1915) (fictional)

A local building authority was sued when structural damage occurred in a residential building block. Although the building's plans had been approved by the authority, it was discovered that the block had not been constructed in conformity with the plans. Anders, the lessee, alleged that the building authority had a duty to ensure that the building was constructed in accordance with the plans, and that it had been negligent in not inspecting it. The Court of Appeal found that the authority owed a *prima facie* duty of care to the lessees of the building based on the relationship between them; that is, that there was "a sufficient *relationship of proximity* or neighbourhood such that, in the reasonable contemplation of the former, carelessness may have been likely to cause damage to the latter".

R. v. Dorse Boat Co. (H.L., 1930) (fictional)

Several prisoners escaped from custody and stole a yacht, and while escaping collided with the yacht of the plaintiffs. It was alleged that the officers in charge of the prisoners' custody had been negligent in their supervision. The majority of the courts found that the fact that the damage had been caused by third parties did not exempt the officers from a duty of care towards the plaintiffs because of the *foreseeability* of the damage caused as a result of their negligence in supervising the prisoners. A concurring majority decision found that the duty of care arose from the *special relationship* between the officers and the prisoners due to the former's *control* over the latter.

Hall v. Chief Constable of West Sheffield (H.L., 1969) (fictional)

An action was brought against the police by the estate of the last victim of the "Yorkshire Ripper", on the grounds that it was foreseeable that this criminal would commit further offences against young women in Britain in the future. The court found that the police did not owe a general duty of care to individual members of the public absent a special *relationship of proximity* between the victim and the police, and that the identification of the victim as a young woman was not sufficient to locate her in a special class of persons to whom a private duty was owed. The court further held that the police should not be liable in such a situation.

Air Alaska Disaster Claimants v. Air Alaska (Ont. Dist. Ct., 1988) (fictional)

An action was brought against the police for not preventing, through proper security measures, an aircraft disaster caused by a bomb. The court held that, although a private law duty to the public generally could not be imposed on the police (as decided in *Hall*), this did not exclude the possibility of a duty of care to a more *limited* class of individuals such as the passengers of the aircraft. The court went on to suggest an expansion of the special relationship criteria to include such factors as the *control* that the defendants had over the situation (*i.e.*, the passengers and baggage allowed on board the aircraft), and the fact that they *knew or ought to have known* of the danger to Air Alaska flights.

Step 1: Determining Relevance of Statutes and Cases

The *Police Act* is relevant because it applies to all police officers in Alberta. The particular section of the statute has not been amended or repealed.

The relative relevance of the cases can be determined from the jurisdiction, dates, and court level of each of the cases. The only binding case is the Alberta Court of Appeal Decision, *Anders*. However, it is factually different (and fairly old), so may be fairly easily distinguished. Although two cases are from England, they are persuasive because they discuss duty of care. Therefore, although they are not binding, the court will likely apply them to Janet Smith's situation. *Air Alaska* is the most recent Canadian case and carries some weight in terms of precedent because it is a Canadian case — although an Alberta court is not bound by decisions from Ontario. The case that is most similar in fact to Smith's situation is *Hall*.

Step 2: Synthesizing the Law

Statute law and case law can be restated in a simplified form as follows:

The *Police Act* imposes on police a public duty to protect the public. In this role, the police are immune from liability. However, the common law has established that public officials can be found to have a private law duty of care to members of the public. This occurs in situations in which: there is a prior knowledge of the danger; harm is foreseeable; a special relationship of proximity exists between the police and that particular group or segment of the public; and the police have control over the situation.

In establishing the existence of a private law duty of care for police officers, the law appears to require four main elements: the foreseeability of harm; prior knowledge of the danger; the existence of a special relationship between the police and the member of the public; and control of the situation.

Step 3: Applying the Law to the Facts

An application of the law to Janet Smith's situation looks like this:

It is likely that the police constables owed a duty of care to Janet Smith. The police constables should have foreseen the possibility of another assault on a single woman in Smith's neighbourhood because they knew of the conditions surrounding the previous assaults and of the danger to women in the neighbourhood. The foreseeability of harm caused to a segment of the public is likely enough to establish a "special relationship" between the constables and the women in that neighbourhood, including Smith.

In addition, it is likely that there was a special relationship between the police and Ms. Smith based on Smith's membership in a small and identifiable group of potential victims. Smith and other women like her would likely be recognized by a court as being a sufficiently narrow class of potential victims and, as such, they may fit into the rule outlined in *Air Alaska*. Janet Smith's case can, therefore, be distinguished from *Hall*, for, unlike the "Yorkshire Ripper", for whom all young or fairly young women in Britain were targets, the assailant in this case targeted only single, white women living alone in second- or third-floor apartments with balconies, in Smith's neighbourhood.

There is no "control" factor in Janet Smith's case. No public authority exercised direct control over Smith's attacker. However, it seems unlikely that the lack of control over the assailant will affect the duty owed by the constables, given the extent to which the other elements apply.

Appendix 10A: Sample Case Brief

Style of Cause

Christie v. Davey, [1893] 1 Chancery Division 316.[1]

Procedural History

No previous judicial action.

Facts

Christie worked as a music teacher and had pupils in her home 17 hours per week. Her daughter, son, and a boarder frequently sang and practised their instruments. Davey had lived in the adjoining semi-detached house for the past three years. He worked out of his home as an engraver and had a musical evening once a week. Davey came to object to the noise from Christie's home and wrote a letter of complaint to Christie. Christie did not respond and the next day Davey began to make shrieking, banging, whistling, and pounding noises whenever Christie commenced musical activity.

Christie filed an action for an injunction to prevent Davey from making noises to annoy or injure Christie. Davey filed a counterclaim to prevent Christie from constant music to injure Davey.

Issue

May the occupier of property engage in an ordinarily legitimate activity on the property if the sole purpose for engaging in the activity is to deliberately annoy the neighbour?

Decision

The court allowed the claim by Christie and an injunction was issued restraining Davey from making noises in his house to annoy Christie, except for noise which resulted from of his engraving trade or his weekly musical evenings, which existed before the dispute.

The court disallowed the counterclaim by Davey, finding that Christie's music lessons were not unusual or malicious.

---

[1]   1 Ch. 316, 62 L.J. Ch. 439, 3 R. 210.

Reasons

The court held that Christie was making reasonable use of her home, evidenced by no complaints by Davey in the past three years. Davey was making unusual noises to annoy and disrupt in a deliberate and malicious manner. Davey was not permitted to complain about a legitimate use of Christie's home.

Ratio Decidendi

An occupier of property may not engage in an activity on the property in a manner ordinarily legitimate if the sole purpose of the activity is to deliberately annoy the neighbour.

Comments

No dissenting opinions. The history of the situation and reasons for the noise (*i.e.*, pleasure or intentional annoyance) are important factors. No cases with which to compare.

Legal Writing

11

The final stage in the research process involves writing the results. Writing is a skill that develops over time. With practice, all writers can become more accurate, brief, and clear.

This chapter discusses the basics of good legal writing and introduces a three-stage process of legal writing. It then describes the format of legal writing and discusses two devices by which the law is communicated: the legal memorandum and the opinion letter.

LEARNING OBJECTIVES

At the end of this chapter you will be able to:

- Name a few rules of good writing
- List the three stages in the legal writing process
- Describe the five parts of a memorandum of law
- Explain the order in which to revise writing
- Describe the form of a typical opinion letter

GOOD LEGAL WRITING

Good legal writing is accurate, brief, and clear. Good writers use plain English and target their writing to their readers. Although a lot has been written about the use of plain language in the law, the essential ideas are well articulated by Richard Wydick in his book *Plain English for Lawyers*.[1] Wydicks' six basic rules are as follows:

1. Omit surplus words.
2. Use familiar, concrete words.
3. Use short sentences.
4. Use base verbs and the active voice.
5. Arrange words with care.
6. Avoid language quirks.

---

[1] Durham, N.C.: Carolina Academic Press, 1985.

Legal writing involves not only good basic writing skills, but, more specifically, the ability to write about the law. This may sound self-evident, but many lawyers who are good writers and knowledgeable about the law are still often unable to convey the law in a clear and concise manner.

Because legal writing is the articulation or written expression of legal thought, it requires all of the skills of good writing plus an ability to put the law in a form that is understandable. As researchers learn more about the law, their ability to communicate it improves: clearer thinking leads to clearer writing. However, before researchers can put pen to paper, they should have a general understanding of the process of legal writing and the way in which the law is usually articulated (*i.e.*, the form of legal writing).

THE PROCESS OF LEGAL WRITING

The process of legal writing, like other writing, has three basic stages:

1. Planning
2. Writing
3. Revising

Stage 1: Planning

Planning involves the following four steps:

Step 1: Identify the reader;
Step 2: Determine the purpose of the writing;
Step 3: Gather, analyze, and organize the information; and
Step 4: Prepare an outline.

The following situation provides an example of the four-step planning process:

Scenario
A biology professor is deciding which first-year biology textbook to purchase and use in her first-year university biology class. You are a Ph.D. candidate in biology and the professor has asked you to review the available books and recommend one. She wants a book that is easy to read, inexpensive, and includes all of the topics that should be taught in a first-year biology course.

Step 1: Identify the Reader. The reader of your response is a biology professor who is very busy. It is likely that she expects thoroughness as

well as conciseness. She will be familiar with the language of biologists and may even be familiar with some of the more popular biology textbooks.

Step 2: Determine the Purpose. The purpose of the project is to select a textbook to be used in a first-year biology class. The textbook should be easy to read, inexpensive, and cover all first-year biology topics. You must provide enough information to enable the professor to make an informed decision.

Step 3: Gather, Analyze, and Organize the Information. It is likely that you will go to a book store and contact publishers to gather information about first-year biology books available. Once you have gathered this information, you will be able to formulate a list of all of the books and organize and summarize the information. This information could then be organized into a schedule indicating the differences between the various options.

Step 4: Prepare an Outline. Once you have summarized all the information, you must decide how you will present it. Drafting an outline will enable you to put your ideas in order.

The following are samples of two potential outlines for the above example.

Sample Outline A:

1. Introduction
2. Body
   a. Book 1: Ease of reading, cost, and topics covered
   b. Book 2: Ease of reading, cost, and topics covered
   c. Book 3: Ease of reading, cost, and topics covered
3. Conclusion

Sample Outline B

1. Introduction
2. Body
   a. Ease of reading: Books 1, 2, and 3
   b. Cost: Books 1, 2, and 3
   c. Topics Covered: Books 1, 2, and 3
3. Conclusion

Beginning researchers often do not spend enough time on planning. New researchers should avoid the temptation to begin writing before the planning process is complete. Each of the four steps of planning are described here in more detail as they relate to legal writing.

Step 1: Identify the Reader

Writers should always keep in mind who their readers are. Identifying the audience enables a writer to focus on an audience's particular wants and needs and adjust the content, organization, and style accordingly. It also gives specific purpose and direction to writing. Some questions that might be asked in order to identify readers are:

- Who are the potential readers?
- How much do the readers already know about the subject?
- What do the readers want or expect in the writing?
- How busy are the readers?
- What are the readers' ages, gender, language, education, *etc.*?

Step 2: Determine the Purpose

Determining how writing will ultimately be used and why a topic is being researched enables writers to convey the information in ways that are practical and useful. For example, if the writing is to be used in preparation for a trial, it will be written persuasively, whereas if the writing is to be used to advise a client, it will be written objectively and informatively. The following examples of audiences and purposes of writing indicate how the audience and purpose affect writing:

Types of Writing, Audiences, and Purposes				
	Poetry	**Exams**	**Legal Memo**	**Opinion Letter**
Audience	Public	Professor	Lawyer	Client
Purpose	Inspire	Assess	Inform	Advise

Each purpose requires a different type of writing in terms of content, form, and organization.

Although readers of legal writing will often be other lawyers, it is advisable not to assume that these lawyers are knowledgeable about the research topic. As you delve into the law, you become somewhat of an expert. Therefore, it is good practice to always introduce the subject at a basic level and work towards the more complicated, as if you were giving instruction about the law. There is some skill involved in deciding in how much detail of the basics should be discussed.

Step 3: Gather, Analyze, and Organize the Information

After identifying the purpose of the writing and the readers, researchers should gather together the law, read it, and attempt to make sense of it.

At this stage, relevant statutes and cases should be briefed and important concepts and quotations should be noted. The cases should be organized in terms of importance and relevance. This step is described in detail in Chapter 9 (How to Find and Update Cases).

Step 4: Prepare an Outline

The use of an outline cannot be overemphasized.

Researchers who develop comprehensive outlines spend significantly less time later at the writing stage. Although it is often difficult to hold back from writing, the benefits of doing so are numerous. Without an outline, your thoughts are less organized and it is difficult to be objective about them. Using an outline will encourage you to be more critical of your words and ideas. Outlines have other advantages. Drafting an outline:

- Highlights gaps and overlaps in information and discussion;
- Indicates where each case and statute will be discussed and the connections between each;
- Shows logical inconsistencies; and
- Forces you to stay on track and to be systematic and logical.

An outline should include all issues, ideas, and law in tabulated form. It should, ideally, fit onto one page and refer to cases and statutes in support of each proposition.

Stage 2: Writing

Writing involves describing the law and its application to the facts in a comprehensive and concise way. If you prepare a solid outline, you will know prior to writing what you generally want to say and how it will be organized. Therefore, the focus at the writing stage is on putting thoughts into words and connecting the thoughts together into a whole.

The first attempt at writing should be a fast, rough draft and should not take as much time as either planning or revising. Lawyers often dictate a first draft. This enables them to quickly get thoughts down and recite quotes from the actual text of cases without rewriting entire quotations. It is recommended that the entire first draft be written in one sitting — even if in point form — so that there is some flow to thoughts.

It is not necessary to wait until your analysis of the law is perfect before beginning your writing. Often thoughts become clearer as they are put into writing. It is important not to get caught up in words at this particular stage. Instead, focus on content and organization. Put everything you want to say in writing and edit it later.

Content

What you decide to include in your writing will obviously depend on a number of factors, such as time, complexity of the law, and the nature of the problem. For example, if a researcher has only one hour to find an answer to a legal problem, the written response may be only one page. However, if a researcher has a week and the law is particularly complex, it is likely that a comprehensive analysis will be more than just a few pages.

How Many Cases to Include

One of the most common questions of the novice researcher is: How many cases should I include and how much should I say about each case?

You should include as many cases as are necessary to describe the law in a clear and concise manner. Although this may sound elusive, once you begin your research you will begin to recognize cases that are critical and those which are subsidiary.

Try not to include cases that say almost the same thing. At a point in your research, certain cases begin to be repeatedly referred to in other cases. This is one of the first clues that your research is beginning to gain focus. Another key turning point in research is when you find a case that refers to a number of other key cases related to your topic. These cases are particularly helpful because they often summarize the law from the other cases. To ensure brevity, legal researchers should refer to the most recent cases and only mention cases separately if they are foundation cases, are critical to the analysis, or have particularly relevant facts.

Deciding on the number of cases to include is always a balancing act. Often novice researchers, in a desire to include all of the research, include cases that are not necessary. One of the most difficult tasks of legal writing is paring down the law so that just enough, but not too much, information is included. It is said that a famous writer once wrote, "I would have written you a shorter letter but I didn't have time."

You can be sure that judges are bombarded with cases in trials, yet their decisions include only those that are important to the outcome of the case.

How Much Information to Include about Each Case

There should be enough said about each case to indicate to the reader why the case is important to your situation. In other words, what does the case add to the analysis?

When including cases, researchers must make decisions about whether to include the following components of each case:

- Name of case and citation;
- How the case fits into the analysis;
- Brief outline of facts;
- Issues; and
- Holding or reasoning.

There is no "right" amount of information to include. The amount and type will be different in each situation, but there are some general patterns. For example, typically a discussion of the law begins with a general overview of the law and moves towards a more detailed description of particularly relevant cases. In other words, the discussion usually moves from the general to the specific, like a funnel:

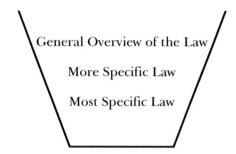

General Overview of the Law

More Specific Law

Most Specific Law

The general overview is a broad statement of the law. It often includes the principles of a few foundation cases and includes only a few facts from each of those cases. In some areas of the law, in which the law is relatively settled, there may be no need to include the facts of a well-known case. Providing the rule of law or the principle resulting from this case may be sufficient.

As researchers begin to go into more detail about particularly relevant cases, the discussion of the cases expands. At this stage, the facts and issues of each case are important for purposes of distinguishing cases and, therefore, should be included in the discussion. At the same time, the writer should try to link each case to both the prior case and the following case, so that the reader is able to see how the law developed.

Organization

Organization is critical to legal writing and the successful communication of thoughts. Lack of organization is the most frequent cause of miscommunication in legal writing. Organization means putting thoughts in an order that permits ideas to flow smoothly from the beginning of the writing through to the conclusion. The reader should be led from one idea to the next and never stumble over ideas. Keep the following rule in mind: "State where you are going; go there; and then state where you have been."

Always provide introductions to new thoughts and conclusions at the end of these thoughts. It is the writer's responsibility to lead the reader through the discussion.

The order of your discussion will depend on the area of law discussed, the particular set of facts, the audience, and your personal style. There is no single, right way to organize, but here are a few tips.

Discuss Each Legal Issue Separately

The most important organizational tip in legal writing is: discuss each legal issue separately. For each issue there should be a discussion of:

- The law pertaining to that issue;
- How that law applies to the particular facts; and
- A conclusion.

This method of organization is not always as simple as it looks. Most cases include several issues, so one of the more difficult tasks in legal writing is deciding how to divide the issues and where and how often to mention a case. This is discussed further below under The Legal Memorandum heading.

Organize Issues Logically

Dividing the law into separate issues requires deciding how to divide the issues clearly and logically.

Many legal problems have natural divisions. For example, in criminal law, two necessary components to a criminal offence are the *actus rea* and the *mens rea*. Therefore, the first issue may be: Was there a criminal act? And the second issue may be: Was there intent? Researchers should avoid falling into the trap of categorizing legal matters in the same way that legal textbooks do. Textbook writers often divide legal issues into those categories that are easiest to teach. These divisions are not always applicable to real-life situations. Some sense of how to organize legal issues can be elicited from the cases being researched.

Theoretically, there may be a different way to organize the legal issues in every new legal problem. Your task is to search for the one that explains the law to the reader in the clearest fashion.

Select a Specific Order for Statutes and Cases

You must make a decision not only about what cases and statutes to include, but also how you will include them and where. Regardless of how you decide to order the cases and statutes, there must be some logic to the order. It should never be random.

For example, it may be desirable to discuss the statute first and the cases second. It may also be preferable to mention the oldest cases first and work forward, or mention the most recent case first and work backwards. Each decision about organization must be rational. Some logical legal patterns are chronological, historical, or general to specific.

When drafting an outline, some of the questions you might ask yourself are:

- Why did I put the cases in that order?
- Do the cases flow logically from one to the next?
- Why did I put the statute where I did?

Your decisions should be driven not only by the subject matter, but also by the expectations of your readers and the rules of good communication.

Stage 3: Revising

Revising involves ensuring that the content, organization, paragraphs, sentences, words, and style are effective at conveying thoughts and information.

Revision is a long and sometimes tedious process. A significant amount of time should be spent on revision. It is recommended that the original draft be revised up to five times — each time for a different purpose. Revising requires the writer to amend what has already been written and then walk away and come back later for further revisions. The writer must be particularly rigorous at this particular stage and be prepared to edit seriously. The recommended way to revise legal work is in the following order:

1. Content
2. Organization
3. Paragraphs
4. Sentences
5. Words
6. Style
7. Form

A writing checklist is included in Appendix 11C, which summarizes the things to look for when editing and revising.

Content

Revising content primarily involves scaling the work down to that which is relevant. This first edit should focus on the bigger concepts and not on the words. Some questions you might ask yourself are:

- Have I covered all the main legal issues?
- Have I included the key statutes and cases for each issue?
- Did I include any cases that basically say the same thing?
- Is there a reason why each case is included?
- What does each case add?

Organization

Revising organization involves ensuring that the facts, brief answers, issues, analysis, and conclusion are in an order that best conveys and expresses your ideas. You should ask yourself the following questions after you have completed your memorandum to ensure that your organization is appropriate:

- Have I explained my organization to my reader?
- Have I told my reader where I am going?
- Is the organization I have selected easy to follow? Does it flow?

- Is there a reason why I have put these issues in this particular order?

Paragraphs

Revising paragraphs involves ensuring that your thoughts flow logically from paragraph to paragraph. Recall that the main rule of organization is to state where you are going; go there; and state where you have been. In order to do this, the writer must provide the reader with "sign posts". Often, new legal writers do not articulate each of the steps in their analysis because they are so immersed in the subject that they forget that the reader needs to know each step that led to the analysis. To assist the reader, it is a good idea to make use of transitions between paragraphs and to tell the reader in the first sentence of each paragraph what that paragraph will include. Transitions provide the reader with directions. They state where the writer has come from and where the writer is going.

The following are examples of transitions. Select the one you like the best.

Examples of Transitions Between Paragraphs

1. In *Brooks v. Goet* a purchaser of a doll sued a toy manufacturer after her child swallowed one of the doll's eyes.
2. Another case involving liability of a manufacturer was *Brooks v. Goet*. In that case, the purchaser of a doll sued ...
3. Several other cases held toy manufacturers liable for faulty construction of dolls. One of theses cases was *Brooks v. Goet*. In that case ...
4. The issue of liability for faulty toys was considered most recently in the case of *Brooks v. Goet*. That case involved ...

You should ask yourself the following questions to ensure your paragraphs are appropriate:

- Have I provided "sign posts" for the reader?
- Would a lay person who knows nothing about the law be able to pick up my writing and understand it?
- Does the first sentence in each paragraph tell what the paragraph will be about?
- Does the last sentence in each paragraph tell what the next paragraph will likely include?

Sentences

Revising sentences involves eliminating excess words, ensuring sentences are short, and using an active rather than passive voice. Although variation in sentence structure keeps the writing interesting, too much variation can be unsettling to a reader.

Words

Revising words involves selecting words that are clear and understandable to the reader. This means using plain English, avoiding Latin, using gender-neutral language, and avoiding jargon. Correct spelling and punctuation are also very important.

Style and Form

The last edit involves revising the style and form of writing. Revising style involves detecting tones that may emerge in your writing. The most important rule with regard to style is to remain objective. The purpose of a legal memorandum is to provide a summary of the law in an impartial manner. While the tone of a memorandum should be objective, there is another style of legal writing besides the informative — the persuasive style.

To achieve objectivity, it is important to avoid identifying too closely with a particular client's concerns. It is better to try to anticipate the other party's position. Even if required to answer to one party in a dispute, researchers should avoid the compulsion to argue in their favour, or the temptation to make their case sound better than it is. Phrasing a letter or memorandum in terms of an argument can unnecessarily split the law into pros and cons and often does not describe the law as a whole. Students who use an argumentative style tend to find it difficult to come to a final decision because the argument necessarily fragments the law and the discussion.

Generally, it is improper in informative writing to include personal opinions about the law. For example, words such as "promising" or "unfortunately" should be saved for persuasive writing. Your writing, even if friendly, should always have a professional tone. For example, you should not use slang and you should never be flippant.

Form and presentation are also very important. The look of the print and the use of divisions and subheadings should invite the reader to read on.

FORMAT

Most legal writing, including judgments, case briefs, letters to clients, and legal memoranda, tends to follow a particular format. This is not the only way law can be communicated, but this particular format has become an acceptable and commonly used means of discourse in the law.

Many readers of law, such as lawyers and judges, expect legal writing to follow a particular format. The format allows them to read the law much more effectively because they know ahead of time where the information they are looking for will be located in the text. It is therefore important to recognize the format when reading and writing about the law.

Other types of writing follow their own particular formats as well. For example, newspaper articles tend to follow a pyramid format: providing the most important information in the first paragraph and expanding on this information in sequential paragraphs. The pyramid format allows readers to move quickly through newspapers selecting the information needed. Newspaper readers have come to expect this type of format and can become frustrated if the format is not followed.

The format used most frequently in legal writing is called FILAC (Facts, Issues, Law, Application, and Conclusion). You will note that the FILAC format of writing is similar to the five-step process recommended for researching the law. In legal writing, however, it looks like this:

Facts — State the legally relevant facts
Issues — State the legal issues
Law — Describe the law (cases and statutes)
Application — Describe how the law applies to the facts
Conclusion — Conclude and state the likely outcome

There are several benefits to dividing the discussion into these five components. First, the reader can quickly select what to read. Second, the reader can see the separation between the law and the application of the law. This is important because the description of the law is totally objective. The application of the law, on the other hand, necessarily includes the opinions of the writer, since it is an estimation of how a judge will apply the law to a particular circumstance. If the reader does not agree with the application, he or she can still benefit from the objective description of the law and attempt an alternative application.

FILAC is not the only format of legal discourse. Legal writers should understand why it is an effective format and strive to improve it by adding their own particular style and creative touches.

The Legal Memorandum

A legal memorandum is a written document that expresses the results of legal research. It is a summary of the law and the application of the law as it applies to a particular situation. It is used as a basis for advice to a client. Although clients rarely see legal memoranda, the memoranda are used to assist lawyers throughout the entire life of the file. Decisions such as whether to proceed, settle, or abandon a claim will be made on the basis of the information and analysis provided in the memorandum. Based on a memorandum, lawyers will often write letters to clients providing opinions about the merits of a case and the likelihood of success.

Before describing how best to put a legal memorandum together, imagine the following situation:

Situation

You are a judge. The two lawyers in the case before you have provided you with about 60 cases and one statute, which they suggest is the law pertaining to the case before you. You have heard the witnesses in the case and have a good idea of the facts involved. Your task is now to write a decision. This means you must restate the facts as you see them, summarize the law as you read it, and tell the parties how the law applies in this particular case. You must then come up with a decision that makes some sense and is clear and concise. How will you do this?

A judge's job is very similar to a legal researcher's, except that, instead of coming to a decision, researchers predict the likely outcome of the case. A legal memorandum, if properly written, will look very similar to a well-written judgment. Although each judge has a particular style, readers can quickly detect which judgments are easiest to follow and get to the point quickly. The same qualities you appreciate as a reader of cases should be incorporated into your own legal writing.

Format of a Legal Memorandum

There is no required format for a legal memorandum. Since memoranda are usually law office documents, the format will usually be dictated by the particular law firm or legal department. The format recommended here is one used in a number of law firms. It is designed to communicate the law in the most useful way for a busy lawyer. Researchers, however, should remain flexible with the format and be as creative as a particular situation may require. The recommended format is as follows:

1. Facts
2. Issues
3. Brief answers
4. Analysis (law and application)
5. Conclusion

You will note that this format follows both the research process and the common discourse in law, which was described earlier. Each component is discussed below.

Facts

The facts in a legal memorandum are the legally relevant facts of the problem presented. A recital of the facts in a legal memorandum should look much like those facts found in judgments. Although the way in which facts can be articulated is unlimited, the goal is to include only relevant facts. This is discussed in more detail in Chapter 2 (Factual Analysis).

Often a first attempt at summarizing the facts is incomplete. As researchers become more familiar with the law pertaining to their case, they begin to recognize the importance of the facts that have been taken into consideration in other cases. Therefore, the facts should be reviewed periodically as research progresses. Any necessary assumptions should also be stated.

Issues

The issues are the legal questions to be answered. Proper drafting of issues enables a reader to know exactly where the writer is headed. Drafting issues is discussed in more detail in Chapter 3 (Issue Determination).

Drafting issues is not a one-time task. Ideally, the issues should be redrafted as the research and writing progress. It is always good practice to review the legal issues at the very end of writing to ensure that these are the specific questions that have been answered in the legal memorandum.

Some tips when drafting issues are as follows. Legal issues should:

- Be drafted as a single question;
- Include both facts and law;
- Use the actual names or roles of the parties in the issue (*e.g.*, not "plaintiff" or "defendant"); and
- Be divided into sub-issues where possible.

Brief Answers

The brief answers in the memorandum are the likely outcome of the case supported by reasoning. A sample brief answer is as follows:

It is likely there is no contract between Mr. Job and Type Company because there was no consideration flowing from Mr. Job when Type Company forwarded merchandise that was not included under the original contract.

It is advisable to use words such as "likely" or "probably" in the brief answers since there is rarely a situation where the outcome of a case is guaranteed. It is also good practice not to include references to specific statutes or cases in the brief answer unless they are critical to the outcome of a case.

Analysis

The analysis part of the memorandum is the bulk of the memorandum. It includes an analysis of the law and a determination of how the law applies to the facts.

Organization is critical to the analysis. As indicated above, it is important to keep each legal issue separate. It is also important to keep the description of the law separate from a description of how the law applies to the facts. For each issue, state the relevant law first (*i.e.*, cases and statutes), synthesize this law into a paragraph or two, and then apply this law to your particular facts. This is discussed in more detail in Chapter 10 (Introduction to Legal Analysis).

Any discussion of policy should appear at the end of the analysis.

Conclusion

The conclusion in a legal memorandum summarizes the information contained in the memorandum. It essentially gathers all of the conclusions reached under each of the issues into one or two concise paragraphs. It is important not to include any new information in the conclusion. Nothing in the conclusion should surprise the reader, since it is simply a brief restatement of what has already been said. Often a reader will only read the issues, the brief answer, and the conclusion of a memorandum. Therefore, the conclusion should include the likely outcome of the case and the reasoning.

It is rare to include case names in the conclusion unless they are very important to the analysis. Mention of policy for the first time in the conclusion should be avoided.

The Opinion Letter

An opinion letter is a letter to a client advising about the state of the law and how it applies to a situation.

Opinion letters are usually written on the basis of legal memoranda and include the same components as the legal memorandum: the facts, the law, the application of the law to the facts, and a conclusion. However, the format is much more flexible. The ultimate aim is to answer the client's question.

Both the format and the language used should enhance understanding. If the law does not support the client's position, this should be made clear and alternatives should be briefly considered. To test the clarity and conciseness of a letter it is a good idea to ask a layperson to provide feedback. A layperson should be able to understand what you have written.

The suggested format of an opinion letter is as follows:

Part 1: Introduce yourself (if necessary) and define your task. State where you are going and what you are going to say. Sometimes it is good to state the conclusion right up front.

Part 2: Introduce the subject at hand generally and give a simple overview of the relevant area of law. Then describe the law in more detail by focusing on the specific wording of statutes or the factors that the courts have taken into consideration in determining past cases. You may want to refer to a specific case if it is very similar to your client's situation.

Part 3: Apply the law to the client's situation and describe the likely outcome of the case if it were to go to trial.

Part 4: Conclude and describe the next steps to be taken.

SELF TEST

The answers to these questions are found at the end of the book in the "Answers to Self Tests" section.

1. Name a few basic rules of good writing.
2. List the three stages in the legal writing process.
3. Name the four steps involved in planning.
4. What are five parts of a legal memorandum?
5. In what order should you revise your writing?
6. What is the form of a typical opinion letter?

Appendix 11A: Sample Memorandum of Law

The following memorandum of law was prepared by a first-year law student. It is only an example and should be critiqued by students.

To: M.F. Fitzgerald
From: Michael Lee
Re: Ravi and May — Liability of Partners
Date: November 24, 2006

STATEMENT OF FACTS

Ravi, May, and Jan formed the law partnership of "JMR Legal Services" to provide traditional legal and mediation services. Their partnership agreement stated that all profits from the law practice were to be shared and the firm's name and facilities were only to be used for activities related to the law practice.

In building their practice, Ravi and May regularly referred clients requiring mediation work to Jan. However, Jan eventually decided that since her mediation work was separate from the traditional law practice she would keep the profits generated from this work. Consequently, she started "Jan's Mediation Services" (JMS), set up her own bookkeeping, banking, and advertising, and met her mediation clients at home. Although Jan tried to keep the two areas of her practice separate, she occasionally asked the secretary at JMR to type correspondence relating to her mediation work. It is assumed that the secretary did not use JMR letterhead.

Viewing the mediation services as integral to the firm's practice, Ravi and May wrote a protest letter to Jan stating that the mediation profits should be shared. However, before this dispute was resolved, Jan was charged with theft for misappropriating $30,000 from the Regal Bank, which had retained Jan to provide mediation services. During the mediation process, Jan had held the money in a trust account under the JMS name. Since Jan had no assets, the bank sued Ravi and May as partners in JMR. It is assumed that there was no previous relationship between Regal Bank and JMR and that the bank did not know that Jan was a lawyer.

ISSUES

The main issue of whether Ravi and May are liable for Jan's misappropriation of funds may be divided into two issues: (1) Was Jan's provision of mediation services to Regal Bank and subsequent misappropriation of funds within the ordinary course of the business of the firm? (2) Was Jan acting within the scope of her apparent authority when she provided mediation services to Regal Bank and misappropriated the funds?

BRIEF ANSWER

Under the *Partnership Act* of B.C., a partner is liable for the wrongful act of another partner if he or she was acting in the ordinary course of the firm's business, or within the scope of his or her apparent authority. Case law identifies the following factors as acting in the ordinary course of business where: (1) there is no agreement excluding the activity from the firm's business; (2) the firm's staff and facilities are used; and (3) the profits from the activity are shared. Acting in the scope of apparent authority can be defined as when: (1) a partner uses the firm's name and its facilities to hold himself or herself out as acting with the approval of the other partners; and (2) a client is under the impression that the individual is acting within his or her authority as a partner in the firm. Most of these factors were not present in this case, so it is unlikely that Jan could be viewed as having acted either in the ordinary course of the firm's business, or within the scope of her apparent authority. Consequently, Ravi and May likely will not be found liable.

ANALYSIS

Issue 1: Ordinary Course of the Firm's Business

The Law

The applicable statute law is s. 12 of the *Partnership Act*[1] of B.C., which states:

> Where by any wrongful act or omission of any partner acting in the ordinary course of the business of the firm, or with the authority of his co-partners, loss or injury is caused to any person not being a partner in the firm, or any penalty is incurred, the firm is liable for that loss, injury or penalty to the same extent as the partner so acting or omitting to act.

---

[1] *Partnership Act*, R.S.B.C. 1979, c. 312.

In *Patchett v. Oliver*,[2] the Supreme Court of B.C. applied the *Partnership Act* to find Oliver's law partner liable for Oliver's wrongful acts, because he was acting within the ordinary course of the business of the firm and within the scope of his apparent authority. From the case it may be inferred that the important factors in making this determination were Oliver's acting as a solicitor and using the firm's bookkeeper and accounts to carry out his wrongful acts.

In *Public Trustee v. Mortimer* ("*Mortimer*"),[3] the Ontario High Court of Justice applied the *Partnership Act* of Ontario, which is similar in language to the B.C. Act. The defendant, Mortimer, a solicitor in a law firm, acted as an executor and trustee of an estate. Using the staff and facilities of his law firm to administer the estate, Mortimer stole money from the estate. The court found the defendant partners liable for Mortimer's wrongful acts because he was acting within the ordinary course of the firm's business. To reach this decision, the court outlined several *indicia* as possible ways to separate a partner's activities as an executor of an estate from the ordinary course of the firm's business [p. 413]:

> There would probably be an agreement between the partners to that effect, and one might expect to find that the partner would not charge the estate on an account issued in the firm's name, would personally keep any fees and compensation paid, rather than treat them as revenues of the firm, would keep the funds of the estate in an account separate from his firm's trust account, and would keep a set of accounting records from the estate separate from those of his firm. If he wanted to be careful to make it clear that his work as an executor was not part of the firm's business, he would not use the firm letterhead when writing as an executor.[4]

None of these *indicia* were met by Mortimer and his firm. In addition, Mortimer used a junior solicitor and the firm's management company for the typing and bookkeeping work on the estate. The executor's fees were also directed into the firm's revenues. Consequently, the court concluded that Mortimer's activities as an executor were within the ordinary course of the business of the firm.

In *Tomiyama v. Riley* ("*Tomiyama*"),[5] the defendant, Riley, asked his client, Mrs. Tomiyama, for a personal loan in exchange for a mortgage on three residential lots owned by Riley. He asked her to make separate discharges of the mortgage, then sold the lots, but failed to repay her. The Supreme Court of B.C., in applying the *Partnership Act* of B.C., found that Riley's firm was liable for Riley's wrongful act, because he was acting within the ordinary course of the business of the firm. This finding was based on Riley's use of his secretary, the firm's facilities, and his position as a partner in the firm to carry out these transactions. For example, the court

---

2   [1977] 5 W.W.R. 299 (B.C.S.C.).
3   (1985), 16 D.L.R. (4th) 404 (Ont. H.C.).
4   *Ibid.*, at 43.
5   [1978] B.C.J. No. 1942 (B.C.S.C.).

cites that Riley applied for the releases of the mortgage as a member of the firm and used his firm's business address. In not separating his activities from the firm, the court inferred that these releases were secured in the ordinary course of the business of the firm.

In *Korz v. St. Pierre* ("*Korz*"),[6] Korz, a solicitor in a law firm, entered into a business agreement with two clients to form a company and serve as its directors. He did not contribute his share of the financing, nor did he help his two clients settle the debts when the company went bankrupt. The Ontario Court of Appeal, applying the *Partnership Act* of Ontario, found Korz's partner liable for Korz's wrongful acts because he was acting in the ordinary course of the business of the firm. This finding was based on Korz acting as the solicitor to the company and, by extension, the directors, and on his long record of solicitor work for both clients prior to the company's formation. In addition, all meetings of the company's directors were held in Korz's law offices.

Synthesis

From these cases, the factors defining when a partner is acting in the ordinary course of business of a law firm are where: (1) there is no agreement excluding the activity from the firm's business; (2) the firm's staff (including lawyers, secretaries, and bookkeepers), facilities (including accounts and offices), and name (including letterhead) are used; and (3) the profits from the activity are shared.

Application of Law to Our Situation

These factors must now be applied to determine whether Jan's activities were in the ordinary course of the business of the firm. As in *Mortimer*, there was no agreement excluding mediation work from the firm's business. Rather, the partners had an understanding, reaffirmed in Ravi and May's protest letter, that the practice was to include mediation work.

However, Jan separated her mediation activities from the business of the firm. Meeting several of the key *indicia* laid out in *Mortimer*, Jan kept separate accounting records and bank accounts and did not share the profits from her mediation work. Although Jan occasionally used the firm's secretary for correspondence related to her mediation activities, this use of the firm's staff was minor compared to Mortimer's use. Jan did not use a junior solicitor of the firm or employees of the firm's management company for bookkeeping. In addition, unlike the *Korz* case, Jan did not use the offices of the firm to conduct meetings with clients regarding mediation services. Jan also did not conduct her mediation activities under the firm's name, as opposed to the *Tomiyama*

---

[6]   (1988), 43 D.L.R. (4th) 528 (Ont. C.A.); leave to appeal refused (1988), 62 O.R. (2d) ix (S.C.C.).

case. As a result, it is unlikely that her activities would be found as having taken place within the ordinary course of the business of the firm.

Issue 2: Apparent Authority

The Law

The applicable statute law is s. 13(*a*) of the *Partnership Act* of B.C., which states:

> where one partner acting within the scope of his apparent authority receives money or property of a third person and misapplies it … the firm is to make good the loss.

In *Mortimer*, the Ontario High Court of Justice, in considering the claim of the managing partner that Mortimer's activities were not in the course of the firm's business, also reviewed the use of apparent authority. Despite the managing partner's claim, Mortimer was allowed to use the facilities of the firm to carry out his activities as an executor. The court held that the firm: "by permitting Mortimer to use the stationery, accounts, staff and other facilities of the firm in connection with his activities as executor and trustee, had vested Mortimer with apparent authority to receive the money or property of the estate which he subsequently misapplied".[7] In this way, through his use of the firm's accounts, letterhead, and staff, Mortimer's activities appeared to be authorized by the partners in his firm.

In *Tomiyama*, the Supreme Court of B.C. applied the decision from the *Mortimer* case regarding apparent authority to suggest that Riley's use of the "trappings of the firm" to carry out his fraud was analogous to Mortimer's activities. The court found that Tomiyama was under the impression that Riley was acting within his authority as a senior partner in the firm. This impression was in part based on her long history of dealings with Riley in a solicitor-client relationship. Tomiyama was also under this impression because Riley carried out these activities using the firm's facilities and staff, such as his secretary. The court summed up Riley's use of his apparent authority: "[w]ithout the aid of his secretary and the trappings of the firm Riley could not have accomplished fraud upon her in the manner that he did. Theoretically perhaps he could have perfected the fraud personally and outside the scope of his firm, but he did not."[8] In this way, Riley by using the firm's name and facilities took advantage of his apparent authority.

---

[7] *Supra* note 3 at 414.
[8] *Supra* note 5 at 5.

Synthesis

From case law, the factors defining acting within the scope of apparent authority are: (1) when a partner uses the firm's name and its facilities to hold himself or herself out as acting with the authority of the other partners; and (2) when the client is under the impression that the individual is acting within his or her authority as a partner in the firm.

Application of Law to Our Situation

These factors must now be applied to determine whether Jan was acting within the scope of her apparent authority. Jan had the authority of her partners to carry out her mediation work, because of the partners' understanding that their practice was to include mediation work. She also did not sever her partnership with JMR. In addition, like the *Mortimer* case, her partners permitted her to use the firm's facilities to carry out her mediation work.

However, in forming JMS, Jan separated her activities from the firm and did not use her authority as a partner in JMR. Unlike both *Mortimer* and *Tomiyama*, Jan did not use the facilities of the firm to give the appearance that her activities were authorized by her partners. In using her own promotional materials and facilities, Jan carried out her mediation activities under a separate business name — unlike Riley, who acted as a partner of his firm. Consequently, it is unlikely that Jan will be found to have been acting within the scope of her apparent authority.

CONCLUSION

It is likely that Ravi and May will not be held liable for Jan's misappropriation of funds from the Regal Bank because Jan was not "acting in the ordinary course of the business" of the firm and not likely acting within the scope of her apparent authority. She had effectively separated her mediation work from the firm's practice. She did not use the firm's facilities or her position as a partner in the firm to give the impression to the bank that she was acting with the authority of her partners. In short, the action against Ravi and May is likely to fail. A recurrent policy theme in case law is holding partners responsible for their partners' wrongful acts where there is a sharing of profits. Should this policy consideration be given more weight, the argument in Ravi and May's favour would not be weakened because Jan kept her mediation work profits separate from those of JMR.

Appendix 11B: Sample Opinion Letter

The following is a sample opinion letter written by a first-year law student. It is only an example and should be critiqued by students.

November 14, 2006

Ravi and May
JMR Legal Services
Victoria, B.C.

Dear Ravi and May:

Re: <u>Liability in Jan's Misappropriation of Funds</u>

I have been assigned your case by Ms. Fitzgerald, and am responding regarding your potential liability in Jan's misappropriation of funds from the Regal Bank. Ms. Fitzgerald gave me the facts of your case and, based on this information, the following letter outlines the issues, case law, and application of the law to your situation.

Under the *Partnership Act* of B.C., you would be liable for Jan's wrongful acts if she was either acting in the ordinary course of the business of the firm, or within the scope of her apparent authority.

The factors used by the courts to define acting in the ordinary course of the firm's business are: (1) there is no agreement excluding the activity from the firm's business; (2) the firm's staff and facilities are used; and (3) the profits from the activity are shared. The factors defining acting in the scope of apparent authority are: (1) a partner uses the firm's name and its facilities to hold himself or herself out as acting with the authority of the other partners; and (2) a client is under the impression that the partner is acting within his or her authority as a partner of the firm.

In applying these factors to your case, it is likely that, although there was an understanding that the firm's practice included mediation work, Jan effectively separated her mediation activities from the law practice. She informed JMR, made arrangements for separate bookkeeping, banking, and advertising, and kept the profits separate from JMR. Although Jan may have had your authority to do mediation work as part of the firm's practice, she did not use the firm's staff, facilities, or name to make it appear as though her activities were authorized by you, her two partners. Rather, Jan used her own facilities and conducted her mediation activities under her own company name.

Therefore, it is likely that the court will find that Jan was neither acting in the ordinary course of the firm's business, nor acting within the scope of her apparent authority. In our opinion, it is unlikely that a court would find you liable for Jan's wrongful act.

Should you wish to discuss this opinion further, please contact me.

Yours sincerely,

Student

Appendix 11C: Legal Writing Checklist

The following checklist summarizes many of the tips provided in Chapter 11. It can be used as a guide for legal writing or as a checklist on completion of your writing to ensure that you have written in an accurate and concise manner.

Content

❑ The purpose is clearly stated.

❑ All relevant facts are identified and necessary assumptions are stated.

❑ The main issues and sub-issues are identified and worded as questions.

❑ The probable outcome is briefly summarized.

❑ The law is synthesized and applied to the facts.

❑ The analysis reconciles or distinguishes conflicting case law.

❑ The conclusion briefly summarizes the law and states the probable outcome.

❑ The text is consistent with the stated purpose.

Organization

❑ The information is presented in logical order.

❑ Topics are discussed in a logical sequence.

❑ There are smooth transitions.

❑ The conclusion summarizes the discussion.

❑ Issues are discussed separately.

Paragraphs

❑ Each paragraph explains no more than one main idea.

❑ The main idea is stated at the beginning of the paragraph.

❑ Each paragraph flows logically from one to the next.

Sentences

❑ Sentences are short, accurate, and clear.

❑ Each sentence is connected to the surrounding sentences.

❑ Complex sentence structure is avoided.

❑ Active rather than passive voice is used.

❑ Sentence structure varies.

Words

❑ Language is concise (*e.g.*, no repetition or wordiness).

❑ Language is precise, and concrete words are used (*e.g.*, no ambiguity or vagueness).

❑ Language is consistent and objective.

❑ Language and tone are suitable for the purpose of writing and the reader.

❑ Legal jargon is avoided.

❑ Legal terms are explained where necessary.

❑ Gender-neutral language is used.

❑ Correct punctuation and spelling is used.

Style and Form

- ❑ Headings and definitions are used effectively.

- ❑ A suitable format is adopted.

This Legal Writing Checklist is adapted from: Modern Writing for Lawyers (Continuing Legal Education Society of British Columbia, 1992) Writing Guide, p. 3. Used and adapted with permission.

A Research Plan

12

Legal research should be done as quickly and inexpensively as possible. This means that researchers should devise ways to conduct research effectively and efficiently. Time is money — the time cost of research has to be taken into account just as costs to do online research must be.

There are many ways to conduct legal research. There is no single, best way. The research method used will depend on a number of factors, such as the nature of the problem and the researcher's abilities. Because legal research is as much an art as a science, the ability to research the law will develop with practice. As lawyers become more familiar with legal sources and more proficient with the research process, they learn shortcuts. Solving legal problems effectively and efficiently, however, should be done in a systematic way. Irrespective of ability and knowledge, researchers are continually confronted with new problems and issues. In these situations, it is advisable to go "back to the basics" of research.

Regardless of the approach taken, each researcher must have a plan prior to beginning the research process. Before heading to the library or logging onto an online resource, researchers should plan where they intend to look and what they hope to find. This gives some direction to the research and keeps researchers from sinking in the myriad of books and databases. Developing a plan eliminates wasted effort in looking at irrelevant sources and provides a checklist indicating steps taken.

This chapter explains what a research plan is, describes some practical considerations, lists some research tips, and describes how to develop a research plan. Appended to this chapter is a sample research plan.

LEARNING OBJECTIVES

At the end of this chapter you will be able to:

- Explain what a research plan is
- Explain why a research plan is necessary
- Name a few practical considerations in preparing a research plan
- Describe the basic parts of a research plan
- Describe some advantages to note-taking

WHAT IS A RESEARCH PLAN?

A research plan is a written plan describing how research will be conducted. As soon as a problem is presented, a researcher will begin to think about possible ways to solve the problem. Some problems will be easy to solve and require little research, whereas others will require extensive research. Each legal problem requires a unique research plan.

At a minimum, a research plan should consist of the five broad steps of the legal research process: Factual analysis, Issue determination, finding the Law, Analyzing the law, and Communicating the law (FILAC). However, the details of how each step is accomplished will vary from problem to problem.

Although there is no magic plan, all research plans should indicate, in as specific terms as possible, where the researcher intends to go and what she or he hopes to find. A research plan evolves as the research progresses and, thus, should remain fairly flexible.

PRACTICAL CONSIDERATIONS

When devising a research plan, some practical factors must be taken into consideration.

Before diving into the research process, researchers must know something about the persons requesting the research (audience), why the research is necessary (purpose), and limitations on the research, such as time and cost. All legal research depends on these factors.

The audience and the purpose of the research are very important considerations when defining the scope of the research. The most typical purpose of research is to advise a client, in preparation for trial or in preparation for negotiation. Although the research process will be similar in either case, the purpose of the research will define exactly how deeply a researcher may delve into a particular area. For example, if the research is being done for a knowledgeable client or a lawyer, the researcher may decide not to include some very basic information on a particular area. However, if the research is being prepared directly for a less sophisticated client, then the researcher may want to include more general or basic information about the particular legal subject.

There will almost always be constraints placed on researchers. Typically, there are time or financial constraints. If, for example, a client is disputing a contract with a value of $100, it would not be practical or proper to spend days researching the issue, especially if the extensive use of online resources is contemplated.

Researchers are also often limited by availability of information. Many libraries do not carry information that could be useful, but the rapidly expanding array of commercial online providers and products opens up new ways to conduct research, even if you work or live quite far from a law library. A researcher must be aware of what information is available and at what cost. One of the first things a new researcher should always do is to familiarize himself or herself not only with the online services available in the workplace but also with whatever physical law collections are handy, such as academic or courthouse law libraries. Within those libraries, the researcher should ask about the kinds of locally prepared tools that are likely to be on hand, such as an index to a local law society newsletter, or a collection of local municipal bylaws, or a listing of cases that have interpreted provincial statutes. Often, these kinds of aids can save hours of time.

RESEARCH TIPS

The following are some tips for legal researchers. The first group of tips deals with the legal research process. The second group deals with note-taking, and the third deals with knowing when to stop.

The Legal Research Process

These tips will assist legal researchers during the legal research process.

- *Think through the whole research process.* It is very important to thoroughly think through the entire research process before beginning research. Although this may seem like an obvious task, time spent here will save you time and effort in the long run.

- *Move from broad to specific.* Researchers should almost always move from the broad to the specific when conducting research. This means that research should begin at the general level and move towards research of more specific legal issues. It is important not to get trapped into a narrow category of law early in the research. Think of this process as an inverted triangle — start at the top with a very broad legal topic, such as torts. Then work your way toward more and more specific subdivisions of that topic, until you arrive at the bottom, at a narrow and manageable specific level. For example, when perusing indexes for a legal topic, do not consider your search complete if you find one relevant topic. Often legal subjects span a number of legal areas.

- *Try not to jump back and forth between sources.* It is usually not efficient to interrupt your review of one source and immediately go to another source. It is best to use one source completely so that you do not have to go back to it and wonder how far you have read in that particular source. If you feel compelled to jump ahead, make detailed notes about where you are so that you can return to the source without retracing steps. When using physical materials in a library, it is a good idea to make a note of exactly where in the building the materials are, to avoid having to relocate things later.

- *Look for "meaty" quotes.* Often court cases are well written and include excellent summaries of the law. Therefore, when reading cases, researchers should be on the lookout for "meaty quotes", which can ultimately be included in the final written product. A good habit is to photocopy important quotations. Handwritten quotations leave room for error when transcribed. Photocopies can also be used to proof the final product.

- *Stay flexible.* Perhaps the most important tip is to stay flexible. If you find yourself off on a tangent, be prepared to abandon what you have done and start again. Try not to be narrow in focus, and continually ask yourself whether the route you are taking is the most effective and efficient. Remain open to new ideas as they present themselves.

Note-Taking

Since legal research can often take weeks or months and uncover vast quantities of information, researchers must be organized and devise systems to record research steps taken. Some of the suggestions made below should assist researchers in doing this.

- *Summarize the facts and issues on one page.* It is a good idea to summarize the facts and legal issues on a separate page. This page can be carried into the library and referred to as necessary and revised as the research progresses. You might also jot down the relationships among the parties in a fact situation, such as physician – patient, or parent – child.

- *List the key words that you search.* Listing the words or phrases that are searched is particularly important because these words are often forgotten later. It is helpful to dedicate a specific page for a list of descriptive words that could be searched. This way the list can be lengthened or shortened. This list is particularly helpful when narrowing down the legal issues and later in the research process when computer searches are conducted.

- *Devote a separate page to each legal issue.* It is recommended that a separate page be devoted to each legal issue. This ensures that the legal issues are dealt with separately and thoroughly. If the information on legal issues is combined, it is very difficult to separate the legal issues later.

- *Record citations as you conduct your research.* It is always a good idea to record the full citations of cases, statutes, and secondary sources as you are conducting your research. This cannot be over-emphasized. Many researchers know how frustrating it is to have to search for a citation of a source later, when only a scrawl has been recorded. Another suggestion is to also record references to material that you considered to be irrelevant at the time and why you thought so. You opposition may present these to the court and you will have to defend yourself regarding your decision **not** to use them as authorities.

- *Photocopy statutes.* When referring to statutes it is critical that the exact numbering, wording and format of the statute be maintained. Therefore it is best to photocopy the relevant sections of the statute or bookmark them within your web browser.

- *Record particular insights.* Often as research progresses, researchers are struck by particular insights. It is a good idea to jot down the ideas you may have, although they need not be researched at that particular moment. These insights often provide the basis for policy discussions later in the analysis.

- *Photocopy key cases.* It is recommended that very important cases that are referred to repeatedly be photocopied or printed out from databases. This is to enable researchers to re-read cases a number of times and highlight the important parts. These cases often include citations and summaries of other relevant cases.

- *Devote a separate page to a list of sources referred to.* It is a good idea to keep a separate page listing authorities referred to. This will be your bibliography. Sometimes researchers will be asked to produce this list to ensure that the research is complete and that all relevant sources have been canvassed. It is recommended that a specific coloured page be devoted to the bibliography because of the importance of keeping a record of the sources referred to. Again, you may wish to keep a separate list of authorities you decided not to use, in case you are questioned about them.

- *Date every page.* Often, dating pages of notes serves as a reminder of the series of steps taken. It can also trigger a researcher's memory so that tracks can be retraced if necessary.

Knowing When to Stop

There is no simple way to know when to stop. If you are consistent and thorough, you will begin to see your research coming into focus. The most obvious clue is discovering that the sources you are referring to refer you back to the same ones you have already examined. If you are getting no new leads or no new references to new legal sources, the research is nearing completion. When you get the sense that you are repeating steps or that the sources are becoming exhausted, you can stop your research.

DEVELOPING A RESEARCH PLAN

Although a research plan will constantly evolve, the framework of each plan should ideally remain constant. In other words, the five-step process (FILAC) should remain the same, although the steps taken within each of those steps might vary.

In earlier chapters, a number of other steps are recommended within this five-step process. These steps are summarized in a sample research plan and are appended to this chapter.

The step that requires significant advance planning is finding the law in the law library. There are two fundamental steps in finding the law: refer to secondary materials, and then refer to primary sources. The way in which secondary materials and primary sources are found and used will vary. However, each researcher should have an idea about which secondary materials will be reviewed and which primary sources he or she hopes to find in the library.

SELF TEST

The answers to these questions are found in the back of the book in the "Answers to Self Tests" section.

1. What is a research plan?
2. Why is a research plan necessary?
3. Name a few practical factors to consider when preparing a research plan.
4. Describe the basic parts of a research plan.
5. Describe some advantages to note-taking.

Appendix 12A: Sample Research Plan

The exact steps taken to research a legal problem depend on a number of factors. The following plan is a guideline consisting of the basic steps in the process of legal research. It should be adjusted to the particular needs of the research and researcher.

Name of Researcher:_____   Date Assigned:_____

Research For: _____   Date Due: _____

File number (if applicable):_____

Preliminary Step: Identify Audience, Purpose, and Limitations

❑ Determine the purpose of the research, who the research is for, and any limitations on the research, such as time and cost. At this stage, you should estimate how much time should be spent on the total research. A record should be kept of all steps taken.

STEP 1: ANALYZE THE FACTS

❑ Gather and organize the facts (*e.g.*, identify the parties, events, and possible claims).

❑ Identify the legally relevant facts by reading generally about the law in secondary materials such as textbooks, the *Canadian Encyclopedic Digest,* or *Halsbury's Laws of Canada.*

❑ Summarize and formulate the relevant facts.

❑ Reformulate the facts later in the research process as the legally relevant facts become clearer.

STEP 2: DETERMINE THE LEGAL ISSUES

❑ Determine applicable areas of law by brainstorming, word association, and/or using the subjects of law courses.

❏ Identify the general legal issues by consulting secondary materials such as journal articles, *Halsbury's Laws of Canada,* the *Canadian Encyclopedic Digest* or textbooks and reading about the law generally. When reading about the law, move from general to specific.

❏ Formulate the specific legal issues by reading about the law in more detail. Articulate the issues as questions of law and fact.

❏ Reformulate the legal issues later in the research process as they become clearer.

STEP 3: FIND THE LAW

Refer to Secondary Materials

Locate and read secondary materials to gain an overview of the law. While reading, record references to specific cases, statutes, and other secondary materials. Here are a few secondary materials:

- Go to *Halsbury's Laws of Canada or the Canadian Encyclopedic Digest* (*Western* or *Ontario*): Locate the first few volumes or the volume that covers your topic. Look in the indexes and keys for relevant subject areas or titles. Go to the relevant volumes and read generally at first. After you have focused your research, record cases and statutes that are referenced. If you have access to an electronic version, scan the table of contents first, then read the text.

- *Textbooks*: Look in a computer catalogue to locate textbooks or go to library shelves and browse. Scan the textbook's table of contents or index first. Read the relevant sections and record the relevant cases and statutes that are referenced. Some researchers photocopy relevant pages from textbooks for future reference. If you have access to electronic textbooks, scan the table of contents or index before conducting a word search.

- *Legal Periodicals*: Locate electronic journals or articles on your topic by looking in any of the following indexes. Journal articles include references to statutes and cases.

    - LegalTrac (<http://www.galegroup.com/pdf/facts/legal.pdf>).

    - HeinOnline (<http://www.Heinonline.org>) or other electronic collections of journals.

- *Online service providers* such as LN/QL or WL*e*C that provide full texts of many journal articles.

- Periodical indexes — in print or online — to locate the titles of articles by subject. Then find and read the texts of the articles.

STATUTES AND CASES

Statutes: Find and Update Relevant Statutes

❑ If you know the **title** of the statute, look in:

- Government websites, <http://www.CanLII.org> or law library websites

- Commercial online providers such as WLeC or LN/QL

- Print versions of the federal, provincial, or territorial tables of public statutes. Statutes are listed alphabetically and direct you to the printed source.

❑ If you are researching by **subject**, you can locate statutes in the following sources:

- Secondary materials, such as *Halsbury's Laws of Canada*, the *Canadian Encyclopedic Digest*, textbooks, and periodicals (above). Those sources refer to relevant statutes.

- Federal or provincial subject indexes of statutes. Search these indexes for descriptive words that will lead you to the statues that pertain to your subject.

❑ Ensure the statute is effective (CIF) by determining whether it has a delayed effective date. If there is a commencement clause (*i.e.*, it is brought into effect at a later time), you must determine the effective date of the statute (see Chapter 7).

❑ Determine whether a statute has been amended by looking in the federal, provincial, or territorial tables of statutes or tables of legislative changes. Statutes can also be updated unofficially by looking in commercially published statute citators, which include not only amendments to the statutes but also cases that have considered statutes. Not all researchers will have these commercial citators readily available.

❑ To further update a statute and its amendments, look in the most recent gazettes or similar publications from the various legislatures (see Chapter 7).

❑ Look for cases that have considered statutes by looking in statute citators — in electronic or print form. For example, the *Canadian*

Abridgment Canadian Statute Citations lists all cases alphabetically, the history of each case, and judicial considerations. Alternatively, use this citator feature online in WL*e*C.

❑   If necessary, search for regulations pertaining to the relevant statutes (see Chapter 8).

Cases: Find and Update Relevant Cases

❑   If you know the **title** of a case, look in electronic collections of cases from any of the following:

*   Provincial, territorial, and federal courts websites.
*   Commercial online providers such as LN/QL or WL*e*C.
*   *Canadian Abridgment Consolidated Table of Cases*, which lists all cases alphabetically along with their parallel citations (also available on WL*e*C).

❑   If you are researching by **subject**, the most direct way to locate cases is through secondary materials such as the following:

*   *Canadian Encyclopedic Digest, Halsbury's Laws of Canada*, textbooks, and periodicals (above). Locate and read those cases cited and note other cases that are referred to in those cases.

*   *Canadian Abridgment Case Law Digests*. Look at the first few volumes of the set and figure out how your subject is categorized in the "key classification scheme". Find the volumes of case digests on that subject. Read the digests and record the citations of relevant cases.

❑   Check if the relevant cases have been appealed or considered in other cases (*i.e.*, note up the cases) through the following sources:

*   Electronic citators through commercial online providers such as LN/QL or WL*e*C.
*   *Canadian Abridgment Consolidated Table of Cases*, which lists all cases alphabetically along with the history of each case (in print and on WL*e*C).
*   *Canadian Abridgment Canadian Case Citations*, which lists all cases alphabetically, the history of each case, and judicial consideration of each case (in print and on WL*e*C).

STEP 4: ANALYZE THE LAW

❏ Read the secondary materials and primary sources.

❏ Analyze and brief cases and identify which cases are similar and whether they are mandatory ("binding") or merely persuasive.

❏ Analyze the relevant statutes.

❏ Synthesize the law (distinguish and analogize cases and merge with statute law).

❏ Apply the law to the legal problem.

STEP 5: COMMUNICATE THE LAW

❏ Consider options or ways to communicate the results of the research (*e.g.*, legal memorandum or opinion letter).

❏ Plan your writing:

1. Identify the reader;
2. Determine the purpose;
3. Gather, analyze, and organize the information, selecting the best authorities from among all you have found; and
4. Prepare an outline.

❏ Write a first draft focusing on content and organization.

❏ Revise your writing in the following order:

1. Content;
2. Organization;
3. Paragraphs;
4. Sentences;
5. Words; and
6. Style and form.

Answers to Self Tests

CHAPTER 1

1. The five steps of legal research are:

   - Facts — Analyze the facts
   - Issues — Determine the legal issues
   - Law — Find the relevant law
   - Analysis — Analyze the law and apply it to the facts
   - Communication — Communicate the results of the research

2. Factual analysis involves gathering the facts and determining which facts are legally relevant.
3. Issue determination involves determining what the legal issues or questions are.
4. Legal analysis involves three tasks: reading the law, synthesizing the law, and applying the law to the facts.

CHAPTER 2

1. The three steps of factual analysis are:

   - Gather and organize the facts
   - Identify the legally relevant facts
   - Formulate the facts

2. PEC stands for Parties, Events and Claims.

CHAPTER 3

1. The three steps in determining legal issues are:

   Step 1: Determine applicable area of law
   Step 2: Identify the general legal issues
   Step 3: Formulate the specific legal issues

2. Some methods that might assist you in thinking about applicable areas of law are: first-year law courses; brainstorming or word association; or

using library sources such as the *Canadian Encyclopedic Digest* and text-books.

3. Library sources that might assist in determining legal issues are the *Canadian Encyclopedic Digest*, textbooks, and legal periodical indexes.
4. Correctly formulated legal issues include both facts and law.
5. Yes, legal issues should be drafted as questions.

CHAPTER 4

1. The two types of law are legislation or government-made law, and case law or judge-made law.
2. The term "common law" originates from the travelling courts in England.
3. Legislation is law made by federal and provincial legislatures and municipalities. It includes statutes, regulations, and municipal by-laws.
4. The law-making process consists of governments making laws (legislative powers), governments enforcing laws (executive powers), and courts interpreting the laws through specific cases (judicial powers).
5. Primary sources are the law. Secondary materials are aids in understanding and locating the law.

CHAPTER 5

1. Door 1: general materials such as textbooks; door 2: journals and periodical indexes; door 3: legislation; and door 4: cases.
2. Two benefits of using computers are speed and access to unreported cases. Three limitations of using computers are that sometimes databases are not complete; searches can be costly; and the search is only as effective as the researcher.
3. Canadian commercial online providers include LN/QL, WL*e*C, Canada Law Book Online, CCH Canadian Online, Maritime Law Book (MLB) Online, SOQUIJ, and CHRR (Canadian Human Rights Reporter) Online.
4. The four steps of computer research are:

   - Plan your research;
   - Select a data source;
   - Select a database; and
   - Formulate a search.

5. A literal search means that a computer will search for the exact words that you have requested.

CHAPTER 6

1. A textbook can be located by using a library computer catalogue and searching by author, title, keyword(s), or subject.
2. To locate journal articles by subject, you could do three things: 1. Go to the library and look in a print-based periodical index. 2. Do an electronic search of an electronic index online. 3. Do a search of full-text electronic database such as HeinOnline.
3. The *Canadian Encyclopedic Digest* is an encyclopedia of all of the law in Canada, arranged by subject.
4. A book of words and phrases includes alphabetical lists of words and phrases that have been considered by the courts.
5. A case digest is a brief summary of a case. These digests are compiled in periodic publications and sorted by subject area.
6. A citator is an annotation of the law. There are case and statute annotators. They include information about whether the law is still current and accurate and they list cases that have interpreted statutes and prior cases. Most citators *do not contain the text* of cases or statutes but are helping tools that list these.

CHAPTER 7

1. Statutes can be located for free on public websites via the Internet on provincial government websites, law library websites and <http://www.CanLII.org>.
2. Statutes are located in one area in a law library, sorted by jurisdiction.
3. A table of statutes is an alphabetic listing of statutes. There is usually one for each set of statutes published by each jurisdiction and they are usually consolidated.
4. Two commercial service providers who provide access to electronic statutes are WL*e*C and LN/QL.
5. A statute citator is a book that lists statutes, their revisions, and any cases that have considered these statutes.

CHAPTER 8

1. A regulation is law that is created through delegated authority. It is also called subordinate legislation and is made pursuant to a statute.
2. Regulations become law by order-in-council.
3. A consolidation of regulations contains all of the regulations in place up to a particular point in time. It consolidates prior regulations so you need not look "behind" a consolidation.

4. A regulation can be found through use of consolidated indexes of regulations, either by title of the statute that empowered it or by the title of the regulation.

CHAPTER 9

1. A case report is a series of books that contain decided cases.
2. A few case reports are: *Supreme Court of Canada Reports* (S.C.R.), *Dominion Law Reports* (D.L.R.), and *British Columbia Law Reports* (B.C.L.R.).
3. To locate a case by name, go to the *Canadian Abridgment Consolidated Table of Cases* or the tables of cases in individual case reports.
4. To locate a case by subject, use the *Canadian Encyclopedic Digest*, a textbook, or the *Canadian Abridgment Case Digests*.
5. Updating a case means ensuring that the case is "good law". This involves finding its history and any judicial considerations of it at any levels of appeal.
6. To update a case you can use the *Canadian Abridgment Canadian Case Citations*, or individual case report research aids.

CHAPTER 10

1. The doctrine of precedent means that courts use precedents or prior decisions as examples or authorities to assist in deciding cases. The doctrine of precedent is designed to promote consistency in law and provide a tool to predict the likely outcome of a case.
2. The doctrine of *stare decisis* means "to stand by the decision". This doctrine means that courts must follow prior decisions of certain other courts.
3. The three basic levels of court in Canada are trial, appeal, and court of last resort.
4. The three steps in case analysis are: determining relevance of cases, reading cases, and synthesizing cases.
5. "Synthesizing the law" means merging all the law from the relevant cases and statutes into one general statement of law.
6. The "Golden Rule" of statutory interpretation means that the plain meaning of the words in a statute are to be applied unless it leads to some absurdity or inconsistency. If so, the statute should be interpreted to avoid this.

CHAPTER 11

1. A few rules of good writing are: omit surplus words, use short sentences, use the active voice, arrange words with care, and avoid language quirks.
2. The three stages of the legal writing process are: planning, writing, and revising.
3. The four steps of the planning process are: identify the reader; determine the purpose; gather, analyze, and organize the information; and prepare an outline.
4. The parts of a legal memorandum are: facts, issues, brief answer, analysis, and conclusion.
5. Revisions should take place in the following order: (1) content, (2) organization, (3) paragraphs, (4) sentences, (5) words and style, and (6) form.
6. A typical opinion letter has four parts: introduction, description of the law, application of the law to the facts, and conclusion.

CHAPTER 12

1. A research plan is a written plan of how research will be conducted. Each legal problem requires a unique research plan.
2. A research plan is necessary to give some direction to the research and keep researchers from sinking in the myriad of books. Developing a plan eliminates wasted effort and provides a checklist indicating steps taken.
3. A few practical factors to take into consideration are audience, purpose, cost, and time.
4. The basic parts of a research plan are FILAC: factual analysis, issue determination, finding the law, legal analysis, and communicating the results.
5. The main advantage of note-taking is that it provides a record of steps taken. This enables researchers to interrupt research without losing position and provides a reminder of what has been done to avoid gaps and repetition.

Index

Note: The abbreviation "i" in index entries refers to illustrations in the text.